ASSESSMENT OF NIH MINORITY RESEARCH AND TRAINING PROGRAMS

PHASE 3

AF764041

Committee for the Assessment of
NIH Minority Research Training Programs

Oversight Committee for the Assessment of NIH Minority Research Training Programs

Board on Higher Education and Workforce

Policy and Global Affairs

NATIONAL RESEARCH COUNCIL
OF THE NATIONAL ACADEMIES

THE NATIONAL ACADEMIES PRESS
Washington, D.C.
www.nap.edu

THE NATIONAL ACADEMIES PRESS 500 Fifth Street, N.W. Washington, DC 20001

NOTICE: The project that is the subject of this report was approved by the Governing Board of the National Research Council, whose members are drawn from the councils of the National Academy of Sciences, the National Academy of Engineering, and the Institute of Medicine. The members of the committee responsible for the report were chosen for their special competences and with regard for appropriate balance.

This study was supported by Contract/Grant No. N01-OD-4-2139 between the National Academy of Sciences and the National Institutes of Health, Department of Health and Human Services. Any opinions, findings, conclusions, or recommendations expressed in this publication are those of the author(s) and do not necessarily reflect the views of the organizations or agencies that provided support for the project.

International Standard Book Number 0-309-09575-1
Library of Congress Catalog Card Number 2005931207

Additional copies of this report are available from the National Academies Press, 500 Fifth Street, N.W., Lockbox 285, Washington, DC 20055; (800) 624-6242 or (202) 334-3313 (in the Washington metropolitan area); Internet, *http://www.nap.edu.*

Printed in the United States of America

THE NATIONAL ACADEMIES

Advisers to the Nation on Science, Engineering, and Medicine

The **National Academy of Sciences** is a private, nonprofit, self-perpetuating society of distinguished scholars engaged in scientific and engineering research, dedicated to the furtherance of science and technology and to their use for the general welfare. Upon the authority of the charter granted to it by the Congress in 1863, the Academy has a mandate that requires it to advise the federal government on scientific and technical matters. Dr. Ralph J. Cicerone is president of the National Academy of Sciences.

The **National Academy of Engineering** was established in 1964, under the charter of the National Academy of Sciences, as a parallel organization of outstanding engineers. It is autonomous in its administration and in the selection of its members, sharing with the National Academy of Sciences the responsibility for advising the federal government. The National Academy of Engineering also sponsors engineering programs aimed at meeting national needs, encourages education and research, and recognizes the superior achievements of engineers. Dr. Wm. A. Wulf is president of the National Academy of Engineering.

The **Institute of Medicine** was established in 1970 by the National Academy of Sciences to secure the services of eminent members of appropriate professions in the examination of policy matters pertaining to the health of the public. The Institute acts under the responsibility given to the National Academy of Sciences by its congressional charter to be an adviser to the federal government and, upon its own initiative, to identify issues of medical care, research, and education. Dr. Harvey V. Fineberg is president of the Institute of Medicine.

The **National Research Council** was organized by the National Academy of Sciences in 1916 to associate the broad community of science and technology with the Academy's purposes of furthering knowledge and advising the federal government. Functioning in accordance with general policies determined by the Academy, the Council has become the principal operating agency of both the National Academy of Sciences and the National Academy of Engineering in providing services to the government, the public, and the scientific and engineering communities. The Council is administered jointly by both Academies and the Institute of Medicine. Dr. Ralph J. Cicerone and Dr. Wm. A. Wulf are chair and vice chair, respectively, of the National Research Council.

www.national-academies.org

Committee for the Assessment of NIH Minority Research Training Programs

John Bailar III, *Co-chair,* Professor Emeritus, Department of Health Studies, University of Chicago
Willie Pearson, Jr., *Co-chair,* Professor and Chair, School of History, Technology and Society, Georgia Institute of Technology
David Gordon, Professor of Pathology and Associate Dean for Diversity and Career Development, University of Michigan School of Medicine
Marigold Linton, Director of American Indian Outreach, University of Kansas
Craig Love, Senior Research Director, Westat
Barbara Lovitts,[1] Senior Research Analyst, American Institutes for Research (2001-2002), Research Associate, University of Maryland (2002-2004)
Catherine Miller,[2] Senior Associate, Hampshire Research Institute (2001-2002)
Javier Rojo, Professor of Statistics, Rice University
Terrence Russell, Executive Director, Association for Institutional Research
Charles Vela, President and Chief Scientist, Expertech Solutions; President and Chief Executive Officer, Center for the Advancement of Hispanics in Science Engineering Education (CAHSEE)

Study Staff
Joan Esnayra, Study Director
Peter Henderson, Board Director (Acting Study Director, April-May 2004 and August-November 2004)
George Reinhart, Senior Program Officer (Acting Study Director, June-July 2004)
Herman Alvarado, Research Associate
Denise Grosshans, Senior Program Assistant
Elizabeth Briggs-Huthnance, Senior Program Assistant
Stacey Kozlouski, Research Assistant
Patricia Santos, Senior Program Assistant

[1] Resigned to take position at National Academies in 2004.
[2] Resigned for family health reasons in 2002.

Oversight Committee for the Assessment of NIH Minority Research Training Programs

Carlos Gutiérrez, *Chair*, Professor, California State University, Los Angeles
Freeman Hrabowski, III, President, University of Maryland, Baltimore County
Georgine Pion, Professor, Vanderbilt University

Staff
Peter Henderson, Board Director
Elizabeth Briggs-Huthnance, Senior Program Assistant
Patricia Santos, Senior Program Assistant

Board on Higher Education and Workforce

Richard A. Tapia, *Chair*, Rice University
Burt Barnow, Institute for Policy Studies, Johns Hopkins University
Donald L. Bitzer, North Carolina State University
Nancy Cantor, Syracuse University
Ronald G. Ehrenberg, Cornell University
Carlos G. Gutiérrez, California State University, Los Angeles
Nancy B. Jackson, Sandia National Laboratories
Donald L. Johnson, Grain Processing Corporation (retired)
Claudia I. Mitchell-Kernan, University of California, Los Angeles
Michael T. Nettles, Educational Testing Service
Debra W. Stewart, The Council of Graduate Schools
Tadataka Yamada, GlaxoSmithKline

Staff
Peter Henderson, Board Director
Evelyn Simeon, Administrative Coordinator

Acknowledgments

The committee would like to thank the following National Institutes of Health staff for critical input to the study process: Elias Zerhouni, John Ruffin, Vincent Thomas, Walter Schaffer, Clifton Poodry, Bob Moore (retired), Lawrence Agodoa, Nelson Aguila, Fred Altman, Nell Armstrong, Robin Barr, Karen Bashir, Lula Beatty, Terry Bishop, Susan Buyer, Faye Calhoun, Mark Chavez, Janita Coen, Michael Commarato, Mary F. Curvey, Irene Eckstrand, Vivian Faden, Julia Freeman, Walter Goldschmidts, Pamela Goodlow, Alfred W. Gordon, Bettie Graham, Taylor Harden, Sandra Hatch, Karin Helmers, Milton Hernandez, Robert Huebner, Chyren Hunter, James Hyde, Lorrayne Jackson, Morgan Jackson, David Jett, Walter Jones, Henry Khachaturian, Steven Klein, Mary Leveck, Enid Light, Flair Lindsey, James Lipton, Belinda Locke, Richard Lymn, Robert Mays, Cindy Miner, Helena Mishoe, Traci Mondoro, Antonio Noronha, John Norvell, Janice Phillips, Judith Podskalny, Cynthia Pond, Suman Rao, Ann Rothgeb, Carol Shreffler, Lorraine Silsbee, Daniel Sklare, Sanya Springfield, Sidney Stahl, Carolyn Strete, Sandra Talley, Adolphus Toliver, Tina Vanderveen, Debra Wynne, and Hinda Zlotnik. Thanks also to Mary Look, Vaishali Joshi, Susan Akin, Jim Craver, Leslyn Hall, Jessica Peters, Cherie Butts, and retired Board on Biology Director, Ralph Dell, who was the inspiration for this report.

This report has been reviewed in draft form by individuals chosen for their diverse perspectives and technical expertise, in accordance with procedures approved by the National Research Council's Report Review Committee. The purpose of this independent review is to provide candid and critical comments that will assist the institution in making its published report as sound as possible and to ensure that the report meets institutional standards for objectivity, evidence, and responsiveness to the study charge. The review comments and draft manuscript remain confidential to protect the integrity of the deliberative process. We wish to thank the following individuals for their review of this report: James Chromy, Research Triangle Institute; James Donaldson, Howard University; James Gavin, Emory University; Chris Golde, Carnegie Foundation; Carlos Gutiérrez, California State University, Los Angeles; Freeman Hrabowski, III, University of Maryland, Baltimore County; Manuel Martinez-Maldonado, Ponce School of Medicine; Joel Oppenheim, New York University; Jeanine Wiener-Kronish, University of California, San Francisco; and James Wyche, University of Miami.

Although the reviewers listed above have provided many constructive comments and suggestions, they were not asked to endorse the conclusions or recommendations, nor did they see the final draft of the report before its release. The review of this report was overseen by Lyle Jones, University of North Carolina, Chapel Hill, and Georgine Pion, Vanderbilt University. Appointed by the National Research Council, they were responsible for making certain that an independent examination of this report was carried out in accordance with institutional procedures and that all review comments were carefully considered. Responsibility for the final content of this report rests entirely with the authoring committee and the institution.

Contents

Appendixes

List of Tables and Figures

Tables

Figures

Summary

Origins of the Study

As part of the Minority Health Initiative launched by the National Institutes of Health (NIH) in 1992, the Assessment of NIH Minority Research Training Programs was initiated by the Office of Research on Minority Health (ORMH) in the Office of the Director at NIH.[1] The goal of this study was to answer a fundamental question: Do the NIH minority research training programs work? The study was implemented in three phases with ORMH conducting phases 1 and 2.

Phase 1 was completed in 1993. It presented an overview of NIH extramural research training programs and summarized available information and trend data for each of the major NIH minority research training programs.[2] Phase 1 findings also documented an overall pattern of minority underrepresentation[3] in the biological, behavioral, and clinical sciences (hereafter referred to as "biomedical" sciences). Phase 2 was completed in 1997. It assessed the feasibility of a trans-NIH assessment of minority research training programs and provided a potential scope for that endeavor. Research questions and potential data sources useful to that assessment, which would be phase 3 of the study were identified.[4]

In 2001, the National Center on Minority Health and Health Disparities (NCMHD, formerly ORMH) contracted with the National Academies to undertake the phase 3 assessment as an independent study that would draw on the findings of ORMH's earlier work. NCMHD chose the National Academies based on its independence, its ability to collect and integrate quantitative and qualitative data from NIH institutes and

---

[1] In 2000, ORMH became the National Center on Minority Health and Health Disparities.
[2] Office of Research on Minority Health, National Institutes of Health. 1993. Assessment of NIH Minority Research/Training Programs: Phase 1. Bethesda, Md.: U.S. Department of Health and Human Services.
[3] The definition of "underrepresented minority" used in this study includes Native Americans, African Americans, and Hispanics. Pacific Islanders are excluded from this definition because historic NIH data aggregate "Asian/Pacific Islander," and the vast majority of these are Asian Americans, a group well-represented in the sciences.
[4] Office of Research on Minority Health, National Institutes of Health. 1997. Assessment of NIH Minority Research/Training Programs: Phase 2. Bethesda, Md.: U.S. Department of Health and Human Services.

centers, and its ability to convene national experts who could analyze and assess these data in an objective manner.

Study Charge

In order to assess and analyze NIH minority trainee educational and career outcomes, the study committee was charged with addressing the following questions to the extent that they could be addressed using available data from NIH:

1. Do the NIH minority research training programs work?
2. Which minority programs and which features of minority programs have been most successful in helping individual students and faculty members move a step forward toward productive careers as research scientists?
3. Which minority programs have been least successful and why?
4. What additional factors contribute to minority trainee success, including characteristics of individual participants and the academic institutions at which they received NIH research training support and/or obtained their terminal degree?
5. How can a system be set up that would better address assessment questions in the future?

In addition, the study committee was charged with developing policy recommendations for an improved coordinated tracking information system that would do the following:

1. Provide NIH administrators a means for obtaining improved annual feedback on minority research training programs;
2. Assist the development of future goals;
3. Assist the development of performance measures; and
4. Assist the improvement of program effectiveness.

Assessing Program Outcomes

To answer the question, "Do the NIH minority research training programs work?" the committee developed three metrics for assessing program success which it applied in the course of its work. First, the committee undertook a thorough analysis of historic NIH program announcements for these programs in order to identify their stated goals. This analysis established that the foremost goal of NIH minority research training programs is, and always has been, to increase the number of Ph.D.-level minority biomedical researchers. However, success in reaching this goal was not quantified among any of the program announcements. Second, the committee considered the work of phases 1 and 2 of this study which recommended examining whether or not trainees had advanced to the "next step" in the science educational and/or career trajectory. Third, the committee also considered the value that participation in the program provides to the trainee. All but one member of the committee also believes that, regardless of whether each trainee advances to the next step in his or her education or becomes a Ph.D.-level researcher, the programs provide important and valuable training experiences for all participants that should be considered in assessing whether a program works.

Given disparities in educational opportunities available to trainees prior to enrollment in any of the NIH programs, it would be inappropriate to expect or demand that minority trainees, as a whole, attain the same average rates of professional success as nonminority trainees. Indeed, the training programs exist because of the need to overcome this gap. An additional and appropriate standard for evaluating minority programs, therefore, is the "value added" by the program to all its participants. This introduces a set of measurement problems as outlined below, but it is a critical foundation of the committee's analysis and recommendations. Thus, the following principles bear upon any discussion of minority research training program success:

- More than one family generation is needed to establish a research training pipeline that is both attractive to minorities and successful at producing large numbers of Ph.D.-level scientists.
- Building capacity and sustaining minority interest in science require the visible promotion of role models. Such persons may include science teachers, professors, medical doctors, entrepreneurs, and others, who open a window to science careers and opportunities to which young minds might not otherwise have been exposed.
- The research training pipeline is necessarily leaky. Those who exit the pipeline early to become part of the scientific workforce are not program failures.
- The research pipeline is not always a straight line. Some will exit the pipeline only to return some years later.
- Programs designed for those who are in early career stages should endorse a broad definition of success. Programs for trainees at later career stages may adopt a more highly prescribed definition of success.

Methods

The study committee was charged with addressing its study questions to the extent that they could be using available data from NIH supplemented by interviews with minority trainees and program administrators. Simply put, the committee was not able to obtain all of the data it wished. While the committee met its charge to the extent feasible, it could not answer all of the research questions in as direct and complete a manner as it would have liked, and it now advocates for a future study. If the advice provided in this report leads to corresponding action, it will improve the programs in the short run and facilitate a more comprehensive study in the future. Indeed, extensive data collection efforts, ongoing deliberations, and analyses allowed the committee to identify critical data elements that should be collected by NIH on a systematic basis, in order to make future assessments of all NIH research training programs feasible.

The committee conducted a census of extramural NIH minority research training programs that were sponsored by the institutes and centers (ICs) at the time the study began in 2001. There were 79 such programs—too many for a feasible assessment, given the project budget and time constraints. Thus, the committee developed rational inclusion and exclusion criteria in order to distill the training programs it could most effectively assess. The committee decided that the time frame for the study would extend from 1970 to 1999 and the study would include the following career stages: undergraduate, graduate, postdoctoral, and junior faculty. Two trainee comparison groups were also identified—minority and nonminority trainees participating in programs that are not targeted specifically for minorities.

The study evaluates 47 of the original 79 minority programs, these 47 being reclassified into 13 program categories that take into account career stages served by the programs and the letter-number designation associated with each program (e.g., F31, T32, K01, etc.). For a summary of the 13 program categories, see Table 2-2.

Another difficulty faced by the committee at the outset of the study was the prohibition against accessing or viewing individual trainee race and gender data in NIH's data sets. Given the need to distinguish minority from nonminority trainees for purposes of carrying out this study, the committee was required to rely on an intermediary NIH-approved contractor that was allowed access to individual trainee race or ethnicity and gender data. Since the National Academies had no direct contractual relationship with the NIH-approved contractor, it had little leverage in terms of the deliverables produced.

The committee is cognizant of the sensitivity of race and gender data and the degree to which the NIH Office of the Director strives to protect the privacy of its trainees and grantees, but in this case it made very difficult the very task the committee was contracted by NIH to conduct. Thus, NIH may wish to reconsider its interpretation of how the Privacy Act applies to the degree of access an outside evaluator has to individual trainee race or ethnicity and gender data when that evaluator has been contracted by NIH to conduct an assessment of minority research training programs. It may also want to revisit the value of having more than one contractor approved for access to individual trainee data.

Trainee Interviews

The committee designed a study approach that called for extensive mining of existing NIH electronic trainee data sets, followed by structured interviews with former NIH trainees and semistructured interviews with program administrators who administer these programs both at NIH and at awardee colleges and universities. The NIH data contractor conducted 732 computer-assisted telephone interviews (CATIs) using a random sample of trainees who were participants in one of these programs prior to 2000. The trainee interviews focused on the following issues:

- Trainee characteristics;
- Trainee educational and career expectations;
- Trainee outcomes;
- Best or worst program features;
- Relationship with head of the laboratory or research group (i.e., principal investigator, or PI);
- Relationship with trainee's mentor; and
- Relationships with other laboratory or research group members.

A few open-ended response items were also included in the survey. These provided trainees with an opportunity to share what they believed to be the strengths and/or weaknesses of the programs and to suggest ways in which NIH could improve its programs.

In the absence of NIH-wide electronic trainee tracking data, the NIH data contractor achieved a very low response rate from its efforts to locate and interview trainees. This was the case despite its use of two commercial and proprietary databases that together maintain credit card-related contact information for millions of Americans and the query of the U.S. Postal Service address-forwarding database. The committee was disappointed but not entirely surprised by the low response rate. As a result of low location and response values, there is a high likelihood of bias among the survey results. Some evidence suggests that the trainees interviewed for our survey were more likely to be among the more "successful" program participants. For example, among those who participated in the Bridges to the Baccalaureate program, survey respondents were more likely to have transferred to a four-year institution and completed a bachelor's degree than program participants in general.[5]

The committee was similarly skeptical about the large numbers of respondents who had at least one family member with a bachelor's or graduate degree. Thus, the committee believes that data from these interviews may not reflect the responses that would have been obtained had the respondents been more representative of the larger universe of program participants. Nevertheless, the data are instructive in a general way and are described qualitatively in the report and summarized briefly below. Respondent data are reported using a variety of nonspecific phrases such as: "nearly all reported," "a majority of respondents said," "a minority of respondents said," "more likely," and "less likely." Such phrases should not be equated with statistical significance.

---

[5] See http://www.nigms.nih.gov/news/reports/bridges.html.

Minority Training Programs: What Is Working?

The committee concludes that underrepresented minorities are entering the biomedical workforce as a direct result of the NIH minority research training programs.

Recruitment

The administrators of these programs mentioned that there are many more applicants to the undergraduate programs than there are available positions. Thus, recruitment appears to be highly effective at this level. At the undergraduate trainee level, attrition from the programs is minimal, due in part to an effective system of oversight and monitoring of trainees' progress.

Research Experience

Among trainee respondents at all career stages, there is profound appreciation for what these programs offer and recognition of the prestige associated with being an NIH research trainee. The "best feature" most often cited by trainee respondents across all career stages is the research experience itself. For undergraduate trainees, the acquisition of laboratory skills was key. For graduate trainees, laboratory experience was important but so were graduate-level coursework, research seminars and workshops, learning how to think critically, learning to make cogent research presentations, and learning to teach science to undergraduates. Among postdoctoral and junior faculty trainees, the opportunity to choose a subspecialty and develop research independence was the most valuable aspect of the training programs.

Mentoring

Among undergraduate trainees, mentoring support was cited as the second most valuable feature of the training programs. Mentoring was most often provided in four key areas:

1. Improving the trainee's research skills,
2. Providing motivation and personal growth,
3. Providing career guidance, and
4. Promoting the trainee for scholarships and other development opportunities.

Mentoring was also very important to graduate, postdoctoral, and junior faculty trainees who reported many positive interactions and support from their mentors.

Funding

Funding support from the training programs was greatly appreciated by undergraduate trainees. Such support came in the form of stipends, summer research positions, and conference travel support. Funding was, for graduate trainees, frequently cited as a best feature. At the graduate level, a funding arrangement exists whereby NIH covers the cost of research training, including stipend and tuition support, research supplies, and benefits. In return, NIH requires that trainees refrain from taking outside jobs in order to devote 100 percent effort to the training experience. For postdoctoral and junior faculty trainees, funding was characterized as "critical and necessary." The "protected time" that funding provided trainees at this level allowed them to achieve research independence, which is the foremost goal of these programs.

Career Development

Other positive program elements that trainees mentioned include the foundation of scientific knowledge that the program provided to undergraduate trainees and the opportunities to network and collaborate with other scientists, which was mentioned by trainees at all levels, but especially graduate trainees. Undergraduate trainees underscored the ability of the programs to help them decide whether to attend graduate school or medical school. Graduate and postdoctoral trainees cited frequently the tremendous value in learning how to prepare a competitive grant proposal. According to junior faculty trainees, the K01 award allowed them to progress to the next step in their careers, namely to obtain an R01 research grant.

Minority Training Programs: What Is Not Working?

The committee concludes that NIH can do a better job in training a large cadre of doctoral-level minority biomedical researchers.

Trainee Characteristics

At the postdoctoral and junior faculty levels, there appears to be a sharp drop-off among minority trainees. An indicator of this is the gender shift from predominantly female at the undergraduate and graduate career stages to predominantly male at the postdoctoral and junior faculty career stages (see Appendix E). Where do the minority female trainees go? This question warrants further study by NIH.

Funding

Although trainees across career stages were extremely grateful for training program funding support, they uniformly stated that the levels of funding are not sufficient and need to be increased. Undergraduates who are already greatly challenged by a demanding research program in addition to a full load of coursework must often take on additional outside work in order to make ends meet. Program administrators call this situation a "recipe for disaster," and it constitutes a barrier against participation in these programs for lower-income minority students.

Graduate trainees complain similarly. They are contractually prohibited from obtaining outside jobs, yet the stipend support is barely above the poverty line. In the context of the uneven health benefits afforded by these programs, this too is a "catch-22" situation that trainees reported with frustration.

Postdoctoral and junior faculty trainees are similarly disheartened by the low stipends afforded by the training programs. This is especially true when trainees have dependents and/or live in major metropolitan areas where the cost of living vastly exceeds what the stipend offers. All trainee respondents were clear and forceful in stating that trainee stipends have to be more in line with market trends; they need to be increased in order to sustain and build student interest in research careers. This sentiment was echoed by numerous program administrators, one of whom stated that the stiffest competition faced in attracting African-American trainees to a research career comes from the salary opportunities provided by advanced health professional programs.

Mentoring

Although highly cited as a positive element of the training programs, mentoring was also criticized as needing significant improvement. Too many trainees reported negative mentoring experiences in the lab. Some minority undergraduate trainees were given mundane administrative tasks to perform in lieu of experiments; others experienced "benign neglect" by their mentors or, at best, a lack of encouragement. One-half of the minority T32 postdoctoral trainees reported having no mentor at all, a trend that was not replicated with nonminority (T32) postdoctoral trainees. This is a red flag to which NIH must pay attention, especially in the context of the scarce numbers of minority trainees at this relatively advanced career stage.

Training in the biomedical sciences historically assumes that if one is trained, one will therefore be a good trainer (mentor), but this is not necessarily so. Mentoring is a skill, one for which academic researchers rarely receive any formal training. Thus, NIH would be wise to assess a variety of research training methods to see which approaches work best in different situations. The old adage, "Do as I did" does not operationalize well in the context of today's diverse trainee populations. Training in the absence of optimization research produces the kind of the homogeneity seen among this study's postgraduate trainee respondents. Those who are just like their mentors are promoted; those who are different from their mentors are not.

Program administrators emphasized that in addition to the lack of mentor training, mentors receive little credit, encouragement, or support for time taken to mentor trainees. Grants do not provide funds that cover mentoring activities and faculty time. Academic departments do not view mentoring as a legitimate activity that counts toward tenure. Yet, mentoring is absolutely essential to the continued growth and sustenance of our biomedical workforce. NIH should examine these issues and consider changing the value it places on this essential activity in some concrete way.

Minority Experiences

Minority respondents to our survey provided additional clues that may bear upon their low numbers at higher career stages. Based on the survey data, which the committee believes are biased toward the most successful NIH trainees, minorities publish fewer papers than do nonminority trainees. They have greater difficulty in securing employment after receipt of the doctoral degree. They report less social integration in their laboratories, and this was experienced more by minority trainees at institutions using nonminority training mechanisms. Finally, a large fraction of minority trainees believe that their minority status in some way affected their training experience. Given that one-half of the minority postdoctoral survey respondents reported having no mentor at all, one wonders what factors are at play in these training environments that affect minority trainee outcomes so profoundly.

Recommendations

By the end of 2005, the NIH director should articulate a set of clear and measurable training goals and objectives specific to minority training. The director should take into account the mission of NIH and the integral role of research training in attaining both societal goals (e.g., health and well-being, the ability to support oneself and one's family, community development) and research goals. Such a policy should be responsive to society's workforce needs in their broadest sense, with an understanding that contributions to society derive from all parts of the career stage pipeline.

NIH should commit to the continued funding of minority-targeted research training programs. Although the committee cannot substantiate this recommendation in quantitative terms for reasons described throughout this report, it does so in qualitative terms, using survey data that were collected from trainees and program administrators who are the programs' primary informants. The following reasons underlie this recommendation:

- These programs have added many minorities to our science workforce.

- The elimination of these programs would likely diminish the number of new minority scientists entering the scientific workforce.
- The trainees interviewed indicate overwhelmingly that these programs benefited them. These programs provided research experiences, financial support, and mentoring that were critical to their career success.
- Mentoring is a critical part of the career development of all scientist, and is particularly important for minority trainees. Trainee survey data suggest that the diversity of mentors is greater in the minority-targeted programs than in the nontargeted-programs. Atkinson et al.[6] found that, when rating mentoring relationships, both mentors and mentees rated their relationships more positively when they were matched for race or ethnicity.

The committee recognizes two distinct and valid approaches to the development of minority research trainees. **The training policy of the NIH institutes and centers (ICs) in conducting these programs should emphasize the development of trainees who have already demonstrated promise in the sciences, so that they can overcome the barriers to becoming productive investigators**. Two examples of minority training programs that emphasize talent "harvesting" include the National Institute of Mental Health Training and Education (NIMH) Career Opportunities in Research (COR) and the Minority Access to Research Careers (MARC) Undergraduate Student Training in Academic Research (U*STAR) programs. Harvesting talent in this context means supporting trainees who probably would have, for a variety of reasons, "made it" regardless of support from the targeted programs. **The NIH training policy should also emphasize the development of other trainees—those without demonstrated science promise—in order to add to the pipeline of trainees interested in pursuing science careers**. An example of a minority training program that emphasizes "growing" talent is the Bridges to the Baccalaureate program. Growing talent in this context means the promotion of science and science careers for individuals and communities that may not otherwise have entered science.

NIH should more vigorously monitor the use of racial or ethnic eligibility criteria for these programs. Survey data from trainees and program administrators indicate that non-underrepresented minorities are participating in minority-targeted training programs.

NIH should examine gender differences among its trainee participants. For example, the minority trainee population at the undergraduate level is mostly female, but this proportion declines at each successive career stage, showing that there is substantially more attrition among women who could have become investigators than among men. This trend is particularly striking at the graduate-to-postdoctoral transition where men, conversely, outnumber women. This trend among females is independent of race.

---

[6] Atkinson, D., H. Neville, and A. Casas. 1991. The mentorship of ethnic minorities in professional psychology. Professional Psychology Research and Practice 22(4):336-338.

Given comments offered by trainees and program administrators, the committee recommends that NIH conduct a review to ensure that the research infrastructure (e.g., laboratory space, laboratory equipment, active faculty research programs) available to minority trainees at the institution level is adequate and, if not, seek ways to further address this programmatically.

The director of each institute should designate a single individual as minority research training programs coordinator for that institute by the third quarter of FY 2005. Some institutes have centralized training coordinators; others do not. This recommendation would provide consistency and make coordinated efforts more feasible.

The NIH training director should convene a meeting of all minority training coordinators on at least a quarterly basis, beginning with the third quarter of 2005. The goal of these meetings would be to coordinate the administration of NIH minority training programs and the collection of relevant program data. Currently, the administration of these programs is fragmented and, as a consequence, external evaluation is difficult. Given the importance of the NIH training programs to the continuation of U.S. leadership in biomedical research, coordinated efforts are needed to develop, manage, and rigorously evaluate research training programs. The collective management of minority training programs, although not intended to supplant IC independence and expertise, requires ongoing communication and cooperation across disciplinary and institutional lines. Agendas for these meetings are expected to change over time as the collaboration improves communication and advances meaningful planning. The meetings should at a minimum address the following issues:

- Clarification of NIH training policies regarding trainee recruitment and documentation of program activities and results,
- Discussion of the range of IC training program characteristics,
- Sharing of trainee recruitment strategies,
- Identification of effective elements of IC training programs,
- Review of IC evaluation results, and
- Development of long-term objectives for addressing workforce needs and for increasing the participation of underrepresented minorities in science.

The committee of minority training program coordinators should establish appropriate guidelines and measures for evaluating NIH minority research training programs. Training program administrators should participate in an ongoing and rigorous evaluation process. By defining program outcomes and monitoring their achievement, the ICs can better manage their programs. NIH should make a commitment to make available all of the data needed for internal or external evaluations of its training programs.

Further study of the relative effectiveness of minority-targeted versus nontargeted programs should be carried out by NIH institutes and centers under coordination from the Office of the Director. The reasons for this recommendation include the following:

- The ICs should establish outcome measures for each training mechanism in a coordinated fashion. To do this, the ICs should identify and document the range of trainee outcomes that result from participation in these programs. Then, the range of outcomes should be codified as either contributing or not contributing to the consensus definition of program success. The committee is cognizant that this recommendation reflects an interactive process.
- Continued integrated study of these programs can identify the best features of the programs and the best practices among recipient colleges and universities.

The director of NIH training should administer the funds for evaluation, data collection, and marketing by FY 2006. Centralized training activities should include a centralized and robust evaluation and planning activity. This approach will empower the director of NIH training to be able to coordinate accountability mandates (i.e., PART, Government Performance and Results Act) with organizational policies and procedures.

The general issues reviewed in this report should be revisited periodically at the NIH level, with the next report submitted by 2009. The Office of the Director at NIH should take the lead on this. The numerous, weighty, and very public issues regarding affirmative action that are raised by targeted research training programs require continuing attention by a consortium of the National Center for Minority Health and Health Disparities, the Office of Extramural Programs, the institutes and centers that fund such training programs, and the NIH Office of the Director. NIH should conduct an independent public review and accounting that will help ensure that the programs remain focused and effective. Doing so will inform both the affected groups and the general public of the success of the programs and ensure that funding is being used effectively, thus yielding a positive return on the nation's investment. The committee believes that five years is a good interval for external review of the program(s), although experience may show that more frequent review would be useful. The committee further believes that the breadth and depth of the issues, compounded by the present fragmentation of many components of NIH, require that the Office of the NIH Director take the lead role.

NIH should develop a relational database that collects a minimum data set (MDS) for all persons who receive funding as trainees, fellows, research assistants, or postdoctorates, including those programs targeted to underrepresented minorities.

- The database should be maintained by the Office of the Director of Extramural Programs, headed by the deputy director and NIH research and training officer. The Office of the Director of Extramural Programs should have the overall responsibility for coordination of the database and its constituent parts.
- The MDS should be a service to all institutes and contain variables that enable rigorous evaluation and assessment of training programs; institutes may add variables at their discretion.

- The MDS should collect data for all trainees, including all those funded through the training mechanisms covered here, as well as for research assistants funded through R and K awards.
- The Office of the Director of Extramural Training, in coordination with institute representatives, should develop a data entry system accessible from multiple sources, including external data entry points such as grant-specific progress reports. In addition, the Office of the Director of Extramural Training should develop a user-friendly data entry form for the MDS that is web accessible. The database and data coordination in the deputy director's office will emulate that of a coordinated data center. Considerations of personal privacy and confidentiality must be high on the list of necessary attributes.
- The Office of the Deputy Director of Extramural Training should identify data elements that help in tracking persons who received training funds—both directly and indirectly. These tracking data should be obtained at the time of initial NIH funding and should be updated periodically.
- Development of the MDS, database, and data entry system should begin immediately and be completed no later that FY 2008.

1

Introduction

Over the last decade, the National Institutes of Health (NIH) funded on average about 15,000 trainees per year at various stages in their careers. In 2002, the number of trainees exceeded 16,000, reflecting a spending level of approximately $650 million.

NIH initiated minority-targeted research training programs in 1972, when it created the Minority Biomedical Research Support (MBRS) program[7] to provide support for biomedical research at minority institutions. In 1975, NIH established the Minority Access to Research Careers (MARC) program to enable faculty at minority institutions to develop undergraduate curricula in the biomedical sciences and to provide opportunities to attract undergraduates to biomedical research. In 1977, MARC established the Honors Undergraduate Research Training program and, over time, it added programs to fund predoctoral, postdoctoral, and junior faculty trainees. During subsequent decades, the expansion of programs designed to enhance the number of minority biomedical and behavioral scientists showed modest but continuous increases in both the number of institutes and centers (ICs) offering them and the types of research and training covered.

Today, NIH supports training opportunities for underrepresented minorities beginning at the secondary school level and continuing through postgraduate training and research. The MBRS and MARC programs reside within the Minority Opportunity in Research (MORE) Division of the National Institute of General Medical Sciences (NIGMS). NIGMS provides a focus for minority research training; however, most of the ICs have one or more minority-targeted research training programs. A census of extramural NIH minority research training programs conducted by the committee in 2001 revealed that the ICs offered 79 different minority-targeted training programs in support of the NIH goal of increasing the number of minority biomedical and behavioral scientists. This study examines the use of 13 of those programs at the undergraduate, graduate, postdoctoral, and junior faculty levels.

---

[8] Originally named the Minority Schools Biomedical Support (MSBS) program.

Origins of the Study

As part of the Minority Health Initiative launched by NIH in 1992, a trans-NIH study—the Assessment of NIH Minority Research Training Programs—was initiated by the Office of Research on Minority Health (ORMH) in the Office of the Director at NIH. The goal of this study was to answer a fundamental question: Do the NIH minority research and research training programs work? Specifically, have they been successful in helping minority students and faculty members move a step forward toward productive careers as research scientists? In addition to answering the basic outcome question, the core of the assessment was to identify which features of minority programs are most effective in helping students and faculty advance to the next step in their careers.

The study was implemented in three phases. ORMH conducted phases 1 and 2. The National Center on Minority Health and Health Disparities (NCMHD), the successor to ORMH,[8] then asked the National Academies to conduct phase 3, as an independent study that would draw on the findings of ORMH's earlier work. Phase 1 focused on presenting an overview of NIH extramural research training programs and summarized available information and trend data for each of the major NIH minority research training programs.[9] In 1993, ORMH completed phase 1 and documented an overall pattern of minority underrepresentation in the biological, behavioral, and clinical sciences (hereafter referred to as "biomedical" sciences). Despite moderate improvements in recent years in the number and proportion of Ph.D. degrees earned by underrepresented minorities, there has not been a marked increase in the number of minorities who have been successful in securing mainstream NIH research grants not specifically targeted for minorities.

In 1997, ORMH reported on phase 2 of the study, which assessed the feasibility of a trans-NIH assessment of minority research training programs (phase 3) and determined the appropriate scope of that endeavor. Research questions and potential data sources useful to phase 3 of the study were identified.[10]

In 2001, NCMHD contracted with the National Academies to undertake the phase 3 assessment. NCMHD chose the National Academies based on its independence, its ability to collect and integrate quantitative and qualitative data from NIH ICs, and its ability to convene national experts who could analyze and assess these data in an

---

[8] In 2000, ORMH became the NCMHD. Congress specified in Public Law 106-525 that the purpose of NCMHD is ". . . the conduct and support of research, training, dissemination of information, and other programs with respect to minority health conditions and other populations with health disparities." Furthermore, Congress empowered NCMHD to ". . . make awards of grants or contracts to designated biomedical and behavioral research institutions, . . . for the purpose of assisting the institutions in supporting programs of excellence in biomedical and behavioral research training for individuals who are members of minority health disparity populations or other health disparity populations."

[9] Office of Research on Minority Health, National Institutes of Health. 1993. Assessment of NIH Minority Research/Training Programs: Phase 1. Bethesda, Md.: U.S. Department of Health and Human Services.

[10] Office of Research on Minority Health, National Institutes of Health. 1997. Assessment of NIH Minority Research/Training Programs: Phase 2, Bethesda. Md.: U.S. Department of Health and Human Services.

objective manner. To that end, National Research Council Chairman, Dr. Bruce Alberts, appointed a study committee to address the specific charge outlined below.

Study Charge

The goals of the study are (1) to assess and analyze NIH minority trainee educational and career outcomes to the extent feasible with the existing data and information at NIH, supplemented by interviews of minority trainees, and (2) to recommend improvements to the NIH coordinated tracking and information system of minority research training programs and their participants.

In order to assess and analyze NIH minority trainee educational and career outcomes, the study committee was charged with addressing the following questions to the extent that they may be addressed using available data from NIH supplemented by interviews with minority trainees and program administrators:

1. Do the NIH minority research training programs work?
2. Which minority programs and which features of minority programs have been most successful in helping individual students and faculty members move a step forward toward productive careers as research scientists?
3. What additional factors contribute to minority trainee success, including characteristics of individual participants and the academic institutions at which they received NIH research training support and/or obtained their terminal degree?
4. Which minority programs have been least successful and why?
5. How can a system be set up that would better address assessment questions in the future?

In addition, the study committee was charged with developing policy recommendations for an improved coordinated tracking information system that would do the following:

1. Provide NIH administrators a means for obtaining improved annual feedback on minority research training programs;
2. Assist the development of future goals;
3. Assist the development of performance measures; and
4. Assist the improvement of program effectiveness.

Minority Underrepresentation

The Problem of Underrepresentation

A diverse research workforce in the biomedical sciences broadens scientific inquiry and knowledge, has enhanced potential to solve population-specific health problems, and more fully exploits a valuable human resource. Although the biomedical sciences are flourishing in the United States, these fields have faced critical workforce supply problems over the last decade.[11] In particular, there is severe underrepresentation of Native-American, African-American, and Hispanic individuals. In 1997, underrepresented minorities comprised only 4.2 percent of the doctoral-level biomedical workforce.[12]

Access to higher education creates opportunities for individuals to enjoy professional careers and upward mobility. Historically, individuals from underrepresented groups have not had the same kind of access to educational opportunities and higher-paying professional positions that individuals from nonminority groups have, although the efforts on the part of higher education institutions to promote diversity in their student populations over the last four decades have made a significant difference.

Bowen and Bok (1998)[13] and Prewitt (2002)[14] have shown that in response to the civil rights movement, key Supreme Court cases, and the Civil Rights Act of 1964, colleges and universities began to actively recruit minority students—Native American, Hispanic, and African American—in the 1960s and became more aggressive in subsequent decades. Indeed, higher education embraced diversity as a mission, recognizing, as Prewitt argues that "it had a special obligation. It had to amend for its own complicity with past racist practices. It was also strategically placed and thus had unique responsibilities . . . . It had always been the route to leadership in law, politics, medicine, and commerce. If it had unfairly kept parts of the population from these roles, it could now accelerate their mobility."[15]

Bowen and Bok (1998) report that these efforts have paid off, particularly in the professions. These trends have led to striking gains in the representation of minorities in the most lucrative and influential occupations. By 1996, African Americans made up 8.6

---

[11] National Research Council. 2000. Addressing the Nation's Changing Needs for Biomedical and Behavioral Scientists. Washington, D.C.: National Academy Press

[12] National Science Foundation, Division of Science Resources Statistics. 2002. Doctoral Scientists and Engineers: 1999 Profile. Arlington, Va.: National Science Foundation.

[13] Bowen, W. G., and D. C. Bok. 1998. The Shape of the River: Long-Term Consequences of Considering Race in College and University Admissions. Princeton, N.J.: Princeton University Press.

[14] Prewitt, K. 2002. Higher education and the diversity agenda. Speech given at the Annual Meeting of the Council of Graduate Schools in San Diego, Calif., in December 2002.

[15] *Ibid.*, p. 4.

percent of all male professionals and 13.1 percent of all female professionals (up from 3.8 and 6 percent, respectively, in 1960). They also accounted for 8.3 percent of all male executives, managers, and administrators and 9.6 percent of all females in such positions (up from 3 and 1.8 percent, respectively). From 1960 to 1990, African Americans almost doubled their percentage of the nation's physicians and almost tripled their share of attorneys and engineers.[16] These gains are indeed impressive, but African Americans remain underrepresented in most of these professional occupations, as do Hispanics and Native Americans relative to their prevalence within society, as a whole.

In fields of science, particularly at the graduate level, the underrepresentation of minorities remains even more severe. In 2001, minorities for all three underrepresented groups earned just 5.7 percent of all doctorates in science and engineering, even though together they comprise more than 25 percent of the total U.S. population. (African Americans earned just 2.8 percent of doctorates in science and engineering, Hispanics earned 2.7 percent, and Native Americans earned 0.3 percent.) Underrepresented minorities earned 9.2 percent of doctorates in the social and behavioral sciences, but only 5.6 percent of all doctorates in the biological sciences.[17] Table 1-1 lists the number of doctorates in biological sciences awarded between 1994 and 2003. In contrast to the gains made by underrepresented minorities in the professions, the percentage of underrepresented minorities earning doctorates in the biological sciences improved approximately 2 percentage points over a 10-year period.[18]

For behavioral scientists, the situation is only slightly better. Table 1-2 shows that between 1994 and 2003 the number of psychology doctorates awarded to underrepresented minorities (as defined by this study) increased by approximately 4 percent.[19]

Clearly, opportunities for underrepresented minorities to participate in the biomedical sciences at the doctoral level are as yet unrealized. The numbers are so low, even after decades of effort to increase minority participation in higher education generally, that one must conclude that barriers to participation persist, to the detriment of individuals who might seek these careers as well as to the detriment of science and of society. It is to these latter two that we now turn.

---

[16] Bowen, W. G., and D. C. Bok. 1998. The Shape of the River: Long-Term Consequences of Considering Race in College and University Admissions. Princeton, N.J.: Princeton University Press, p. 10.

[17] NSF/NIH/NEH/USDA/NASA, 2001 Survey of Earned Doctorates.

[18] Data from Table 1-1 were recalculated and the Asian/Pacific Islanders category was removed from the definition of minority because Asians are not underrepresented in science. The percentage of underrepresented minorities receiving doctorates in the biological sciences are recalculated as follows: 1994: 5.5; 1995: 5.8; 1996: 5.7; 1997: 6.2; 1998: 6.8; 1999: 7.5; 2000: 7.2; 2001: 7.5; 2002: 7.7; 2003:7.3.

[19] Data from Table 1-2 were recalculated and the category of Asian/Pacific Islanders was removed for purposes of comparison with recalculated data from Table 1-1. The percentage of underrepresented minorities receiving doctorates in psychology are recalculated as follows: 1994: 8.6; 1995: 9.7; 1996: 10.6; 1997: 10.9; 1998: 12.1; 1999: 12.8; 2000: 13.1; 2001: 12.1; 2002: 13.3; 2003:12.6.

TABLE 1-1 Doctorates in Biological Sciences Awarded to U.S. Citizens or Permanent Residents by Race or Ethnicity and Major Field of Study: 1994-2003

Year	1994	1995	1996	1997	1998	1999	2000	2001	2002	2003
American Indian or Alaskan Native	16	15	20	7	12	20	17	15	12	11
Asian or Pacific Islander	719	920	885	721	657	608	539	558	581	542
Black	78	107	98	112	111	116	118	139	124	108
Hispanic	131	127	131	146	168	175	173	165	182	175
Total minority biological sciences doctorates	944	1169	1134	986	948	919	847	877	899	836
Minority doctorates as a percentage of total	24.05	28.04	27.36	25.80	24.65	24.15	22.49	23.29	24.18	24.56
White	3,105	3,115	3,170	3,158	3,246	3,128	3,308	3,255	3,117	3,053
Total	4,088	4,329	4,364	4,256	4,308	4,124	4,268	4,243	4,111	4,047

SOURCE: NSF/NIH/NEH/USDA/NASA, 2003 Survey of Earned Doctorates.

TABLE 1-2 Doctorates in Psychology Awarded to U.S. Citizens or Permanent Residents by Race or Ethnicity and Major Field of Study: 1994-2003

Year	1994	1995	1996	1997	1998	1999	2000	2001	2002	2003
American Indian or Alaskan Native	12	14	17	18	31	35	22	17	15	22
Asian or Pacific Islander	108	121	121	126	113	132	145	122	128	125
Black	124	149	152	152	158	172	189	174	171	168
Hispanic	133	146	173	171	208	215	211	175	185	169
Total minority psychology doctorates	377	430	463	467	510	554	567	488	499	484
Minority doctorates as a percentage of total	12.02	13.51	14.32	14.94	15.58	16.83	17.55	16.09	17.86	17.01
White	2,729	2,722	2,744	2,523	2,645	2,701	2,607	2,454	2,228	2,254
Total	3,136	3,184	3,233	3,125	3,274	3,292	3,231	3,033	2,794	2,846

SOURCE: SOURCE: NSF/NIH/NEH/USDA/NASA, 2003 Survey of Earned Doctorates.

Ensuring a High-Quality Scientific Workforce

Increasing the participation of underrepresented minorities is critical to ensuring a high-quality supply of scientists and engineers in the United States over the long term. This is so for at least three reasons: First, if some groups are underrepresented in science, we are very likely not attracting as many of the most talented individuals to what is a key activity in our knowledge economy. If nothing is done, this problem will become even more severe as minority groups increase as a percentage of the U.S. population. Second, minority scientists' general knowledge and understanding of their communities can facilitate the resolution of population-specific health problems. Third, the resolution of health problems associated with minority populations, such as obesity, heart disease, and diabetes, will help solve similar problems prevalent in nonminority communities.

The diversity of societal scientific problems is best addressed by a diverse science workforce with vested interests in these issues. The participation of minorities broadens and deepens science as individuals with diverse backgrounds address familiar and new problems, formulate novel questions, and employ alternative strategies for solutions. Scientists tend to work on areas that are of most interest to them. Although not uniformly a desire, many minority scientists focus their efforts on issues of critical importance to minority communities, frequently as a result of their own backgrounds. This is seen especially in clinical and public health research areas, such as health disparities and medical care, and in targeted efforts at specific diseases. It is perhaps no accident that the recent upsurge in the biomedical sciences focused around women's health issues has occurred concomitantly with an increase in the number of women scientists and physicians in this country. Female biomedical researchers are likely to promote research in these areas and to have personal insights into the causes of these problems and about barriers to their prevention or eradication.

The scientific challenges that we face (e.g., making sense out of the human genome) are enormous and difficult. In order to overcome these challenges, NIH must attract and develop creative, innovative, and knowledgeable practitioners of science across a wide range of biomedical disciplines. To the extent that much of the as-yet-untapped talent resides with minority individuals, high-quality research training opportunities must continue to be made available. Even this is not enough. A welcoming and tolerant scientific workplace environment is also essential in cultivating biomedical workforce diversity.

This is well recognized in other aspects of our society. For example, many corporations have discovered the value of diversity not only in sales and marketing functions, where a wide base for customer appeal is important but also in other operations where the best talent is needed. Minority trainees need role models as much as they need efforts to develop them as new entrants. They also need to see organizational goals that are shared by their communities (e.g., the reduction of health problems that affect minority individuals). Conversely, organizations need such individuals not only for their talent, but also to best educate them and aid them in making these environments truly nurturing. They also need such individuals in key leadership positions (e.g., professors, department chairs, heads of key committees, and national advisers) in order to better serve the function of role model and promote policies that effect truly best practices for all segments of society. Thus, it can be argued that a research institution that is not diverse is likely not bringing the best talent to the table.

In addition to issues of talent, there are issues of supply.[20] For one thing, demographic trends suggest an important emphasis on recruiting underrepresented minorities to science and engineering simply because those groups are increasing as a proportion of the U.S. population and are expected to reach 49.9 percent in the near future.[21] As the National Science and Technology Council (2000) related:

> Demographic trends inspire concern about the nation's ability to meet its future ST&E [scientific, technical, and engineering] workforce needs. Historically, non-Hispanic white males have made up a large fraction of U.S. scientists and engineers. However, in the 21st century this portion of the U.S. population is projected to decrease significantly. Other populations groups, such as Hispanics and African Americans, form a much smaller part of the ST&E workforce, but their populations are expected to increase markedly in the next 50 years. This implies that the ST&E fraction of the total workforce may decline if the relative participation rates of these different groups remain at the present values.[22]

If anything, this message is even more important today. Recent data on graduate enrollments in science and engineering have shown a long-term decline in the number of white males enrolling in NIH research training programs over the last decade. Moreover, the number of international trainees participating in U.S. science and engineering graduate and postdoctoral training programs is also in danger of sharp decline, given recent world events. Minority

---

[20]Some reports have argued additionally and strongly that we either already have, or will soon be facing, a shortage of scientists and engineers in the United States, particularly a shortage of domestic scientists and engineers. These reports include the following: National Science Board. 2003. The Science and Engineering Workforce: Realizing America's Potential. Arlington, Va.: National Science Foundation; Congressional Commission on the Advancement of Women and Minorities in Science, Engineering and Technology Development. 2000. Land of Plenty: Diversity as America's Competitive Edge in Science, Engineering and Technology. Arlington, Va.: National Science Foundation; and Jackson, S. A. 2004. The perfect storm: A weather forecast. Speech given at American Association for the Advancement of Science Annual Meeting in Seattle, Wash. They argue that we need to address this crisis by recruiting more U.S. citizens to science, technology, engineering and mathematics (STEM) fields, and as part of this effort increase the participation of minorities. There are dissenters from the view that we have or will soon have such a general shortage: see Mervis, J. 2003. Down for the count. Science 300(5622):1070; Fechter, A., and M. S. Teitelbaum. 1997. A fresh approach to immigration. Issues in Science and Technology. 13 (3):28-32; National Research Council. 2000. Addressing the Nation's Changing Needs for Biomedical and Behavioral Scientists. Washington, D.C.: National Academy Press; for examples of analysts who do not believe there is, at least now, a shortage.

[21] U.S. Census Bureau, Projected Population of the U.S. by Race and Hispanic Origin: 2000 to 2050, http://www.census.gov/ipc/www/usinterimproj/natprojtab01a.pdf.

[22] National Science and Technology Council. 2000. Ensuring a Strong U.S. Scientific, Technical, and Engineering Workforce in the 21st Century, Washington, D.C.: Executive Office of the President of the United States, p. 4.

groups, therefore, are largely untapped populations that can help to remedy a significant and growing problem.

Regardless of the debate about the accuracy of future labor market projections, Fechter and Teitelbaum (1997) explain:

> Some policy issues may be independent of the current or projected state of the labor market. A notable example is underrepresented groups—women and members of underrepresented racial/ethnic groups—underrepresentation in part reflect barriers that prevent qualified individuals from these groups from pursuing scientific careers. Therefore, underrepresentation is an indicator of talent that is not exploited to its fullest potential. Such underutilization, which can exist simultaneously with situations of abundance, represents a cost to society as well as to the individuals in these groups. And policy formulation aimed at reducing this underrepresentation should not be totally based on market conditions.[23]

Addressing Underrepresentation

What are the roots of this problem with recruiting, retaining, and promoting minorities in science? There are no single answer and no single remedy. The preparation of students during their pre-K-12 years for science, technology, engineering, and mathematics (STEM) higher education and careers is certainly an important foundation that determines whether students will be able to meet the challenges of courses and careers in these areas. Many have argued that much work must be done to improve K-12 science and mathematics education in general, and for underrepresented groups in particular. Remedies at this level include improving teacher quality, introducing pedagogical methods that include inquiry-based learning, and implementing improved curricula that map to national science and mathematics education standards.[24]

Postsecondary education has many principles that provide guidance to institutions in their efforts to help minority students succeed regardless of field. Building Engineering and Science Talent (BEST)[25] recently outlined eight key design principles to expand minority participation in higher education:

1. Institutional leadership: commitment to inclusiveness across the campus community;
2. Targeted recruitment: investing in and executing a K-12 feeder system;
3. Engaged faculty: developing student talent as a valued activity among faculty;

---

[23] Fechter, A., and M. S. Teitelbaum. Spring 1997. A fresh approach to immigration. Issues in Science and Technology 13(3):28-32.

[24] National Research Council. 1999. Selecting Instructional Materials: A Guide for K-12 Science. Washington, D.C.: National Academy Press.

[25] Building Engineering and Science Talent (BEST). 2004. A Bridge for All: Higher Education Design Principles to Broaden Participation in Science, Technology, Engineering and Mathematics. San Diego, Calif.: BEST. See http://www.bestworkforce.com.

4. Personal attention: addressing, through mentoring and tutoring, the learning needs of each student;
5. Peer support: student interaction opportunities that build support across cohorts and allegiance to institution, discipline, and profession;
6. Enriched research experience: beyond-the-classroom, hands-on opportunities and summer internships;
7. Bridging to the next level: institutional relationships that help students and faculty to envision pathways to milestones and career development; and
8. Continuous evaluation: ongoing monitoring of process and outcomes that guide program adjustments to heighten impact.

BEST goes on to note that even with all of these design principles in place, the key role of socioeconomic status in determining success in higher education will require comprehensive financial assistance for low-income students.

For many of the children and young adults in underrepresented groups, the long years of schooling are daunting and the costs of this education (both direct costs and forgone income from delaying entry into the workforce) seem prohibitive. These, coupled with a lack of encouragement and expectation by their peers and some counselors that they can become successful, are just some of the barriers faced by minority and low-income students.

The availability of role models and mentors is of paramount importance. The ability to see and interact with individuals much like themselves who have "made it" thus becomes key for nurturing future generations of scientists. The lack of minority faculty and senior scientists translates to a lack of critical role models for minority trainees at these institutions. From an educational and professional development standpoint, inclusive promotion of science professions in our society will require that all segments of this society see role models for themselves—successful professionals who come from their backgrounds. This is particularly important for those groups that are underrepresented in the sciences.

The probable effects of improving professional development of underrepresented minority and disadvantaged individuals are not widely appreciated. Although minorities and disadvantaged individuals still experience racism and stereotypical prejudices in our society, many of the hurdles of professional development are also faced by nonminority individuals. For example, even though a higher percentage of minority trainees may cite a lack of a good mentor as a significant barrier, on a numerical basis more nonminority trainees are likely to experience the same shortfall since they outnumber the minority individuals in science severalfold. In general, many of the training and professional development barriers are accentuated among minority individuals, in part because they often come to the table feeling isolated, having fewer professional contacts, possibly fewer financial resources (e.g., for books and supplemental materials). This may be compounded if they are also surrounded by the doubts of others about their abilities, especially if any affirmative action has been in evidence. The latter remark is based on numerous open-ended comments received from minority trainees in the course of administering the trainee survey.

Assessing Program Outcomes

The study committee was charged with answering the general question, Do the NIH minority training and research programs work? To address this question, the committee undertook a thorough analysis of historic NIH program announcements for minority research training programs, in order to identify the stated goals of the programs. This analysis established that the goal of NIH minority research training programs is, and always has been, to increase the number of Ph.D.-level minority biomedical researchers. In no instance, however, was success in reaching this goal quantified among the program announcements. As a second step, the committee also considered the work of earlier phases of this study to determine additional benchmarks for program success. Phases 1 and 2 of the study recommend that evaluation of minority research training programs employ, as a metric for assessing program success, whether or not trainees had advanced to the "next step" in the science educational and career trajectory.[26]

The committee determined to apply each of these—increasing the number of minority Ph.D.-level biomedical researchers and advancing trainees to the next step—as metrics for assessing program success. Yet all but one member of the committee also believed that regardless of whether each trainee advances to the next step in his or her education, or becomes a Ph.D.-level researcher, the programs provide important and valuable training experiences for all participants that should be considered in assessing whether a program works. Given disparities in the educational opportunities available to trainees prior to enrollment in any of the NIH programs, it would be inappropriate to expect or demand that minority trainees, as a whole, have the same average rates of professional attainment and success as nonminority trainees. Indeed, the training programs exist because of the need to overcome this gap. An additional and appropriate standard for the evaluation of minority programs, therefore, is the "value added" that the program provides to all of its participants. This introduces its own set of measurement problems as outlined below, but it is a critical foundation of the committee's analysis and recommendations. Thus, the following principles bear upon any discussion of minority research training program success:

- More than one generation is needed to establish a research training pipeline that is both attractive to minorities and successful at producing large numbers of Ph.D.-level scientists.
- Building capacity and sustaining minority interest in science require the visible promotion of role models. Young people who see that others like them have

[26] Office of Research on Minority Health, National Institutes of Health. 1993. Assessment of NIH Minority Research/Training Programs: Phase 1. Bethesda, Md.: U.S. Department of Health and Human Services. Office of Research on Minority Health, National Institutes of Health. 1997. Assessment of NIH Minority Research/Training Programs: Phase 2. Bethesda, Md.: U.S. Department of Health and Human Services.

made it are more likely to believe that they can make it too. Role models in science may include teachers, professors, doctors, entrepreneurs, and others. Every role model in science counts toward building each group's capacity for sustaining science and ultimately producing biomedical research Ph.D.s.

- The research training pipeline is understandably leaky (see Figure 1-1). Some trainees will exit the pipeline, never to return, after completing a bachelor's degree in science, for example. Some of these may take a job in the biotech industry. Others may go on to practice medicine or become science writers. The committee believes these are all successful outcomes for underrepresented groups that do not yet have a strong and visible presence in biomedical science.
- The research pipeline is not always a straight line. Some will exit the pipeline but return some years later. Time taken to raise a family, care for a family member who is ill, gain valuable experience, or rescue personal and family finances is a manifestation of cultural values. This should be respected.
- Leakiness in the research training pipeline diminishes with each career stage progression. Trainees further commit as they progress through their training. Therefore, programs designed for those who are in early career stages should endorse a broad definition of success. Programs for trainees at later career stages may adopt more highly prescribed definitions of success.

Program Success Viewed from Three Perspectives

In summary, the committee decided to consider program outcomes in a broader context and the success of minority training programs from three complementary perspectives: (1) increasing the number of Ph.D.-level minority research scientists; (2) advancing minority trainees to the next step in their education; and (3) the value-added of scientific enrichment, in general. Figure 1 shows that there are a number of different outcomes for NIH training programs, depending on the specific segment of the training pipeline in question. For example, a bachelor's-level program is expected to result in more minority individuals who pursue graduate and/or professional education and/or enter technical research careers. A program for graduate trainees should result in an increase in the number of successful scientists, teachers, research administrators, and those individuals interested in science policy.

In addition to examining minority research training programs relative to these outcome metrics, the committee also identifies features of minority programs that have or have not been successful in helping individual students and faculty move a step forward toward productive careers as research scientists. It explores a variety of factors that contribute to minority trainee success, including the characteristics of individual participants and the academic institutions at which they received their NIH support.

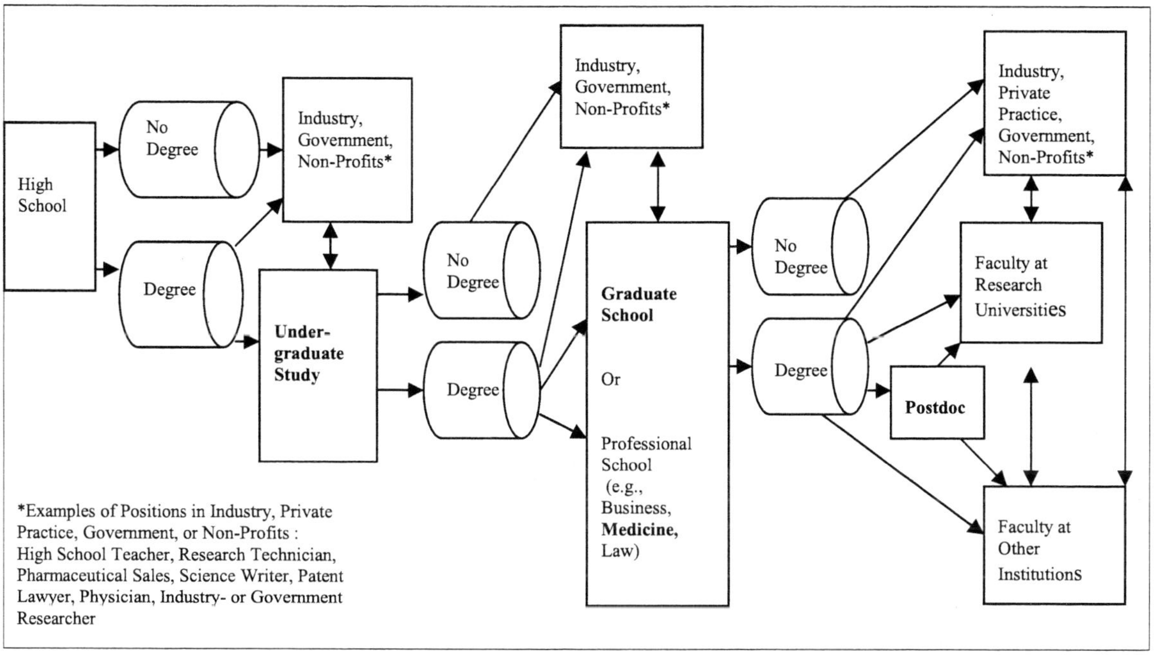

Figure 1-1 The NIH training pipeline.

Organization of the Report

This report contains seven chapters. This Introduction, is followed by Chapter 2, a discussion of methods. Chapters 3, 4, and 5 focus on, analyze, and assess research training programs geared toward each of the four research training career stages—undergraduate, graduate, postdoctoral, and junior faculty. Chapter 6 describes the perspectives of numerous NIH research training program administrators who were interviewed as part of the committee's data-collection process. Chapter 7 synthesizes findings across the four career stage levels and concludes with specific policy recommendations for NIH. These recommendations suggest ways to enhance NIH's minority research training programs and provide guidance to NIH for future data collection efforts designed to enhance the ability of evaluators to assess the success of these programs at regular intervals.

2

Methods

The committee was charged with addressing the study questions to the extent that they could be using available data from National Institutes of Health (NIH) supplemented by interviews with minority trainees and program administrators. This chapter describes the committee's approach to obtaining and analyzing these data. It describes the extent to which the committee was successful in obtaining useful data, problems encountered along the way, and instances in which requested data did not materialize. Indeed the committee was not able to obtain all of the data it wished to have in order to conduct its assessment. Although it met its charge to the extent feasible, the committee could not answer all of the research questions in as direct and complete a manner as it would have liked, which it now advocates for the future. The advice provided in this report, if it leads to corresponding action, will both improve the programs in the short run and facilitate more comprehensive study in the future. Indeed, extensive data-collection efforts, ongoing deliberations, and analyses allowed the committee to identify critical data elements that should be collected by NIH on a systematic basis in order to make future assessments of all NIH research training programs feasible.

Definitions

The committee began its work by defining key terms used in its work that appear throughout this report. Three terms—biomedical, trainee, and underrepresented minority—stood out as central to the task and, to be clear, they are defined here.

The term "biomedical" is used broadly in this report. It is intended to include the biological, behavioral, and clinical sciences. In certain instances, such as when drawing from official program descriptions, the phrase "biomedical and behavioral sciences" is used.

The term "trainee" is used throughout the report to describe any person engaged in higher education science studies or training, with the intention of building a career in the biomedical sciences. Trainees may be undergraduates, graduate students, postdoctoral fellows, or junior faculty. The term trainee is also used to describe an individual who is or was a participant in any NIH-supported research training program.

The term "underrepresented minority" is used narrowly, focusing on those groups that have suffered a historical pattern of discrimination in the United States and are also underrepresented in science. NIH has determined these groups to be African-Americans, Hispanics, Native-Americans and Alaskan Natives, and Pacific Islanders. For analytical purposes, however, the definition has been narrowed further. While Pacific Islanders are viewed by NIH as an underrepresented minority group, this study could not include them as such, because Pacific Islanders are aggregated with Asians across the data sets.

Universe of Programs

The NIH supports minority-targeted research training programs at all educational and career stages—high school, undergraduate, graduate, postdoctoral, and junior faculty. Determining which of these programs the committee would focus on, in order to meet its charge and to render the study manageable, involved several steps. First, the committee decided to focus exclusively on active extramural research training programs. Retired programs were not included, so that the assessment could focus on providing useful information about existing programs. Intramural minority programs were not included because NIH was conducting an internal assessment of those programs at the time this study began. The committee cannot speak to whatever results may have come from that effort. Second, the committee conducted a census of minority research training programs and established inclusion-exclusion criteria to determine the set of programs it would assess.

Conducting a census of extramural NIH minority research training programs was a staff-intensive effort. National Center on Minority Health and Health Disparities (NCMHD) staff provided the National Research Council (NRC) with a comprehensive list of minority research training programs that served as a starting point for the census. This list was updated in 2001with help from NCMHD staff, the NIH extramural training officer, 23 institute or center (IC) liaisons who were appointed by their IC directors to assist the study, and numerous health science administrators across the NIH campus. Although most ICs responded positively to the committee's request for program data, a few ICs did not respond and are therefore unaccounted for in terms of the minority programs they support. In addition, the committee searched through the NIH website for information on minority programs, focusing on specific IC websites, IC health disparity strategic plans, and NIH Guide program announcements. The resulting census listed 79 programs utilized to greater or lesser degrees by 17 of the 27 ICs at NIH.[27] Some of these programs are duplicated across ICs, such as the minority (F31) National Research Service Award (NRSA) predoctoral fellowship award, which is supported by most ICs. Nonetheless, each instance of a program was counted in the tally of total programs regardless of how many ICs participated.

[27] Specific census data are found in Appendix B.

TABLE 2-1 Reasons for Excluding Minority Training Programs from the Study

Exclusionary Rationale	Number of Programs
Program was less than 5 years old in 2001	11
Program was for capacity building at minority-serving institutions (MSIs)	8
Program was less than 5 years old in 2001 and was for capacity-building at MSIs	4
Program funded conferences and workshops	2
Program focused on senior faculty outside the scope of study	1
Program was originally included but random sampling for trainee interviews produced no respondents from this program	1
Program information provided by the IC was incomplete	3
Program was outside of study scope because its goal is not to increase number of minority Ph.D.s in biomedical research and program information provided by the IC was incomplete	2
Total Excluded Programs	32

While there are 79 targeted minority programs across the ICs (inclusive of duplicated mechanisms), this study examines 47 of them. The committee established inclusion-exclusion criteria for the minority research training programs in order to reach this smaller number and then reclassified them into 13 unique program categories (i.e., without duplications) based on career stage served and mechanism number.[28] In general, the minority research training programs included in the study were active extramural minority research training programs that had existed for five years or longer in 2001.

Table 2-1 lists the reasons programs were excluded and the number of programs excluded for each reason. In brief, programs were included or excluded for two reasons. First, a set of programs were included in the study because they met criteria that established a significant benefit to assessing them and excluded if they did not. The following criteria were used:

- Extramural programs in existence for at least five years by 2001 were included and those in existence for less than five years at that point in time were excluded. The five-year period ensures that for each included program a cohort of program graduates would have had enough time to advance to the next step in their training.
- Extramural programs were included if participation in the program had the significant potential for causing trainee progress through the pipeline. Thus, minority-targeted travel and conference awards were excluded from the study, because of their short-lived nature and the difficulty of ascribing causality or assessing their impact on trainees' progression through the pipeline.

[28] Mechanism number refers to the letter-number designation among programs (e.g., F31, T32, T35, R03).

Second, programs were included if they met criteria that indicated adequate information was available on the program and if there were accessible electronic data on trainees. These criteria were as follows:

- The NRC needed sufficient data on the programs to understand their goals and structures. For a set of programs, the ICs at NIH did not provide sufficient information to the NRC to allow the committee to understand these programs and determine whether they should be included, so they were excluded from the study.
- Accessible electronic data on the program would be necessary. Thus, programs focused on minority high school students, capacity-building awards (institutional awards made primarily to minority-serving institutions), and minority supplementary awards were excluded because information on the trainees in these programs was not available to the committee in electronic form.

In addition to determining which targeted programs to include, the committee identified programs that would provide for trainee comparison groups. These programs were those not targeted to a specific racial or ethnic group. To the extent possible, the nontargeted programs included in the study were matched closely with targeted programs, in terms of both their sponsoring institutes and the years during which the programs were offered. When this was not possible, the closest proxy was identified. However, there are situations in which a nontargeted comparison program does not exist, such as with all minority undergraduate training programs and the R03 Minority Dissertation Research Grant program. Table 2-2 lists the minority-targeted training programs that fall within the study parameters established by the committee and which were used to draw a sample of minority trainees. Nontargeted comparison programs are also listed in the table.

From the nontargeted programs, two comparison groups were identified, which are also indicated in Table 2-2. The first comparison group is comprised of minority trainees who were trained in a nontargeted program. The second comparison group consists of trainees who do not fall within the study's definition of underrepresented minority, hereafter referred to as "nonminority" trainees. For undergraduate trainees, there are no comparison groups because nontargeted undergraduate training programs do not exist.

Consequently, the committee examined seven clusters of trainees:

1. Undergraduate minority trainees in minority-targeted programs,
2. Graduate minority trainees in minority-targeted programs,
3. Graduate minority trainees in nontargeted programs,
4. Graduate nonminority trainees in nontargeted programs,
5. Postdoctoral/faculty minority trainees in minority-targeted programs,
6. Postdoctoral/faculty minority trainees in nontargeted programs, and
7. Postdoctoral/faculty nonminority trainees in nontargeted programs.

TABLE 2-2 Training Programs Examined in the Study

Training Level	Minorities in Targeted Programs	Minorities in Untargeted Programs	Nonminorities in Untargeted Programs
Undergraduates	(R25) Bridges to the Baccalaureate (T34) Undergraduate Student Training Academic Research (T34) Career Opportunities in Research		
Graduate trainees	(R25) Bridges to the Doctorate (R03) Dissertation Research Grant		
	(F31) NRSA Predoctoral Fellowship	(F31) NRSA Predoctoral Fellowship	(F31) NRSA Predoctoral Fellowship
	(T32) NRSA Institutional Research Training Grant	(T32) NRSA Institutional Research Training Grant	(T32) NRSA Institutional Research Training Grant
	(T35) NRSA Short-Term Institutional Research Training Grant	(T35) NRSA Short-Term Institutional Research Training Grant	(T35) NRSA Short-Term Institutional Research Training Grant
Postdoctoral or faculty	(T32) NRSA Institutional Research Training Grant	(T32) NRSA Institutional Research Training Grant	(T32) NRSA Institutional Research Training Grant
	(T35) NRSA Short-Term Institutional Training Grant	(T35) NRSA Short-Term Institutional Training Grant	(T35) NRSA Short-Term Institutional Training Grant
	(K01) Mentored Research Scientist Development (Post-doctoral)	(K01) Mentored Research Scientist Development (Postdoctoral)	(K01) Mentored Research Scientist Development (Postdoctoral)
	(K08) Mentored Clinical Scientist Development	(K08) Mentored Clinical Scientist Development	(K08) Mentored Clinical Scientist Development
	(K01) Mentored Research Scientist Development (Junior Faculty)	(K01) Mentored Research Scientist Development (Junior Faculty)	(K01) Mentored Research Scientist Development (Junior Faculty)

NOTE: NRSA = National Research Service Award

Approach to Data Collection

The study committee sought data that would allow it to answer the questions in its charge and provide evidence to support findings and recommendations about the NIH minority research training programs included in the assessment. The committee identified four types of data that could provide input to the study:

1. Existing data on science and engineering higher education and, more specifically, on NIH trainees in the biomedical sciences,
2. Computer assisted telephone interviews (CATIs) with trainees who were supported by these NIH research training programs,
3. Interviews with individuals who administer these programs at recipient colleges and universities; they are hereafter referred to as trainee "program administrators at recipient institutions" (PARIs), and
4. Interviews with NIH staff who administer these programs on behalf of their NIH institute or center; they are hereafter referred to as "program administrators at the ICs" (PAICs).

The committee decided to use all of these sources to the extent possible. The committee determined to mine existing data to the extent they were readily available in electronic data files. The committee proceeded to conduct simultaneous trainee, administrator, and staff interviews with the assistance of an NIH contractor.

Existing Data

Data Sources

The committee identified the following six extant data sources that could be used assess the education or research outcomes of persons who received training funds from NIH:

1. NIH Information for Management, Planning, Analysis, and Coordination (IMPAC) system. This file contains application and award information for many (but not all) extramural programs, including grants, contracts, and cooperative agreements. Grants and grantee data are extracted from the Statement of Appointment Form (PHS 2271); however, not all data elements can be reliably extracted and converted into electronic format.
2. NIH Trainee and Fellows File (TFF). This file contains data on all individuals who received training support from NIH and other Public Health Service agencies since these programs began in 1938. The file contains information on fellows (i.e., recipients of individual awards) from the IMPAC system and on trainees from the Trainee Appointment File (TAF). The TFF can be linked with data files such as the Doctorate Records File (DRF) and the Association of American Medical College's (AAMC's) Medical School Graduation Questionnaire.
3. NIH Computer Retrieval of Information on Scientific Projects (CRISP) collection. This file contains information on research projects and programs funded by the Department of Health and Human Services (DHHS) from 1972 to the present.

CRISP contains administrative data from IMPAC along with project abstracts and indexing terms.

4. Doctorate Records File (DRF). The DRF is a census of research doctorate recipients from U.S. universities since 1920. Data on individuals receiving doctorates prior to 1958 was collected retrospectively. Since 1958, DRF data has been collected through the Survey of Earned Doctorates (SED) which obtains data on the social, demographic, and educational characteristics of new Ph.D.s and their plans for the year following graduation.
5. AAMC's Medical School Graduation Questionnaire. This file is a census of graduates of American medical schools that has been collected since 1978. It contains demographic characteristics, assessments of clinical experiences, and data on graduate satisfaction with the medical school experience.
6. Prior assessments of minority-targeted programs conducted by ICs within NIH. The committee utilized four assessments of undergraduate programs—three by the National Institute of General Medical Sciences (NIGMS) and one by the National Institute of Mental Health (NIMH). In addition, the committee examined two assessments of graduate training programs both conducted by NIGMS.

The committee viewed the TFF as an especially rich data source. The TFF contains historic data on more than 400,000 trainees who at one time or another received NIH funding. This file includes records on undergraduates, graduate students, and postdoctoral trainees, both for short courses and for multiyear and multicenter program projects. Importantly, the TFF can link multiple numbers and types of awards for recipients. It captures the following data elements reliably: type of grant, identification (ID) or serial number, name, gender, Social Security number, address, date of birth, citizenship, race or ethnicity, dates of award, award amount, and degree sought. In addition, the TFF can be linked to the DRF and the AAMC Medical School Graduation Questionnaire.

Outcomes of Data Queries

Although these data sets had the potential for providing the committee with a wealth of data, in actuality, the data available to the committee were of limited value and utility. First, the committee learned that the level of item nonresponse was very high for many of the variables in the TFF, including data on race or ethnic origin. For example, before 1992, nearly 75 percent of persons who received predoctoral funding from NIH were not classified by race or ethic origin in the TFF. Since 1992, the nonresponse rate for data on race or ethnicity of predoctoral trainees has been reduced to 14 percent. Consequently, even if the committee were able to access TFF files, data from early years could not be used to classify the vast majority of trainees by race or ethnic origin. There was also a high nonresponse rate for a number of other variables including gender, Social Security number, date of birth, degree sought, and permanent address. Finally, four data elements included on the paper form had not been extracted and entered into the TFF or

IMPAC II files, including name of institution, address and phone number of institution, name of program director, and specialty boards.

Second, the committee learned early in its tenure that NIH interpreted the Privacy Act (P.L. 09-25-0112) as prohibiting the NRC study committee and staff from accessing unit record data from the TFF and any other database that contained individual trainee data because these data were deemed sensitive. Therefore, the committee was told that all data queries for trainee data, TFF data, and data linking TFF data to external data sources (e.g., the DRF) would necessarily be handled by an intermediary contractor designated by NIH. Although the committee understands and accepts the reason that NIH should and must protect the privacy of individual trainees, the requirement for an intermediary precluded some potentially fruitful avenues of study.

During the information-gathering phase of the study, the committee developed a series of queries and requests for tabulation of TFF data and from external sources data that can be linked to the TFF. The committee then submitted these requests to the NIH data contractor. Unfortunately this process was far more difficult, cumbersome, and time-consuming than anticipated. The free flow of data and information that had been sought either did not emerge or the deliverables did not meet the committee's specifications. In some cases they were not provided at all. Early in its deliberations, the committee submitted eight queries, designed to assist the committee in developing instrumentation and framing the directions of additional inquiry, as follows:

1. Provide aggregate tabulation of the racial or ethnic identity of the all persons who received initial predoctoral funding between 1970 and 1999 by year.
2. Identify targeted undergraduates who received NIH funding and match these persons with the file of persons who received initial predoctoral funding by year.
3. Match the targeted undergraduates with persons in the DRF and provide all DRF data.
4. Identify the participants in the comparison programs and link them to DRF data by year of degree.
5. Match targeted undergraduates who received NIH funding, with AAMC data on graduation from medical school by year of graduation.
6. Match the file of persons who received initial predoctoral funding between 1970 and 1999 with AAMC data on medical school graduates by year of graduation from medical school.
7. Match the participants in the six comparison programs with the AAMC medical school data by year of graduation from medical school.
8. Match all persons who received minority-targeted K01 awards between 1970 and 1999 by year with the DRF database a retrospective search and then prospectively match with the CRISP database to identify existence of R01 awards.

The committee did receive data on the ethnic identity of persons who received initial predoctoral funding between 1970 and 1999. However, because of the very high levels of missing ethnic-identity data, the committee was unable to use these data to assess whether NIH minority training and research programs work.

In addition, the committee obtained responses to five additional data requests:

1. DRF data for persons who received initial predoctoral funding between 1970 and 1999,
2. The number of undergraduate trainees who ever received NIH predoctoral funding,
3. DRF data for undergraduate trainees,
4. AAMC matched data for undergraduate trainees, and
5. Data linking K01 awards and the DRF.

The committee was disappointed with the results of the data queries. The DRF data on persons who received NIH predoctoral funding were interesting, but because the type and level of funding could not be identified, the results were of little value to the committee's task. The committee did find that there were 103,970 persons who received NIH predoctoral funding. Of these, 41,438 matched against the DRF. Unfortunately, the NIH contractor did not use an updated version of the DRF in responding to the query. The number of matches between NIH predoctoral funding and the DRF fell off rapidly beginning with 1993. This corresponds roughly with NIH's increase in developing funding vehicles that target minorities. Consequently, the committee found that the query did not contribute to its assessment.

The outdated DRF data also plagued the results of the query that sought to match minority undergraduates participating in minority-targeted programs. Nevertheless, the match of undergraduate trainees with NIH predoctoral funding was promising—out of 6,614 targeted undergraduates, 3,914 received NIH predoctoral funding. However, when they were matched against the DRF, only 277 had received a Ph.D. and only 164 had received an M.D. degree as indicated by AAMC data. The committee believes that these results are in doubt in light of the contractor's reliance on outdated DRF data.

Finally, the committee was puzzled by the data linking minority-targeted K01 awards made between 1970 and 1999 with the DRF. Only 575 matches were found, and only 288 of K01 award recipients were also in the DFR. The remaining 287 K01 awardees presumably were M.D.s. The K01 and R01 match was never made. Interestingly, according to the DRF, about two-thirds of the 287 Ph.D.s who received these minority-targeted K01 awards were white.

Following the completion of the four surveys, the committee developed a second series of nine data queries . This second series of queries was developed in order to clarify data issues generated by the four surveys of trainees.

1. Gender, citizenship, and ethnic origin of the 5, 371 trainees included in the sampling plan for the four surveys, classified by program.
2. Number of undergraduate trainees ever funded in seven defined programs and aggregated data on the gender, ethic identity, and citizenship by program and year.

3. Number of undergraduate trainees in the seven programs who ever received predoctoral funding, cross-classified by undergraduate program, predoctoral funding mechanism, and year of initial predoctoral funding.
4. Undergraduate trainees from the seven programs matched against the DRF and classified by undergraduate program and year of initial undergraduate funding.
5. Undergraduate trainees from the seven programs matched against AAMC data classified by undergraduate program and year of initial undergraduate funding.
6. Predoctoral funding recipients between 1970 and 1999, classified by funding mechanism, whether the program was minority-targeted, and year of initial funding.
7. Cross-classification of the listing above by gender and ethnic origin.
8. Initial predoctoral funding recipients between 1970 and 1999, classified by mechanism number (i.e., K01, F31, T32, etc.) and year, matched against the DRF including all DRF data.
9. Predoctoral funding recipients, classified by mechanism number and year, matched against AAMC data including data on age at graduation, gender, ethnic origin, years between matriculation and graduation, and type of medical program.

At the time this report went into peer review, the committee had received answers to none of these queries because of the NIH sponsor's considerable delay in processing contract paperwork that could have allowed the NIH data contractor to run the queries. As a result, some analyses of trainee characteristics and program outcomes that would have been very informative to the study were not completed and other analyses had to be tailored to the data provided rather than in response to the committee's needs. For example, the TFF to DRF match was not provided in the manner specified by the committee and efforts to work with the NIH contractor to create a data set that could be used by the committee did not materialize. Thus, the committee had to forego the use of outcomes data that might have provided more insight about individual and program success.

The committee believes that more and better analyses of extant data would likely have emerged if the TFF and other trainee data could have been accessed directly or if the NIH data could have been supplied directly to the committee, bypassing a third-party contractor. The pattern of request and response between the committee and the NIH data contractor was slow and cumbersome. The ability to analyze data and tailor new queries based on that analysis was absent. The duration between a data request and the response from the NIH data contractor was unnecessarily long, sometimes taking many months for a single request. Consequently, the committee was unable to analyze much of the data that it had planned to use. The committee believes that a rich data resource, that could serve the NIH well in assessing the state of training and research of minorities, lies fallow.

Trainee Interviews

The committee concluded that direct input from trainees would provide a rich source of information for assessing the value of minority training programs to individual participants and the features of these programs that facilitate trainee success. After considering alternative methods of data collection, the committee decided that trainees from each career stage (i.e., undergraduate, graduate, postdoctoral, and junior faculty) would be contacted through a CATI protocol. However, the protocol was complicated by the fact that experiences, attitudes, and outcomes for each career stage would be divergent, thus different questions and response patterns were required. The committee therefore elected to prepare four distinct CATI instruments, each of which was tailored to a specific career stage. The committee also determined that the study would include only trainees whose initial year of funding fell between 1970 and 1999; there were no minority-targeted programs prior to 1970. Trainees whose funding began after 1999 were not included because the committee believes it is necessary for at least five years to elapse from the time of initial funding in order to assess progress.

CATI Instruments

The committee identified the process and outcome variables it should examine as it assessed the success of NIH minority training programs. Because of the different educational levels of the four cohorts of trainees, the committee concluded that the outcome variables should be consistent with the career stage of trainees at the time he or she was funded by one of the programs under study. For example, trainees selected to participate in the interview from the undergraduate strata were asked to recount their experiences while they were undergraduates, regardless of whether they had subsequently been funded for training at the graduate or postdoctoral levels. The 10 categories of questions included in the CATI instruments are listed below:

1. Trainee demographics,
2. Educational expectations,
3. Current educational status,
4. Plans immediately following degree completion,
5. Expectations of program participation,
6. Career goals,
7. Sources of financial support,
8. Research and laboratory experience,
9. Experience with mentor and/or laboratory principal investigator, and
10. Overall assessment of the training program.

The CATI instrument developed for graduate trainees can be found in Appendix C. The other three CATI questionnaires, although similar to the graduate trainee questionnaire have important distinctions. These questionnaires can be found on the National Academies web site at http://www7.nationalacademies.org/BHEW/NIH Minority Codebook.pdf.

TABLE 2-3 Number of Trainees in Program Universe, 1970-1999

Training Level	Minorities in Targeted Programs	Minorities in Untargeted Programs	Nonminorities in Untargeted Programs	Race Unknown in Untargeted Programs	Total Number of Trainees
Undergraduate trainees	6,614	n/a	n/a	n/a	6,614
Graduate trainees	4,115	856	6,364	5,145	16,480
Postdoctoral or faculty	247	738	7,905	5,487	14,377
Total trainees	10,976	1,594	14,269	10,632	37,471

NOTE: n/a = not applicable.

Trainee Universe, Sample, and Response

Building on the census of minority-targeted programs conducted earlier, the committee, assisted by the NIH contractor, constructed a census of the trainee universe. What might have been a straightforward task, if NIH data sets had the right variables, turned out to be extremely time-consuming as the TFF file does not indicate whether a trainee is in a minority-targeted or nontargeted program. Consequently, the only way that this information could be obtained for each trainee was through a time-intensive process that began with the NIH data contractor providing lists of grant numbers for each program and time period by IC. These lists of grant numbers were then distributed to the IC representatives who used "in-house" databases at their disposal to determine which of the grant numbers pertained to minority-targeted awards. This strategy was ultimately successful, but it took months and required much follow up with IC representatives. The trainee universe was 37,471, as shown in Table 2-3.

Once the universe had been determined, the committee established a trainee sampling plan and derived the trainee sample in collaboration with the NIH data contractor. The sampling plan designed by the committee oversampled programs with low numbers of trainees in order to increase their representation among trainee interviews. In the case of very small programs, the entire trainee population was used and every attempt was made to contact these trainees. The total trainee sample size was 5,371. As a target for interview completion, the committee selected a cell size of 100 trainees for each of the 10 combinations of trainee level and program focus as shown in Table 2-3 to ensure adequate power to demonstrate important differences.

Trainee Interview Protocol

The NIH data contractor identified 12 interviewers and supervisors experienced in conducting government-sponsored survey research to assist this study. Each received training specific to this study that addressed the following issues: administration of the trainee CATI protocol, respondent location activities and procedures, the purpose and design of the trainee protocol and its design, relevant characteristics of the sample population, data collection procedures, and an item-by-item review of the four survey instruments. The strategies used to locate trainee respondents are described below:

1. Obtain trainee-identification data consisting of name and Social Security number for each trainee in the sample (n = 5,371).
2. Match these identification data against the data files of two credit bureaus (Experian and Accurint) to obtain address and telephone number for all trainees in the sample.
3. Randomly select and call trainees from each career stage, minority-targeted or non-targeted program category, and minority status, until a quota of 100 completed interviews per cell was achieved.

In total, 5,371 trainees were matched against the Experian and Accurint databases. Ovcr two-thirds of these queries (n = 3,628) produced neither an address nor a telephone number. For the remainder of the trainee sample (n = 1,743), letters of introduction signed by the NIH director were mailed to the addresses obtained from these searches. The introductory letter explained the purpose and importance of the study, encouraged sampled individuals to participate, and invited them to provide updated contact information by returning a prepaid postcard to the NIH data contractor. The CATI sample file was updated with telephone information obtained from returned postcards. In addition, a proprietary contact information management system was used to locate individuals for whom no telephone number or an incorrect number was initially obtained. The system includes data gathered from the U.S. Postal Change of Address database. These efforts were necessary because of initial difficulties in locating individuals who may have dropped out of school, graduated many years ago, left the field, or been otherwise difficult to find.

Interviews were conducted between February 11 and May 10, 2004. The data collection protocol followed by interviewers is summarized below.

- Attempts were made to contact trainees at both home and work telephone numbers as these became available.
- Attempts were made between the hours of 9 a.m. and 9 p.m. local (trainee) time.
- No maximum number of attempted contacts was set for any trainee. The median number of attempts required to complete an interview was between four and five calls; however, up to 70 calls were made to a few trainees. A minimum of nine attempts was made on every verified telephone number in order to complete an interview with a respondent at that number, with the following exceptions:

  - — Some sample records in subgroups with high numbers of completed responses received fewer attempts due to the decision to concentrate on difficult subgroups.
  - — Respondents requesting a set appointment for an interview might be contacted fewer than nine times to comply with their request.
  - — Respondents located very late in the interviewing period (i.e., fewer than nine days left) received fewer attempts.
- No more than one attempt per day was made to contact any individual unless specifically requested by the trainee.
- Trainees who stated explicitly that they did not want to participate in the study were not contacted again. Trainees who were reluctant to participate were contacted subsequently until they gave an explicit refusal or the interview was otherwise resolved. Those identified as "resistant" respondents were contacted less frequently. Despite assurances from the NIH data contractor that all CATI operators were proficient and skillful in conducting CATI interviews, at least one interviewer had difficulty reading and correctly pronouncing the terms used in the survey. NRC staff were monitoring the first few calls when this happened and witnessed the frustration of a trainee respondent, who was a busy M.D., when the interviewer could not read or correctly pronounce essential elements of the survey. The respondent, in this case, nearly hung-up on her.

Interview Outcomes

Table 2-4 shows the distribution of the sample size and various sampling outcomes by trainee level. The outcomes for the CATI process can be summarized as follows:

- Unfortunately, the first strategy for locating trainee respondents did not prove to be effective. In total, 5,371 trainees were matched against the Experian and Accurint databases. More than two-thirds of these queries (n = 3,628) produced neither an address nor a telephone number.
- Of the 1,743 trainees for whom telephone and address information was obtained, 792, or 45 percent, were never contacted despite repeated attempts.
- Of the 951 persons contacted, 21 failed the screener (wrong person) and were dropped from the sampling frame, 141 trainees refused to participate in the interview, and 50 did not complete the interview.
- The final sample of 739 completed interviews included 83 trainees who were funded as undergraduates, 328 trainees funded as graduate trainees, and 328 trainees funded after receiving an M.D. or a Ph.D.

TABLE 2-4 Number in Sample Size and Sampling Outcomes for NIH Minority Research and Training Survey by Trainee Level

Trainee Level	Total in Sample	Number with Phone or Address Data	Number Contacted	Failed Screener	Refused or Terminated Interview	Completed Interview
Undergraduate	1,006	248	122	4	35	83
Graduate	2,464	759	415	9	78	328
Postdoctoral or junior faculty	1,901	736	414	8	78	328
Total	5,371	1,743	951	21	191	739

The committee is disappointed with these outcomes, because the percentage of trainees for whom no contact information could be obtained is sufficiently large that a sampling bias has been introduced and the external validity of the survey has been challenged. Given this, the committee determined the following:

- The sampling bias was sufficiently serious that the survey data could not be used in an explicitly quantitative manner in this report.
- The 739 completed interviews provided sufficient information to allow the data to be assessed, however, and used in a qualitative manner. Thus, data are reported using nonspecific terms such as "a majority of respondents said" or "a minority of respondents said." Such phrases should not be equated with statistical significance.
- The 739 completed interviews provided a wealth of information through a series of open-ended responses, eliciting trainee opinions about the best and worst features of their programs, suggestions for changes to the programs, and a variety of experiences with them. The committee believes that this information was important and useful and, therefore, drew on this information to describe and assess the programs and their value to participants.

Program Administrator Interviews

The committee concluded that direct input from training program administrators at recipient institutions (PARI) and program administrators at NIH institutes and centers (PAIC) would be vital and necessary to the evaluation of these programs. After consideration of alternative methods of data collection, the committee decided that both administrator cohorts would be contacted through an unstructured, ethnographic interview process—by telephone for PARIs and in person for PAICs. The flexibility inherent in ethnographic interviewing was expected to enable the interviewer to quickly target relevant topic areas and probe for information germane to the study charge. All interviews were conducted by NIH data contractor staff who are specially trained in ethnographic interviewing procedures.

Interview Process

The committee developed interview schedules for the ethnographic interviews of PARIs and PAICs that pose questions in five broad domains:

1. History of the program and its role within the host institution.
2. Processes to identify and recruit trainees.
3. Trainee experiences with the program.
4. Administrative program issues.
5. Program evaluations or assessments.

As was the case with the trainee CATI interviews, these interview schedules were tailored to their audiences. The two interview schedules provided a way to assess these five important domains from two different vantage points—that of the training programs themselves and that of the NIH ICs.

The NIH data contractor conducted a pretest of these instruments consisting of three interviews with training program administrators and IC representatives. The pretest resulted in changes that were incorporated into the ethnographic instruments and approved by the committee. Copies of these ethnographic interview guides used for the unstructured interviews are presented in Appendix D.

The committee coordinated the programs used for the trainee sample with those used for the sample of training program administrators, so that there would be three triangulated sources of information for each program—trainees, PARIs, and PAICs.

For the PARI interviews, a sample of recipient institutions (e.g., universities, colleges) was randomly selected from the population of eligible institutions using a selection protocol that identified institutions as either high producers or low producers of underrepresented minority degrees The 47 PARI interviews were distributed among programs as follows:

- 18 targeted undergraduate programs.
- 18 targeted graduate or postdoctoral programs.
- 6 untargeted graduate or postdoctoral programs.
- 1 targeted postdoctoral or junior faculty program.
- 4 targeted institutional awards that covered all levels.

PAIC interviews were identified through random selection and include the following:

- 2 targeted undergraduate programs.
- 12 targeted graduate or postdoctoral programs.
- 4 targeted postdoctoral or junior faculty programs.
- 2 untargeted postdoctoral or junior faculty programs.
- 2 institutional awards that covered all levels.

Interview Outcomes

A total of 47 PARI and 22 PAIC interviews were completed during the winter and spring of 2004. The interviews were transcribed and prepared as structured text files. No quantitative analyses of these interviews were intended. Staff reviewed these files and provided the committee with key observations that were used to inform its analyses at the undergraduate, graduate, postdoctoral, and junior faculty levels as well as the chapter on perspectives of NIH administrators.

Throughout both interview processes, however, interviewers did not always adhere to the study protocol. This was especially true for the PAIC interviews. In some instances, interviewees were told to speak about minority training programs in general, rather than focusing on a specific program or set of programs as the protocol dictated. Despite the committee's request that interviewers review each transcript carefully before transmittal to the committee, it appears that this was also not done with diligence. Thus, despite having taped these many hour-long conversations, the interviews were frequently inaudible and not interpretable by the committee. As a result, potentially valuable information was lost. Unfortunately, time and budgetary constraints prohibited the recovery of these lost data.

3

Undergraduate Programs

Undergraduates in the biological and behavioral sciences have a variety of educational and career goals. Some focus on enjoying a liberal arts education, while others focus on their career aspirations. Even when students take similar courses and have similar interests, they may not share the same career objectives. Substantial numbers seek employment directly after receiving a bachelor's degree. For those who have aspirations for further education, students who major in the biological or behavioral sciences contemplate a clinical career as often as a research career.

For those students who plan a research career, key learning experiences at the undergraduate level might include establishing a foundation for more targeted study in a range of scientific fields at the graduate level; learning about the scientific process and research ethics; and hands-on research experience that includes an in-depth examination of some topic. Programs in these fields may also include work in statistics, informatics, and communication as key elements of a foundation of knowledge for work in the discipline.

Many undergraduates face a variety of challenges. Some students struggle academically. Many are searching for direction in education, careers, and life. Students change majors and a high percentage transfer from one institution to another. Students may have personal or family challenges or issues related to financing their educations that affect how quickly or even whether they complete a course of study.

Undergraduate trainees from underrepresented minority populations face all of these challenges and more. Because, on average, they come from lower-income families, they may face financial and family challenges more acutely. Because they are minorities, they may experience barriers or challenges that are specific to their racial or ethnic group. They may have poorer primary and secondary schooling, less preparation and knowledge of higher education, and inadequate access to and financial support for postsecondary education. They may also face challenges related to the quality of the research infrastructure at institutions that serve minority populations and whether nonminority faculty take minority students as seriously as they do nonminority students.

In order to increase the participation and success of underrepresented minorities, the National Institutes of Health (NIH) has established programs that provide the kinds of support needed to address the challenges that minority undergraduates face and prepare them for graduate work in these fields. These programs provide financial support, classes that include exposure to the foundation of knowledge in their field, hands-on research experience, and mentoring. By selecting bright students who have shown an aptitude and interest in scientific fields and by providing them these kinds of support, NIH intends to increase the pool of minority undergraduates that could continue on to graduate school.

Undergraduate Programs for Underrepresented Minorities

The NIH supports undergraduate education in the biomedical and mental health-related behavioral sciences for underrepresented minorities most directly through a number of programs offered by the National Institute of General Medical Sciences (NIGMS) and the National Institute of Mental Health (NIMH). The study committee decided to focus on three of these programs. The first is the R25 Bridges to the Baccalaureate program; it focuses on the preparation of students in the biomedical or behavioral sciences at two-year institutions, such as community or tribal colleges, in order to prepare them for transfer to a four-year institution. The other two programs, T34 U*STAR and T34 COR, focus on students in their third and fourth years of undergraduate study. All three programs provide only institutional awards and the institutions eligible for these awards are historically black colleges and universities (HBCUs), Hispanic-serving institutions (HSIs), or tribal colleges or universities. (The National Institute of Environmental Health Sciences offers some short-term training for minority undergraduates using the T35 mechanism, but this program is discussed in chapters 4 and 5 since the majority of T35 participants are graduate trainees, medical students, and postdoctoral scholars).

(R25) Bridges to the Baccalaureate

The NIGMS designed the R25 Bridges to the Baccalaureate program, established in 1992, "to make available to the biomedical research enterprise and the nation the intellectual talents of an increasing number of underrepresented minorities."[29] It does so through undergraduate and graduate components that provide support to institutions to help students make transitions at critical stages in their development as scientists. At the undergraduate level, the R25 Bridges to the Baccalaureate program focuses on building partnerships between community or tribal colleges and four-year baccalaureate institutions, with the goal of providing a nearly seamless transition for underrepresented minority students at community or tribal colleges who are interested in careers in biomedical research. It does so by improving the skills and opportunities of these students through coursework and hands-on research experience. The program also guides

---

[29] National Institutes of General Medical Sciences, National Institutes of Health. 1992. Initiative for Minority Students: Bridges to the Baccalaureate (Program announcement, PAR-02-084). See http://grants2.nih.gov/grants/guide/pa-files/PAR-02-084.

these students through mentoring and career guidance and supports them financially so that they may focus their energies on the program and more fully realize its benefits. Ideally, with skills, interest, motivation, guidance, and support, a student may transfer to a four-year institution where a baccalaureate may be earned with support from the four-year institution. After that point, the student will be positioned to pursue further work in the field at the graduate level.

(T34) Undergraduate Student Training in Academic Research Program (U*STAR)

The Minority Access to Research Careers (MARC) program initiated an Honors Undergraduate Research Training program in 1977 to improve the preparation of an increasing number of underrepresented minority students in their junior and senior years for graduate training in the biomedical sciences. In 1996 it replaced the program with the T34 U*STAR program, which shares the same goals but provides institutions with both greater flexibility and the responsibility for self-evaluation. The T34 U*STAR program makes awards to four-year minority-serving institutions. These institutions select trainees who are qualified undergraduate honors students majoring in the sciences. Eligible trainees must demonstrate interest in a biomedical research career and an intention to pursue graduate education leading to a Ph.D., M.D.-Ph.D., or other professional degree combined with a Ph.D. T34 U*STAR also supports program activities designed to improve the overall research training environment for MARC and pre-MARC (freshman and sophomore) students and for science faculty development at MARC-supported institutions.

(T34) Career Opportunities in Research Education and Training (COR)

The T34 COR Honors Undergraduate Research Training Grant program of the NIMH is intended to strengthen research and research training experiences for underrepresented minorities in scientific disciplines related to mental health. NIMH has made awards to institutions since 1979 with the goal of increasing the number of well-prepared students from these institutions who can compete successfully for entry into mental health research career training programs. An applicant institution must propose a two-year T34 COR Honors undergraduate program for which six to ten highly talented third- and fourth-year undergraduate students will be selected. Students will be provided with special research training experiences designed to improve their qualifications for entry into advanced research career training programs leading to doctoral-level or M.D. research career degrees.

Focus of the Assessment

To conduct its assessment of these undergraduate programs, the study committee relied on the following:

1. Analysis of key documents related to these programs, including a review of the R25 Bridges to the Baccalaureate program conducted by an NIGMS working group in 1999; two prior evaluations (1985, 1995) of the MARC Honors Undergraduate Research Training program, which was replaced by the T34 U*STAR program in 1996; and NIMH staff and working group reports on racial or ethnic diversity in mental health research careers conducted in 2001.
2. Interviews by the NIH data contractor of three R25 Bridges to the Baccalaureate and seven T34 U*STAR campus program administrators. (The NIH data contractor did not conduct interviews with T34 COR program administrators.)
3. Interview data from the NIH data contractor, which conducted a computer-assisted telephone interview (CATI) survey of a sample of R25 Bridges, T34 U*STAR, and T34 COR trainees who were participants in one of these programs prior to 2000. These interviews are described in greater detail below.

Trainee Interview Data

Under contract with the National Center for Minority Health and Health Disparities (NCMHD), the NIH data contractor conducted the telephone interviews described in the third item above, drawing from a sample of trainees supported by the three undergraduate programs.

These interviews addressed trainee demographics; program characteristics; the relationships trainees had with principal investigators (PIs), mentors, and laboratory or research group members; and trainee educational and career expectations and outcomes. They also provided trainees with an opportunity to discuss what they perceived to be the strengths of the programs and to suggest program improvements. The NIH data contractor identified a universe 6,614 R25 Bridges, T34 U*STAR, and T34 COR trainees who met the committee's inclusion criteria. A total of 100 interviews with individuals in this pool were anticipated. The NIH data contractor identified a pool of trainees evenly distributed across the three programs to serve as a sampling frame for the CATI interviews (see Table 3-1). Because the difficulty of identifying and interviewing trainees reduced response rates, the pool was expanded to a total of 1,006 trainees; of these, 83 were actually interviewed.

TABLE 3-1 Undergraduate Trainee Universe, Survey Pool, and Interviews

Program	No. of Trainees In Universe	No. of Trainees in Sample[a]	No. of Trainees Interviewed
R25 Bridges to the Baccalaureate	4,027	340	31
T34 U*STAR	1,576	333	19
T34 COR	1,011	333	33
Total	6,614	1,006	83

[a]Number of trainees selected for interview

The 83 completed trainee interviews represent a very small number within the universe; moreover, contact information for most individuals in the pool was unobtainable. Therefore, there is a high likelihood of bias in the survey results. In addition, some evidence suggests that trainees interviewed for the committee's survey were generally likely to be among the more "successful" undergraduate program participants. For example, among those who participated in the R25 Bridges to the Baccalaureate program, survey respondents were more likely to have transferred to a four-year institution and completed a bachelor's degree than program participants in general. In addition, large numbers of respondents had at least one family member with a bachelor's or graduate degree. As a result, the data that from these interviews may not reflect the responses that would have been obtained had the respondents been more representative of the larger universe of program participants. Nevertheless, the data are instructive in a general way and have been used qualitatively to illuminate issues of importance in this report. For example, respondent data are reported using a variety of nonspecific phrases such as "nearly all reported," "a majority of respondents said," "a minority of respondents said," "more likely," and "less likely." Such phrases should not be equated with statistical significance.

(R25) Bridges to the Baccalaureate Program

The R25 Bridges to the Baccalaureate program seeks to assist students in their freshman and sophomore years at community or tribal colleges in moving to programs in the biological or behavioral sciences at four-year institutions. These students differ, therefore, from those in the other two programs at the undergraduate level, T34 U*STAR and T34 COR, which focus on upperclassmen in four-year institutions and prepare them for graduate study in the biological or behavioral sciences.

The R25 Bridges program funds institutional partnerships that involve at least two colleges or universities. The community or tribal college must offer the associate degree as the only undergraduate degree in the sciences within the participating departments and must have a significant enrollment of underrepresented minority students. The partnership may involve a consortium of several institutions and it may include several institutions within a single state system.

Collaborative agreements between the institutions involved in a particular grant are designed to fit local needs and meet local goals. Program elements may include enriching the curriculum at the two-year institution, enabling students from the two-year institution to take courses at the baccalaureate college, developing courses at the two-year college taught jointly by faculty of both institutions, and visiting lectureships at the two-year college by science faculty from the baccalaureate institution. The program typically provides laboratory research experiences at the baccalaureate or other research institution, mentoring, and academic counseling. Programs are structured in different ways and housed in different departments across institutions. One campus administrator interviewed has a program housed in the biology department; another has a joint program of the chemistry and biology departments; and a third said the program was not department-based but, rather, centered in a support program called "science educational equity."

Trainee Characteristics

Most respondents to the trainee interviews who were in the R25 Bridges to the Baccalaureate program were women. Nearly one-half were African American and almost one-quarter were Hispanic, while the rest were Native American, Alaskan Native, Pacific Islander, white, "other," or did not answer the question. A substantial minority of R25 Bridges respondents said they were married or in a long-term relationship. Moreover, R25 Bridges respondents were much more likely than the others to have dependents, with almost one-third reporting them.

R25 Bridges respondents were as likely as their T34 U*STAR and T34 COR counterparts to say they expected the program to provide mentoring. They were only slightly less likely to say they expected to increase their research skills or obtain financial support from the program. R25 Bridges respondents were as likely as the others to say that they expected the program to help them decide whether they were cut out for research and whether to go on to a graduate program or a medical school. Participants in the R25 Bridges program had expectations for themselves and their programs that differed from those in the T34 U*STAR and T34 COR programs—students who are upperclassmen and may already have focused on graduate school. They were substantially less likely to say they expected the program to increase their chances for admission to a graduate program or to medical school.

Indeed, R25 Bridges program respondents reported lower expectations for their highest degree than was reported by participants of the T34 U*STAR and T34 COR programs. R25 Bridges respondents were more likely to report their highest degree expected as A.A. or A.S., B.A. or B.S., or master's degrees and were less likely to report the Ph.D. or M.D. Perhaps because they were still in the first two years of their undergraduate education, R25 Bridges respondents were also far more likely than T34 U*STAR and T34 COR respondents to indicate that they would work or complete a bachelor's degree as their expected immediate next step after completing their program. R25 Bridges respondents were more likely than T34 U*STAR and T34 COR respondents to report that when they were in their program they considered career options other than research. Among R25 Bridges respondents, a majority said they considered working in the health professions and almost one-half said they considered practicing medicine.

The "ideal" students for the R25 Bridges program have several qualities, according to campus administrators who were interviewed. They have good academic track records, aptitude and passion for science, and desire to pursue a career in biomedical science. One campus administrator said an ideal candidate "would be a student who has an interest in one of the natural sciences and the desire to go on for a baccalaureate and perhaps a further degree." Furthermore, students accepted into the program should be "highly motivated" and have "good follow-through."

Other comments by program administrators suggest that, in reality, many students need to be motivated and to increase their confidence and that they still need key skills to help them through the educational process. One administrator said the successful candidate for the program is someone who goes on to earn an M.S. degree. Another administrator cited a person who is now in a Ph.D. program. This trainee "was 'plucked' off the campus sidewalk and given intense mentoring and personal coaching, which raised her self-esteem considerably. She was thereby 'converted' to science . . . by learning to believe in herself." This administrator also said that program strategies should focus on growing rather than harvesting talent. That is, a program should not simply look for talent that exists but, rather, the program should identify potential and work to elicit a positive result from students by working with and nurturing them mentally. Another campus program administrator related that his program goals included assisting students "with the transition [to a four-year institution], by improving time management and study skills."

The reality for most students in the R25 Bridges program seems to be far from the "ideal." Although administrators would like students who are motivated, many community or tribal college students are still sorting out their career goals, may not yet fully understand what a research career entails, and may lack the confidence necessary to embark on a research career. In addition, when asked to describe an unsuccessful trainee, one administrator said "numerous trainees who have difficult personal issues have dropped [from the program]." Two administrators noted that two interrelated challenges facing trainees in the program are economic and family issues (e.g., spouses, children).

There are differences of opinion about how to deal with these kinds of personal issues. One way is to simply avoid them by selecting individuals who are not likely to have them. One program administrator described looking for students who "hopefully would not have gotten into a situation where they have taken on a lot of responsibilities (family, kids) and could survive with work study funds." Another way is to admit these students but invest time and energy in them. Another administrator said that if you want success in these programs "you have to be proactive in their [the students'] lives." Such responses raise the question of how much support any program can give to students facing these types of serious challenges.

Success in the program is the result of a variety of factors. The background, circumstances, and motivation that students bring to the program are critical. However, once students are in the program, providing them with a research experience, guidance and counseling, and a sense of how one's education and career unfold after the program is also critical. Many minority students come into the Bridges program knowing little about biomedical research as a career option. Those with the high grades necessary for graduate training are usually headed for medical school. Hence the argument is that interest in research careers must be "grown" before it can ever be harvested.

Program Recruitment

Campus administrators at two- and four-year institutions use a variety of techniques to make information available about their programs. They post professional-style posters, hand out brochures on campus, visit science classrooms at participating community college(s), and identify potential program participants by talking with faculty and others. One campus administrator also visits local high schools to talk with school counselors who are asked to identify students with interests in the biological sciences who, for financial reasons, were planning to attend community college.

Visiting science classrooms in the community college to promote the program is a particularly key recruitment strategy noted by all of the campus administrators interviewed. This strategy is useful in getting the message out in an efficient manner to a large number of students who could be interested in biomedical or behavioral research. Although this strategy is successful in interesting students, an acknowledged downside is that it will miss students who are not in class when the program is being promoted or discussed. Thus, it must be supplemented by other techniques.

Despite these efforts by program staff, when asked what they would recommend as an improvement to the program, a small number of R25 Bridges trainees suggested that the program could be better advertised. One trainee recommended doing a better job of making the program known to everyone. "I just found out about it by chance," the trainee said, "right place, right time." Another suggested the program get more funding "to promote it more in different ways so people know about it." The respondent went on to suggest that the program then also do a better job of screening applicants for participation in the program. Another recommended extending the program to other campuses, at both the community or tribal college and the baccalaureate levels.

Programs do tend to target their recruitment efforts, which may be a source of the perception among trainees that a program is not as widely advertised as it might be. One campus administrator made an extra effort to recruit certain students who may be particularly receptive to the idea of participating in the R25 Bridges program. These students include, for example, those planning to focus on the health professions, because they have the potential to become interested in a career in biomedical science. Recruitment of these students involves going to the core science classes that they are required to take and providing them with information about program and career options.

Perhaps as a result of these targeted recruitment efforts, however, respondents to the trainee interviews who were in the R25 Bridges program were more likely than their counterparts in T34 U*STAR and T34 COR to report that when they were in their program they considered career options other than research. Among those respondents to the trainee survey who were in the R25 Bridges program, for example, a majority indicated that they considered working in the health professions as a career option, compared to a minority of respondents in the T34 U*STAR and T34 COR programs.

This finding is not at all surprising, given that most minority families are not aware of biomedical research as a career option for their children. Since the number of minority biomedical researchers is so small to begin with, few minority middle and high school students ever make the acquaintance of persons working in biomedical research. It simply is not on their radar, but a career in medicine certainly is. In many instances the medical doctor is an icon of doctoral-level achievement within minority communities. This is why the most promising pool of untapped minority talent at both the community college and the four-year university levels is in the premedical sector. This is where minorities who are good at science often end up.

Funding

R25 Bridges students were generally like other undergraduates in NIH minority programs in terms of their financial support during their program. They were as likely as T34 U*STAR and T34 COR respondents to report having no other financial support than that provided by the program while they were in it, and they just as frequently relied on loans. However, there were areas in which their patterns of support differed from those of upperclassmen. R25 Bridges respondents were as likely as T34 U*STAR but more likely than T34 COR respondents to say that they relied on spousal or family support. They were more likely than respondents in T34 U*STAR or T34 COR programs to rely on wages or salary during the program. R25 Bridges students were less likely to have a scholarship but more likely to have a government grant during the program.

Research Experience

When asked what the best features of the program were, a majority of respondents said the research experience. Many of the respondents noted, moreover, the hands-on nature of the experience. As one respondent put it when asked the best feature of the program, "the ability to go into the lab and do the work." A very large majority of R25 Bridges respondents reported having daily or weekly contact with their laboratory or research group, typically 4-10 people and typically including many minority students. In terms of the influence of laboratory or research groups over their careers, however, respondents were spread evenly across a spectrum from a lot to none. R25 Bridges respondents were most likely to say the influence was "neutral." PIs or lab heads were generally more influential in students' education and careers than were their laboratory mates.

Mentoring

Indeed, R25 Bridges trainees who responded to our survey reported that overall they had very good relationships with their program PIs, but a sizable fraction (more so than respondents in the T34 U*STAR or T34 COR programs) reported having a distant or less helpful relationship with their PIs. A large majority of R25 Bridges respondents had some or a lot of encouragement from their PIs to engage in research, said that their PIs were good or very good to work with, and said that PIs were some or a lot of help with their next step. Moreover, mentoring and support was the second most frequent response to the question, What are the best features of the program? As one respondent said, the best features of the program were "the help of the professors, the projects they gave you to work on, and their overall mentorship to help you really achieve."

Similarly, in response to a question about whether their PIs influenced their careers, the most cited response typically focused on how the PI provided motivation or opportunities for growth. One respondent said simply that the PI "made me believe in myself, that I could do it." Others elaborated further, responding, "She already had been down that road, that path, and I was heading down that path. She saw me as a person trying to follow in her footsteps," and " . . . very enthusiastic person—believed in what she did. Good conviction; told me I needed a personal passion for what I was doing; very encouraging in a seemingly boring field of research." Other responses to the question about best features of the program noted the importance of financial support, networking, motivation, and greater awareness of educational options.

However, a sizable minority reported having little encouragement much more frequently than for respondents in the T34 U*STAR and T34 COR programs. And R25 Bridges respondents were less likely to report that their PIs had some or a great deal of influence on their careers. Similar numbers of respondents across the three undergraduate programs indicated that they had daily or weekly contact with their PIs. R25 Bridges respondents were actually more likely to report that they had daily contact, but despite this frequent contact, these students reported feeling more distant from their PIs.

Other Issues Raised by Trainees

Although financial support, research, and mentoring were critical to trainees, some comments raise questions or suggestions for improvement. For example, the second most cited response to the question, What were the worst features of the program? centered on the time commitment and, in some cases, the quality of the work. One respondent said the worst feature was "my work hours." A second characterized the program as "double work" and indicated "a lot of struggles with home, work, and studying." A third said the program was "a lot to add on to what we were doing [and] the actual duties were mundane," and a fourth even charged that "professors took advantage of free labor." A handful of respondents, however, suggested that the issue for them was struggling to make the most of the experience, especially when experiments were not successful.

Two respondents said the worst feature of the program had to do with writing. One said it was "writing papers and summarization of the data." This is not necessarily a bad thing; rather it may be an important and challenging aspect of the program. Another respondent wanted more from the laboratory experience, saying students "didn't get a lot of work done. We would start an experience and didn't get to finish it. If we did get to finish [and] if something came out wrong, we wouldn't be able to analyze the results."

Other responses to the question about program improvements suggested better preparation of students for the courses they were to take or better preparation for the transition to a university. One respondent asked that programs become "more standardized as to what students and professors should expect from each other."

Does the (R25) Bridges Program Work?

The information available to the committee does not allow it to conduct a direct analysis to determine whether the program is "successful" in strictly quantitative terms. The information does clearly indicate that the R25 Bridges to the Baccalaureate program provides value to many of its participants. It also "works" for some, but not all, participants who complete the program, transfer, and earn a bachelor's degree. The data also indicate that there is variation among programs at the institutional level in the success they have in moving students toward completion of the program and eventual transfer, a matter that is worth probing further.

Value to Students

Respondents were asked two questions about whether and how the program influenced their education and careers. The most often cited responses to these questions were that the program provided students with direction, skills, and research experience. For example, one respondent said, "At the time I wasn't looking for much but a bachelor's." The program made him consider a Ph.D. or M.D. Another respondent said that the program "broadened my horizons. It showed me that there are other opportunities and career goals." Another eloquently summed up his experience, saying the program "gave me a chance. Opened doors that wouldn't be possible. Gave me a chance to expand my analytical thinking. Gave me a chance to enter a field that I wouldn't have gone into." Several other respondents noted that the program inspired them to change their majors or pin down a specific field to focus on.

Several respondents had a contrary experience and noted that, after trying the program, they decided research was not for them. Typically and not surprisingly, given the fields from which program administrators recruit for the R25 Bridges program, these respondents generally went into nursing instead. Yet it appears that the program provided important information for these trainees and they acted responsibly based on that input.

At the very end of the trainee interview, respondents were asked, "What else would you like NIH to know?" In response, most respondents simply offered that the program was a positive experience for them and hoped it would be continued. For example, one respondent said, "Overall, it was a very excellent program. It was very rewarding. I would recommend it to anyone who is pursuing science as a career." Another said, "Ask them to continue to support the [R25 Bridges to the] Baccalaureate [program]. It makes a difference." Similarly, respondents were also asked if they wanted to suggest any improvements to the program. The response given most often was to ensure that as many students as possible knew about the opportunity and to make it available to more people by extending the program to other campuses. This demonstrates a level of satisfaction with the program, at least among those who responded to the interviews.

This discussion requires a further note about race or ethnicity. About one-quarter of R25 Bridges respondents indicated that their race or ethnicity had an impact on their experience in the program. One respondent sensed that his race worked against him, saying, "I feel like if I was white I would have got more attention . . . . The head would have given me research experience [and I] probably would have gotten to follow him around." However, others saw their race or ethnicity as adding a positive dimension to the experience. One respondent noted that the program allows "a lot of minorities [to] enter a field they wouldn't ordinarily get into." A second "realized how few minorities [were] in the program. Challenged me to reach higher for my race." A third said, "I think it made it a lot more meaningful. I got to see other minorities being successful. You usually think of the sciences as old white guys." A fourth "liked that there were minorities in positions of leadership. That would be the number one thing." Two others noted that race and ethnicity were also related to the kinds of questions scientists asked. One of these, for example, noted, "Most research that you look at is predominantly based on the white male middle class. Being African American, you are able to give a different perspective."

Taken together, the information from trainee interviews suggest that respondents to the interviews were in general very pleased with the program, although this finding must be tempered by the fact that the respondents were likely to have been among the more successful in the program. This serves as an indicator that the program provided, at a minimum, important value to its participants.

Meeting Goals for Transfer and Bachelor's Degree Attainment

In 1999, NIGMS convened a working group to examine the current status of the R25 Bridges program and to review and revise program goals for the future.[30] As part of its work, this working group reviewed data from NIGMS staff and found that, as of September 1999, NIGMS could assert that after five years, 70 percent of all R25 Bridges to the Baccalaureate program students had transferred to four-year institutions, and of those who transferred, 45 percent completed the four-year degree. As a result, 31 percent of R25 Bridges trainees achieved the program goal of earning a baccalaureate degree. Since these data derive from a third-party source, it is unclear whether the baccalaureate degrees tabulated were limited to science disciplines. Further, it is unclear whether or not students who transferred earned an associate's degree before transferring. Similarly, the committee does not know how many years each student spent in community college before transferring to a four-year institution. More recent data from NIGMS indicate that, as of 2004, 50 percent of all R25 Bridges students transfer and, of those who do, 41 percent earn a bachelor's degree. Thus, 21 percent of participants now achieve the program goal of earning a baccalaureate degree, compared to 31 percent in 1999. Despite the decline, however, even this lower rate is higher than the national rate at which community college students transfer and complete a baccalaureate. According to the National Center for Education Statistics,[31] the national rate for transfer and completion is 16 percent. It is not possible to tell from the committee's data if these rather highly selected and motivated students would have done as well without R25 Bridges support.

Given that 55 to 60 percent of those R25 Bridges students who transfer do not earn a bachelor's degree, an examination of the backgrounds of these students may reveal whether or not (1) they should have been in the program in the first place, (2) the

[30] National Institute of General Medical Sciences and Office of Research on Minority Health, National Institutes of Health. Undated. Planning and Priorities of the Bridges to the Future Program. Bethesda, Md.: U.S. Department of Health and Human Services, undated. See. http://nigms.nih.gov/news/reports/bridges.html.

[31] See http://nces.ed.gov//programs/coe/.

program prepared them adequately before transfer, or (3) other extenuating circumstances contributed to a failure to complete the bachelor's degree.

One administrator interviewed for this study said R25 Bridges students experience "culture shock" upon transition to the baccalaureate institution. Does this suggest that their experience in a community or tribal college program was not as challenging as it might have been or that the environments at two-year and four-year institutions are substantially different in some other way such that students are not ready for the four-year institution when they arrive? What can be done at the two-year institution to minimize this shock or to maximize preparation to meet the demands on these students as juniors and seniors?

A second issue is what happens to students after they transfer and what can be done to improve the experience for these students at four-year institutions. Indeed, one program administrator commented on the need to worry about students after they transfer saying, "This is a bridge program. Well, what happens to the trainees when they cross the bridge? There is no cognate program that provides continuity for these trainees." Another administrator made nearly the same point, saying, "Students can participate in R25 Bridges, yet never really cross over to the four-year university. There is no 'carrot' awaiting them, such as a small scholarship. So, some of them just 'disappear'." The administrator added, "The one item [that] would really enhance this program is if we were able to support the students after they came to the four-year institution. It would be fabulous if we had an NIH scholarship, even something modest ($1,000)." Beyond that, "NIH does not financially support me [the director] or the students after they have matriculated to the university [so mentoring cannot officially continue]. So what happens when the students transfer?"

This is an important issue, since NIH intends that there will be support for these students after they transfer. As the program is currently structured, the four-year institutions that receive R25 Bridges students should commit to supporting them after they transfer. Moreover, NIGMS instituted two programs in the late 1990s through its Minority Biomedical Research Support (MBRS) program that should also be available to support R25 Bridges students after transfer. These include Research Initiative for Scientific Enhancement (RISE) programs that provide awards to minority-serving institutions to enhance their research environment as a means for increasing the interest, skills, and competitiveness of students and faculty in pursuit of biomedical research careers. They also include the Initiative for Minority Student Development (IMSD) program, which may be awarded competitively to any four-year institution and encourages the development and/or expansion of innovative programs to improve the academic and research competitiveness of underrepresented minority students and to facilitate their progress toward careers in biomedical research.

A third issue is variability in the success with which institutions move students to program completion and transfer. Among the three program administrators interviewed for this study, two indicated the percentage of students that transferred and these percentages indicate a large potential variance among campus programs. One program administrator said that 50 percent will actually transfer to the four-year university and another said that 80 percent complete the program.

Lessons from the Bridges to the Baccalaureate Program

Many students recruited to the R25 Bridges program are new to research, have not decided on their educational and career options, have relatively lower educational and career expectations than minority students who are upperclassmen at four-year institutions, and need to improve their confidence and motivation. The R25 Bridges program is designed to address each of these issues. It provides hands-on research, career guidance, mentoring, and financial support that lead to improved skills, increased exposure to and knowledge of research, and greater awareness of educational and career options. These experiences will help improve the confidence of trainees in their abilities and allow them to envision a research career. At the same time, students who have not had the perspective to dream about research may become motivated to pursue a science career.

If a program's success is judged by examining the percentage of participants who complete it and move to the following stage, then the R25 Bridges to the Baccalaureate program would be a success since at least one-half of the students appear to complete the program and transfer. However, if a stricter definition of success is applied, such as students progressing to and completing the following career stage, then the program "works" for just some percentage of the one-fourth of program participants who transfer and eventually complete a bachelor's degree who would not have done so without the program. Given the natural state of loss through the education pipeline (only a small percentage of individuals with baccalaureate degrees go on to get a Ph.D.), it is, however, an achievement to get even that fraction to complete the bachelor's degree that makes them eligible to continue with graduate studies. Thus, the R25 Bridges program is successful in contributing minorities to the ranks of scientists and science participants.

It is harder to measure whether the program was a success or not for those who did not transfer or who transferred but did not complete a bachelor's degree. The committee has found that the program provides value for students and believes that this is true for both students who do not transfer and those who do. Moreover, as discovered in trainee interviews, some of students who did not transfer gave research a try, decided it was not for them, and returned to what they had originally planned to do, such as a career in nursing or other health professions. This is not necessarily a "failure" of the program, but rather serves as an important part of the process that provides students room to discover whether a career in biomedical or behavioral research is for them. Unfortunately, the survey data do not reveal how a career in research (as opposed to medicine) may have been marketed to trainees during the recruitment process.

To be sure, there are other students who, to use the words of program administrators interviewed, have "personal issues" and drop out or "disappear" before or after transfer. It is not clear to what extent the program has had a beneficial impact for them, nor is it clear how often this happens among students generally, with or without other forms of government support. In any event, these are all natural attrition events in the progress toward the bachelor's degree and occur with some frequency in all institutions of higher learning and with nonminority as well as minority students.

Issues that the R25 Bridges program should explore further include the following:

1. Is the program recruiting widely enough in high schools, community colleges, and tribal colleges?
2. How should programs screen applicants? What criteria should be used? (Some programs are "screening out" or at least avoiding students with "personal issues.")
3. What are the characteristics of students who do not complete their community or tribal college program or transfer? What are the characteristics of students who transfer but do not complete? How can the program be modified to improve selection of trainees or increase the chances of student success while preserving a focus on growing new talent, not just harvesting what is already waiting?
4. How much truth is there to the perception related by some trainees that their PIs provided little encouragement, were of little or no help, had little or no influence, or simply used them as labor for "mundane tasks"? If true, how pervasive are these behaviors in practice?
5. What accounts for variability in the success of programs to transfer students, and is this variability justified? For example, does the size or type (liberal arts, master's, doctoral, or research) of four-year institution matter? Does disciplinary focus or diversity matter? Are there ways to improve programs at low-performing institutions to increase transfer success?
6. What can be done by the receiving four-year institution to improve the success of students after they cross the "bridge"?
7. What data should be collected going forward to help monitor the R25 Bridges program more effectively?

(T34) U*STAR and (T34) COR Programs

The support of NIGMS for underrepresented minorities at the undergraduate level began in 1977 with the MARC Honors program and has continued since 1996 with the T34 U*STAR program that replaced it. Under the T34 U*STAR program, institutional programs average 8-10 new students per year or 16-20 juniors and seniors in a given year. The study committee focused its assessment of the T34 U*STAR program on the period 1996 to 1999. During this time, T34 U*STAR provided support for 1,576 students. Under the T34 COR program, institutions are required to develop programs that have 6 to 10 students each year. The study committee focused its assessment of the T34 COR program on the period 1979 to 1999. During this time, T34 COR provided support for 1,011 students.

The principal objective of both the MARC T34 U*STAR and the NIMH T34 COR programs is to increase the number of competitively trained underrepresented minority students who enroll in programs in their fields leading to the Ph.D. or a Ph.D. combined with another professional degree (e.g.,the M.D.-Ph.D). The two programs do so by emphasizing training and research. The T34 U*STAR program requires institutions to detail a research training program reflecting its mission, physical and personnel resources, and student population. This plan should describe program activities, detail how it will better prepare students academically for graduate school, demonstrate how it will increase the flow of MARC students to Ph.D. programs, and state the anticipated benefits of the program to minority science students (in terms of recruitment, retention, graduation rates, and career outcomes). T34 U*STAR institutions must also describe specific arrangements for extramural research training experiences for the students (during the school year and/or during the summer between junior and senior years). For the T34 COR program, institutions must provide a training plan that demonstrates how trainees will receive high-quality scientific training and research experiences that provide both learning and motivation to pursue research careers in the mental health field. T34 COR institutions must provide a detailed plan for students' summer research and study experiences between the junior and senior years.

Trainee Characteristics

Demographically, those respondents to the trainee interviews who were in the T34 U*STAR and T34 COR program had the following characteristics:

- Women comprised almost three-quarters of those respondents to the trainee interviews who were in the T34 U*STAR program. A similar proportion of T34 COR respondents were women. Interviews with program administrators at recipient institutions indicate that most trainees in most programs are female. One respondent reported having a program that was evenly split between men and women, but one reported that "85 percent of my honors students are female" and two reported they look particularly for black males.
- Respondents who were in the T34 U*STAR program were 42 percent African American, 32 percent Hispanic, 5 percent Asian, and 11 percent Pacific Islander. By contrast, respondents who were in the T34 COR program were 76 percent African American, 12 percent Hispanic, 6 percent Asian, 3 percent Pacific Islander, and 3 percent white. The racial or ethnic make-up of the trainee population, though, varies from institution to institution, depending largely on what geographic region the institution is in. One T34 U*STAR campus administrator, for example, reported that 70 percent of the T34 U*STAR trainees in their program are African Americans.
- In looking at the list of names of individuals in the trainee universe at the undergraduate level, there are a substantial number of individuals whose surnames indicate that they are likely not underrepresented minorities as the

committee has defined them (African American, Hispanic American, Native American, or Alaskan Native). To cite one example, there are many recipients whose surnames are Vietnamese. The committee is unable to estimate the size of this part of the trainee pool but raises this as an important finding about these undergraduate programs as they were originally instituted to focus on students from historically underrepresented groups in the United States. It appears that many participants fall outside these populations.
- A large minority of T34 U*STAR and one-third of T34 COR respondents said that they were married or in a long-term relationship while in the program. Only a very small fraction in either program reported having dependents.

Key expectations that T34 U*STAR and T34 COR respondents had for their respective programs were as follows:
- Nearly all T34 U*STAR and T34 COR respondents expected to improve their research skills.
- A large majority of T34 U*STAR and more than one-half of T34 COR respondents expected their programs to help them to decide whether they were cut out for research.
- All T34 U*STAR respondents and a large majority of T34 COR respondents expected the program to provide mentoring, which in fact it did.
- Nearly all T34 U*STAR respondents and a large majority of T34 COR respondents indicated that they expected the program to increase their chances of getting into graduate school, large majorities of respondents from both programs indicated that graduate school would be their immediate next step after graduating, and just less than one-half expected the Ph.D. to eventually be their highest degree.
- A small but sizable minority in both programs reported they hoped the program would increase their chances of getting into medical school, and a similar size group indicated that medical school would be their immediate next step after graduating. T34 U*STAR respondents were twice as likely as T34 COR respondents to expect the M.D. as their highest degree earned.
- A majority of both groups expected the program to help them decide on whether to go to graduate or medical school, but this was more often the case for T34 COR respondents.
- The majority of T34 U*STAR and T34 COR respondents indicated that they had a variety of academic career goals when they were in their program: T34 U*STAR respondents most often considered clinical research, biological research, and teaching as potential career options; T34 COR respondents most often considered behavioral research, clinical research, and teaching.

Recruitment for (T34) U*STAR and (T34) COR

Programs recruit students through a variety of methods. The primary method, and one cited by most of the program administrators interviewed, is personal contact with minority students in the sciences who have already shown a certain aptitude in their freshman and sophomore years. This typically begins with a process for identifying students. Program administrators often request a listing from the registrar of freshman and sophomore minority students in certain fields who have earned at least a 3.0 grade point average (GPA). They also identify prospects by talking with faculty and the honor society. One respondent indicated that he targets students who perform well in his honors biology class. The program then sends a letter or e-mail to the students and follows up with more e-mails and phone calls. Administrators noted that it is important to begin targeting students early in college. One program, for example, initially focused just on sophomores but now engages in outreach to both high school students and freshmen so that they are already aware of the program when they become sophomores.

Several methods are available for advertising to current students. Campus administrators (and sometimes current T34 U*STAR students) visit classes that potential trainees are taking and use vehicles such as minority science clubs and tutoring programs as means for recruiting. They post information about the program on bulletin boards and web sites on campus. One program advertises in the semiannual campus biology newsletter. According to program administrators, information is also distributed off-campus to high school and community college students. One program targets high school students by distributing flyers to high school counselors. One institution offers a summer colloquium for incoming freshmen called "Careers in Science and Math for Minority Professionals," and the program administrator uses that class as a means of disseminating information to potential students. One administrator noted that the program has recently started targeting community college students, and another indicated a need to reach out to these groups, stating that they "need to do more outreach to communities of color, including faculty at community colleges. If we could recruit the top sophomore students from the area's community colleges we would be in great shape."

Respondents to the trainee interviews were asked a multiple-response question about how they learned about their programs. Most T34 U*STAR respondents heard about the program from a friend and more than half heard about it from a college professor. Slightly less than one-half heard about the program from departmental staff and a small number saw a notice on a bulletin board. Among T34 COR respondents most heard about the program from a college professor and almost one-half heard about it from departmental staff. A small number saw a notice on a bulletin board and a minority also heard about the program from a friend.

There was only one comment among the open-ended responses in which a trainee commented on recruitment. In response to a question about whether the trainee had any improvements to suggest for the program, one T34 COR respondent said, "It needs to be open to more people and help students be aware of this program and others."

Campus administrators also reported the need for greater outreach to broaden the pool of applicants to the program. When asked who is overlooked in recruitment, they noted several important groups. One said simply, "Black males are in short supply." Another noted that gifted students who are noncitizens, many of whom are Hispanic, are overlooked. Another would like to target students who are Cambodian, Vietnamese, and Filipino, but while they may be admitted to the program they do not count toward program "success" because they are not from historically underrepresented groups. Another administrator would like to include students who intend to go to medical school, but the program is explicitly targeted toward students who plan to go into research careers.

Funding

The T34 U*STAR and T34 COR respondents had similar sources of financial support, both generally as undergraduates and while in their respective programs. Most T34 U*STAR and T34 COR respondents had scholarships and most also had support from their spouse or family. More than one-half of T34 U*STAR and T34 COR respondents reported having wages or a salary and more than one-half of each also took out loans. Slightly less than one-half of each had government grants, and about one-third of each group worked as research assistants. Juniors and seniors in the T34 U*STAR and T34 COR programs were less reliant on sources of financial support other than their NIH stipends. During the program, less than one-half of T34 U*STAR and more than one-half of T34 COR respondents had an additional scholarship, and more than one-half of T34 U*STAR and slightly less than one-half of T34 COR respondents reported having support from spouse or family. However, fewer took out loans or earned wages or a salary while in the program, and only small numbers had other government grants or worked as research assistants.

The financial support that the T34 U*STAR and T34 COR programs provide students is important to their success, and many T34 U*STAR and T34 COR respondents noted the importance of the financial support received when asked about the best features of the program. T34 U*STAR respondents noted that the program paid tuition and a stipend, allowing them to focus on their studies and obviating the need for additional student loans. T34 COR respondents noted these as well as the importance of financial support for summer research and travel to conferences. One T34 COR respondent remarked, "Thanks to the money it is possible to do all those wonderful things. The money really matters."

There were also a few T34 U*STAR and T34 COR respondents who suggested improving the financial support provided by the T34 U*STAR program either by increasing the amount of the stipend or by ensuring that the funding arrives in a more timely manner. One program administrator reported that, for some students, the annual stipend of $10,500 was not enough, so they hold other jobs. Another program administrator, however, said that the selection process screens out students who plan to work because it is a "recipe for failure." In reality, about one-third of trainees reported taking loans during the program and about one-quarter reported earning wages or a salary.

Mentoring

An experiential research opportunity is a central feature of both the T34 U*STAR and T34 COR programs for their trainees. The trainees conduct research projects under the supervision of faculty who are PIs or lab heads. Training occurs throughout the school year and during the summer between their junior and senior years. About one-half of T34 U*STAR respondents indicated they discussed their research with their PIs on a weekly basis and another quarter said they did so daily. Almost two-thirds of T34 COR respondents indicated they discussed their research with their PIs on a weekly basis and a small number said they did so daily.

Survey respondents who were in the T34 U*STAR and T34 COR programs reported that, overall, they had very good relations with the PIs of their programs with whom they worked closely. Almost all T34 U*STAR and T34 COR respondents said their PIs were good or very good to work with. Most T34 U*STAR and T34 COR respondents had some or a lot of encouragement from their PIs to engage in research. Only a few reported having no or little encouragement. A large majority from both programs said their PIs were either some or a lot of help with their next step, although a small minority said their PIs were of little or no help in this regard. More than one-half of respondents from both programs said their relationship with their PI was familiar or close. Again, only a small minority said they felt remote or distant.

Both T34 COR and T34 U*STAR respondents were more likely than R25 Bridges respondents to report that their PI had some or a great deal of influence on their careers, more than one-half of them reporting this. When asked how the PI influenced their education or career path, respondents reported they did in so in four key areas: improving the trainee's research skills, providing motivation and personal growth, providing career guidance, and promoting the trainee for scholarships and outside internships. Just as important, as evidenced by trainee responses, is the manner in which the PIs provided this training, motivation, and guidance. They did so by acting as role models and teachers; by listening to, talking with, and nurturing students; by being involved in and encouraging the trainee's research; by providing information about and encouraging students to continue to graduate school and beyond; and by recommending trainees for scholarships. One respondent summed up many of the ways PIs help their trainees saying that her PI "encouraged research, spent a lot of time to help me, helped me get a scholarship, [and] remains in contact . . . always provided support academically and as a mentor."

Another key feature of the T34 U*STAR program is the availability of mentoring for trainees. Respondents to the survey were asked if there was "someone who took a personal interest in you and was supportive of your research and career," in other words, a mentor. All T34 U*STAR and most T34 COR respondents reported having a mentor while in their program. In both programs, most respondents reported that their PI was also their mentor, but a substantial minority had a mentor who was different from the PI in their laboratories. Slightly more than one-half of the mentors for both T34 U*STAR and T34 COR respondents were male. There were greater differences in the race or ethnicity of mentors. More than one-half of T34 U*STAR mentors were white, while less than one-half of T34 COR mentors were. For T34 COR, almost as many were African American as were white.

When asked what the best features of the T34 COR program were, about one-half of the respondents indicated that the research experience was among the best features, but they indicated almost as often that support and mentoring were. By contrast, only a very few T34 U*STAR respondents mentioned mentoring as a best feature and just as many cited it as a worst feature.

One T34 COR respondent detailed how mentoring can be key to the trainee's research experience, saying that the best features of the program were "the opportunity to do undergrad research, opportunity to develop close relationships with faculty members, being able to complete and present a research study and article at a conference." Another comment by a T34 COR respondent presents a different dimension of mentoring—that of a mentor who is influential in the trainee's overall experience and provides motivation for the next step. This respondent reported, "My experience was so positive because the director of the [T34 COR program] was extremely passionate and committed to the student's success, and that kept me connected to the program."

However, a sizable minority of T34 COR respondents cited mentoring as an area in need of improvement and had a variety of suggestions about mentoring in the program. One respondent noted that it was hard to find a mentor generally, and another said it was specifically more difficult to find a mentor who could serve as a bridge between the psychology and anthropology programs. Others asked for "more intensive mentoring" or a mentor (or someone from the program) who was more actively involved in a range of areas, including research, graduate applications, Graduate Record Examination (GRE) preparation, time management, grant writing, and publications. Two T34 U*STAR respondents noted that they had to change mentors in order to find someone with whom they could work.

Trainees and Their Laboratory or Research Group

The trainee survey also asked respondents to comment on the relationship they had with the other members of their laboratory or research group, typically four to ten in number and including three to six minorities. A majority of T34 U*STAR and T34 COR respondents reported having daily or weekly contact with their laboratory or research group, although T34 U*STAR respondents were far more likely than T34 COR respondents to have daily contact. More than one-half of T34 U*STAR and T34 COR respondents indicated feeling close to or familiar with their research groups. Most of the rest indicated feeling "neutral." Only slightly more than one-third of T34 U*STAR and T34 COR respondents reported that their laboratory or research group had much influence over their careers. PIs were more likely to have an influence.

Do the (T34) U*STAR and (T34) COR Programs Work?

The data available to the committee do not allow a direct analysis to determine whether the T34 U*STAR and T34 COR programs are "successful" in strictly quantitative terms. However, the information available indicates that the programs provide value to their participants and clearly "work" for most program participants, because a very high proportion eventually graduates from the program and a reasonably high percentage appears to eventually continue to graduate school. The data also indicate that there is variation among programs at the institutional level in the success they have in moving students toward completion of the program and eventual transfer—an issue worth probing further.

Value of Program to Trainees

Trainees were asked several open-ended questions in their interviews, and their answers reinforce the usefulness of the key features of the program but also raise some important concerns. Among the questions that were posed were what were the best features of the program? what were the worst features of the program? what improvements for the program would you recommend? and do you have anything else you would like to say to NIH? T34 U*STAR respondents tended to be briefer in their responses than T34 COR respondents. However, their responses to these questions provide insights into overall program quality, key program features, the relationship of the program to education and career goals, and diversity.

Program Quality

In response to the question, do you have anything else you would like to say to NIH, a small number of T34 U*STAR and more than one-half of T34 COR respondents commented on the quality of and/or their appreciation for the program. T34 U*STAR respondents who answered this way were effusive, calling the program "a wonderful experience," "an awesome experience," "a great opportunity for kids," and a "really great grant—it opened my mind." T34 COR respondents were equally enthusiastic, with such responses as, "It shaped my career path. I would never have thought of going into the sciences," or "It's a very beneficial program that provides a really good springboard for undergrads to get to a research career." Similarly, when asked, what were the worst features of the program? one-third of T34 COR respondents simply replied that there were none or they could not think of any.

A real sense of the T34 U*STAR respondents' appreciation for the program came in response to the questions about how the program influenced their education and career. In response to these questions, respondents noted the skills that the program gave them. One respondent noted that the program "provided a foundation for research as well as technical skills in research." Another noted that the research experience was "unmatched" and the importance of attending conferences and making oral presentations. Two respondents noted the importance of being able to focus on studies while in the program. One respondent summed this up nicely, saying the program "let me concentrate on school so I didn't have to work. Let me enter graduate school. Exposed me to different science research so I was able to know exactly what I wanted to do in graduate school." The most cited response, however, focused on how the program helped respondents with the educational and career direction. As one respondent put it, "I found my calling, which is research."

Taken together, these responses suggest a high level of satisfaction on the part of T34 U*STAR and T34 COR respondents with their programs and demonstrate the value of these programs to the participants. This value is demonstrated further in respondent comments about specific program features.

Program Features

Research. When asked what the best features of the program were, the feature cited most often, by most T34 U*STAR and one-half of T34 COR respondents, was the research experience, particularly the hands-on, practical experience with laboratory research. A T34 COR respondent summed up the benefit of the research experience and also cited other key program features (mentoring, travel) by citing the "opportunity to do undergrad research, opportunity to develop close relationship with faculty members, being able to complete and present a research study and article at a conference."

In addition, a T34 U*STAR respondent specifically noted the opportunity to travel to another institution to do research during the summer between junior and senior year. This had the advantage of not only allowing exposure to more research, but also of introducing the student "to a lot of professors so we already knew a lot of people before applying to graduate school." A handful of T34 COR respondents also noted the summer research internship in particular as a best feature.

To be sure, there were those who had complaints or suggestions about research, but even these comments show an appreciation for the importance of a meaningful research experience. A T34 U*STAR respondent said that the worst feature of the program was the "lack of lab space." Two others said that the program might be improved by including "more lab opportunities" and less time "doing administrative things." A T34 COR respondent said that the worst feature of the program was, simply, "the mice." Two others made practical suggestions, such as "make research topics more interesting" and provide "opportunities to work in different labs."

Travel. A program feature cited by T34 COR respondents as a best feature almost as often as the research experience was the opportunity to travel to conferences and make either a poster or an oral presentation based on the trainee's research. Numerous respondents commented on this feature, often when also citing the importance of the research experience. Several T34 U*STAR respondents also cited travel to conferences as a best feature, but far fewer than for T34 COR respondents. One T34 U*STAR respondent even cited this as a worst feature, saying "it was a lot of pressure."

Mentoring. When asked what best features of the T34 U*STAR program were, very few respondents mentioned mentoring—a surprising result since almost one-half of T34 COR respondents indicated that mentoring was one. However, when asked how their PIs influenced their education or career path, respondents reported that they were very helpful, particularly in four key areas: (1) improving the trainee's research skills, (2) providing motivation and personal growth, (3) providing career guidance, and (4) promoting the trainee for scholarships and outside internships. They did so by acting as role models; teaching, listening to, and talking with students; being involved in and encouraging the trainee's research; providing information about opportunities; and recommending trainees for scholarships.

The T34 COR respondents were much more likely to cite mentoring as a best feature, but also as an area in need of improvement. Slightly less than one-half of T34 COR respondents cited mentoring as one of the best features of the program. Working with faculty in research provides one important dimension of the mentor-trainee relationship. The motivation that a mentor can provide is another. On the other hand, a sizable minority of T34 COR respondents cited mentoring as an area in need of improvement.

Financial Support. Some T34 U*STAR and T34 COR respondents indicated that the financial support was one of the best features of the program. Respondents noted that because of the financial support they did not have to pay tuition for much of the time they were undergraduates, did not have to work while in the program, and in one case, did not have to take out loans. However, a handful of respondents said that the financial support provided by these programs could be improved either by increasing the amount of the stipend or by ensuring that the funding arrives in a timelier manner. Just as often, however, the suggestion was not for an increase in student support but in funding for other activities (e.g., more mentoring).

Skill. Very few respondents cited "skills," other than those associated with the research experience, when asked about the best features of the program. In response to a question about how the program influenced the trainee's career, however, many T34 U*STAR and T34 COR respondents said that the program provided them with important skills. T34 U*STAR respondents noted such skills as "a better understanding of the principles," the ability to be "objective," technical skills in research, knowledge about research ethics, and making oral presentations. T34 COR respondents noted a wide variety of skills such as writing, presentation skills, critical thinking, academic research, lab techniques, scientific methods, teamwork, networking, discipline, and "the skill that I needed to be able to survive at graduate school." However, respondents wanted additional help with research, graduate applications, GRE preparation, time management, grant writing, and publications. Two respondents specified the need for help with "the transition to graduate school."

Networking. Networking was also important to at least a handful of respondents. The ability to interact with other students and to work with faculty were both cited as key features. One T34 U*STAR respondent noted that the extramural summer research experience introduced the trainee "to a lot of professors so we already knew a lot of people before applying to graduate school." Meeting other researchers at conferences was noted by T34 COR respondents as an important part of the experience in traveling to meetings to make poster or oral presentations.

Program Impact on Education and Careers

Respondents were asked two questions about whether and how the program influenced their education and careers. The most often cited response to these questions was that the program provided students with direction and motivation. Respondents said that the exposure to research made them more interested in it as a possible career path. They noted as well that the program made them more focused on going to graduate school. Others noted that the program exposed them to career opportunities they would not have known about otherwise, and one said, "It guided my career and shaped it."

There were other comments, however, about negative aspects of the program. For example, a substantial minority of respondents noted some aspect of the time commitment involved in program participation. One respondent said the worst feature of the program was "being on a tight schedule—had to give up Saturdays to go to exams." Another said the program "took time away from your studies for your major." Still another complained about "putting in long hours at the lab." Other comments were focused less on the time commitment than on program rigor. While some respondents liked the structure and opportunities the program afforded, one commented, "It was hard."

Issues Related to Race and Ethnicity or Diversity

Respondents provided a range of comments about race and ethnicity or diversity in response to the open-ended questions asked during the telephone interviews. A few T34 COR respondents indicated that some aspect of diversity was among the best features of the programs. One noted, for example, the diversity of mentors, and another noted that the program gave minority students an opportunity they might not otherwise have had. Several T34 U*STAR respondents, however, had complaints related to diversity. One complained that the program was not administered by a minority, and another reported that few participants in the program were minorities from historically underrepresented groups.

Respondents were also asked whether and how their race or ethnicity impacted the experience they had in the program. Significantly more T34 COR respondents than T34 U*STAR or R25 Bridges respondents said their race or ethnicity was a factor in their program experience. Almost one-third of T34 COR respondents noted that their race made them eligible for the program and provided them with opportunities (e.g., travel) that other students might not have had. One respondent said the program made her feel "equal" and another said it made her feel "special." One respondent, however, cautioned that one of the worst features of the program was that "there was a lot of jealousy from other mainstream students who were not in the program." One-tenth of the respondents indicated that their race provided them with a different perspective either on the research they did or on their career path.

Interviews of Program Administrators at Recipient Institutions

Trainee Selection Criteria

Program administrators at recipient institutions (PARIs) were asked what criteria they look for when selecting program trainees. At a minimum, trainees must be juniors, U.S. citizens, and in good academic standing. However, program administrators also look for a certain goals, ambitions, and characteristics. One program administrator, for example, provided this response: "We wish to attract bright, highly motivated people with a good work ethic. We are looking for people who are willing to work hard, who are intelligent, and who are motivated to pursue graduate studies. And we also look for previous research experience." In addition, as one administrator said, trainees "have to be willing to sort of live and breathe science." Key criteria that administrators use for trainee selection are the following:

- ***Academic standing***. Administrators report that they look for students who are bright, intelligent, and in good academic standing. They look as well for creativity, ingenuity, and inquisitiveness. Most programs tend to recruit students with at least a 3.0 GPA, although one program requires at least a 3.2. Several program administrators said they also look specifically at how students have performed in what one called "gatekeeper courses" such as physics, mathematics, and organic chemistry. One administrator said, "If we have a student with weak grades [who] applies, we try to evaluate what the problems were or other issues. We are looking for students who are willing to work hard and not really make excuses."

- ***Hard-working and motivated.*** Program administrators invariably mentioned that they seek students who are "hard working" or have a "good work ethic." They report looking for students who are "highly motivated" or, as one put it, have the "fire-in-the-belly type of thing." They look for people who take initiative, have a sense of themselves, and have enthusiasm. One administrator said trainees must be "mentorable," by which was meant "goal-directed, definitive in their approach to educational decisions."
- ***Commitment.*** One administrator reported that students must be able to commit to a minimum of 10 hours per week in a lab. Another said the applicant should not have plans to hold down a job in addition to working in the program. "This is a recipe for failure."
- ***Interested in graduate study and research.*** Across the board, administrators interviewed were adamant that students must be motivated to pursue graduate studies and should have a strong interest in research. Several specified that applicants have to demonstrate that they want to eventually earn a Ph.D. One program requires participants to sign a statement saying that if, at any point they decide to go to medical school, they must drop out of the program. Another focuses on screening out those who just want the financial aid and those who want to go to medical school.

These responses, on the whole, seem to be intended to involve students what are most likely to succeed in the program. This is appropriate in large measure, but it does shift the focus somewhat from growing new talent to harvesting already apparent talent.

(T34) U*STAR Trainee Challenges

The seven T34 U*STAR program administrators at recipient institutions who were interviewed for this study were asked to discuss the kinds of challenges that trainees in the T34 U*STAR program face. They provided frank insights about academic issues as well as personal issues, faced by trainees, as summarized below. In most cases, the challenges cited present the flip side of the characteristics administrators look for in the ideal candidate. However, in most cases, students eventually succeed in the program, sometimes despite the challenges. One administrator reported that only one trainee had ever dropped out of the program and another reported that only 3 students out of 100 did not complete the program.

Academic Challenges. All of the program administrators cited academic issues as key challenges. They described these variously as "keeping their grades up," "the academic load," and "the demands of research," which can include up to 10-15 hours in the laboratory each week. One administrator noted that, for trainees who are transferring to a four-year institution at the time they join the program, the transition could be challenging. Another administrator noted the demands of the program saying, "Between semesters and during summers, we do not allow the kids to go home. They have to stay on campus, attend extra courses, and work full-time in the lab during the summer, for example. The only time they get off is Christmas." A third noted that, "sometimes they need extra academic support in courses such as chemistry, physics, and math." These are often gatekeeper courses that may be designed as much to weed out students as to help them progress; without appropriate intervention at this stage, unprepared students will be lost. A fourth said, "GRE verbal scores are a real problem for our minority trainees. One guy got a quantitative score in the high 90s and a verbal score in the mid-40s."

Focus. Another set of challenges that program administrators cited was the ability of trainees to focus their efforts and manage their time in the right way. This appears to have several dimensions to it. One administrator summed up all of these concerns saying trainees require "learning time management, learning patience, and the ability to 'stick-to-it.'"

Choices. One administrator noted that some trainees have challenges with maintaining their self-confidence. Another noted that there are distractions or other options. This administrator reported, "There are so many opportunities out there, but people can become overwhelmed by all the opportunities and it becomes difficult to choose." When asked to describe an unsuccessful trainee, three administrators related stories about students who decided that research was not for them and decided to go to medical or dental school instead. In one case, however, an administrator related that a student went to medical school, dropped out after a year, worked for a couple of years, and then went to graduate school, earned a doctorate, did a postdoc, and is now a faculty member.

Personal and Family Issues. A variety of other issues surface for trainees. One administrator said, "In 2 out of 100 cases, I had to move a minority trainee out of a lab, because the faculty member was abusing them in some way." Another noted that "family issues can be a big challenge—certainly, for the Native American students—because their homes are so far away if issues come up. That is probably the biggest." A third administrator noted that financial concerns can also be a challenge. "Financially, you know, paying them $10,500 a year is nice but that's not necessarily enough for a student, and they may still have to work and do some other things."

In response to a question asking administrators to describe an unsuccessful trainee, several administrators noted there were students who had family issues that derailed their studies. In one case, a student had two young children and, because the spouse was unsupportive, was not able to create the time necessary to be successful in the program. Another trainee was "very bright" but left to get married and start a family.

On the other hand, one administrator related the story of a trainee who was "always screwing up." When the program administrator intervened and mediated, he found that the trainee was given custody of a "wild sister whom the parents could not control." The trainee eventually turned things around and earned a Ph.D. from an Ivy League institution.

Race or Ethnicity. Finally, program administrators noted that racial or ethnic relations can also be a challenge for trainees in the program. One administrator stated, "Our minority trainees often have to deal with racist comments from nonminority peers who ostracize them for participating in a targeted program." Another noted, "And, I think probably for the black students, because they are such a small percentage . . . they have their issues of being a minority amongst the minority." A third said, "There is some culture shock for minority trainees who come from rural backgrounds where there is little ethnic diversity."

Despite these kinds of challenges, students can and do succeed. One program administrator, when asked to describe a successful student, described one trainee as "very shy" with a "low confidence level," but a "smart kid, eldest in his Latino family," with an "overwhelming sense of responsibility about things in his family." This trainee "had to leave the program one summer to take care of family matters. Family was in financial ruin." Later, the trainee returned and completed the program but "applied to only one grad school, despite our advice that he do otherwise." The trainee was not accepted, but "persisted in focusing on this one school, enrolled [in] and completed their prep program . . . was admitted. Over time, he developed confidence and determination." He eventually received his Ph.D. in organic chemistry, did a postdoc, and now has a faculty position. The administrator says, "Now he is fierce!"

(T34) COR Trainee Challenges

The T34 COR PIs were not interviewed for this study, but an NIMH staff report summarized the views of T34 COR training directors as they were expressed at an October 1999 workshop. These views provide insight into the challenges that T34 COR trainees face and were summarized as follows:

- T34 COR program leaders report that many undergraduates are excited about the opportunities offered by the program but they do not fully understand what a research career entails. Consequently, even some of those who go on to graduate school become disillusioned and drop out. For minority students, and especially those who have dependents, financial constraints often dictate that they work for several years prior to going on for advanced degrees. This is especially true for many who make it to the Master's degree.
- T34 COR program administrators also note that career advancement has become increasingly more difficult in many respects, for all students, not just minority students. Getting into graduate school is more difficult and getting out is even harder. The length of time it takes to complete the Ph.D. is a deterrent for many students, especially when they learn how difficult it is to get an academic position

and, after that, tenure. Once they get an academic position, they learn how difficult it is to obtain research funding.

- On the other hand, according to some numbers and anecdotal reports from T34 COR program administrators, the majority of the trainees who have been successfully tracked through their graduate training and beyond, are in academic (teaching) settings. The second largest group is employed in academic/research environments followed by industry and government. Program administrators estimate, however, that the number of individuals who have obtained research support from the Public Health Service and other federal entities and private sources is relatively low. Some individuals are able to obtain funds from private foundations, their own institutions and other sources to support research projects, which allow student participation. Many publish despite the fact that they may not have an R01 or similar independent research grant.
- What is needed to ensure that students continue along the research career trajectory requires more focused attention and effort from both the Federal granting organizations as well as those who train and mentor students.[32]

The committee would add to this the need to focus on the value added by the program as well as ultimate attainments.

How to Help Trainees Succeed

When T34 U*STAR administrators on campus were asked to describe a successful trainee, they had no trouble relating stories of students who completed the program, earned a Ph.D. from a prestigious institution, did a postdoctoral fellowship, and went on to a successful career in academic or industrial research. The program elements that appeared to be key to the success of these students were exposure to research, the extramural summer research program, and mentoring. Indeed, when program administrators were asked about what "alerts" there are that a trainee is having difficulties and what they do to help students deal with them, they focused on two key tools they have at their disposal: monitoring and mentoring.

Program administrators monitor the progress of students in a variety of ways. Four administrators noted that they have access to trainee grades and review them periodically. In smaller programs, the administrator meets directly with trainees. In larger programs, mentors provide the administrator with information through phone calls or periodic reports (monthly, quarterly, or at the end of a semester) on student progress in summer research or academics. Student progress can also be gauged by the quality of their work in laboratories, weekly seminars, and presentations.

---

[32] National Institute of Mental Health (NIMH), National Institutes of Health. Undated. NIMH Training Programs for Underrepresented Racial/Ethnic Minorities (NIMH interim staff report). Bethesda, Md.: U.S. Department of Health and Human Services.

When monitoring suggests a problem, keeping students on track typically requires mentoring, and each administrator noted the importance of this. As one administrator put it, "Students . . . do better in a context where there's some peer involvement and where somebody is paying attention to them." Another argued, "I don't think you can ever overemphasize what mentoring is for students—well, for people in general, but certainly for students. So I think that where, in a lot of cases these things may be personal issues, they will not feel comfortable going to a faculty member who's just teaching them in the class. So I think the way we do it is through both initiation from the student . . . [and] being close enough and being involved with the students enough that you just sort of know these things."

The periodicity of meetings with students varies. Some administrators said that mentors meet with students weekly and others every two weeks. One said, "I see the students all the time. Remember, [this institution] is a small place. I am the adviser for the students, academic adviser for the students."

To reinforce the notion that mentoring—and having the right mentor—is important, one administrator also related the story of a trainee who was receiving no guidance from her mentor and was floundering. After she spoke with the administrator about her problem, he . . . "talked to the mentor and came to the conclusion that things were not going to improve. The problem wasn't with the student." So the administrator moved the trainee out of that mentor's laboratory and into another, where she "blossomed like crazy. I think if we would have kept her in the first one, she would have probably darn near dropped out of school. She was really distressed."

Program administrators may act as mentors themselves, but most programs typically have many mentors with whom students work. The level of interaction between administrators and mentors appears to vary. One has "occasional phone calls" with mentors. Another has irregular contact on an "as-needed basis" but, each fall, has a luncheon for all of the faculty mentors. Another organizes a symposium for students and mentors at which the students make presentations. At the other end of the spectrum, one administrator receives a progress report from each mentor and student on the trainee's research progress every semester. Another was a former dean and so knows all of the faculty personally, has a good relationship with them, and knows who is and is not a good mentor. Another meets face-to-face with mentors at the end of each summer and once each semester.

Issues for Improvement

Program administrators did not report many areas for improvement. As noted, one reported that, in response to the program evaluation, they were trying to engage in more outreach to increase the number of program applicants. This did not appear to be an issue at other institutions. Administrators at other institutions reported that there were many more program applicants than slots.

Two program administrators noted issues of concern related to research infrastructure. This administrator at a large institution reported, "One problem we don't have is finding research opportunities here for the students. And certainly, other institutions . . . lot of times, they send their students out elsewhere for the summer." However, another administrator related, "Coming from a research university and being, now, at a teaching university, I certainly recognize the limitations we have at teaching universities in terms of facilities, resources, et cetera. The grants are supposed to help with that. But, at the same time, there has got to be some institutional support . . . . The reviews come back: 'Well, you don't really have the infrastructure to do this.' That's a very difficult thing to deal with because many of the campuses don't have a real strong research infrastructure." Further, valid comparisons with minority students who are enrolled at institutions where there is a substantial research infrastructure are difficult to make under these circumstances, because such institutions are not generally awarded these programs unless they are minority-serving institutions to begin with.

(T34) U*STAR Student Outcomes

The number of T34 U*STAR trainees interviewed was small, and the trainee response data are not likely to be representative of the larger universe of trainees. Still, the committee notes that among T34 U*STAR respondents there was considerable progress, and the outcomes they report are similar to those reported by campus administrators and other sources. At the time they were surveyed, nearly all T34 U*STAR respondents reported that they had graduated from the program and almost one-half of all respondents had already earned either a master's degree or the Ph.D. A third had already authored or coauthored and published at least one academic paper, and one-tenth had already been awarded grants for research.

Similarly, T34 U*STAR program administrators interviewed for this study reported a high level of success among program participants. Administrators reported such success rates for their individual programs as "85-90 percent of trainees complete the program," "almost 100 percent of trainees complete the program (only one has dropped in 24 years)," and "93 percent of our students have graduated." One administrator did not provide a completion rate but did report that 52 percent of trainees who complete the program go on to Ph.D. programs around the country and that MARC students are more likely than other minority undergraduates to go on to graduate school.

In a 1995 assessment of the MARC Honors programs, which MARC T34 U*STAR replaced in 1996, NIGMS found similar rates of student progress. For former MARC students through the 1986 cohort, 94.8 percent had obtained a baccalaureate, a level similar to that reported by T34 U*STAR trainees and program administrators in the current survey. At the postbaccalaureate level, 16.1 percent had obtained a terminal master's degree, 13.0 percent had earned a research doctorate (Ph.D.), 24.9 percent had earned a clinical doctorate (M.D.), and 1.3 percent had earned an M.D.-Ph.D.[33] Thus, 55 percent of MARC Honors participants earned postbaccalaureate degrees, which T34 U*STAR students appear to be on track to equal or exceed.

Almost one-half of those Honors trainees who earned postbaccalaureate degrees earned the M.D., and it is unclear from the data whether or not a similar percentage of T34 U*STAR trainees will follow suit. When asked what they expect their highest degree will be, a sizable minority of T34 U*STAR respondents said the M.D. However, when asked the highest degree received so far, none reported having received the M.D. degree at the time of the survey.

Again, it is not possible to distinguish between growing new talent and harvesting abilities already present, but this sketch appears to confirm the overall success of students in the T34 U*STAR program. However, there appears to be variability in how successful institutions are in moving students to program completion and on to matriculation in graduate school.

(T34) COR Student Outcomes

The number of T34 COR trainees interviewed was small, and the trainee response data are not likely to be representative of the larger universe of trainees. At the time they were surveyed, nearly all T34 COR respondents reported that they had graduated from the program and most respondents had already earned either a Master's Degree or a Ph.D. One-fifth reported they had authored or coauthored papers, and one-tenth reported having obtained one or more research grants.

In May 2001, the National Advisory Mental Health Council's Workgroup on Racial/Ethnic Diversity in Research Training and Health Disparities Research issued a report on racial/ethnic diversity in mental health research careers. This workgroup drew on the findings of an October 1999 Workshop on NIMH Minority Training Programs and NIMH staff analysis of data collected about student progress under NIMH's minority training programs.[34] The data on student progress reported by the working group and staff analysis were particularly impressive, suggesting that at least 85 percent of all participants in the T34 COR program had already completed and graduated with bachelor's degrees. Most of the remaining participants were, at the time, still enrolled.

Moreover, of 895 trainees who had graduated from the 15 programs that had been funded by T34 COR, 60 percent (540) had already earned an advanced degree (master's

---

[33] National Institute of General Medical Sciences (NIGMS), National Institutes of Health. August 1995. A Study of the Minority Access to Research Careers Honors Undergraduate Research Training Program. Bethesda, Md.: U.S. Department of Health and Human Services.

[34] National Institute of Mental Health, National Institutes of Health. Undated. NIMH Training Programs for Underrepresented Racial/Ethnic Minorities, NIMH interim staff report. Bethesda, MD.: U.S. Department of Health and Human Services.

degree, Ph.D., M.D., M.D.-Ph.D., or other.) Although aggregate data on student progress were obtained for all 15 programs, more detailed data were obtained by NIMH staff on 11 programs, 10 of which were old enough to provide a reasonably detailed illustration of student progress. Data on these 10 programs are provided in Table 3-2. For this group of 10 programs, 87 percent of participants had already graduated. Of those who had graduated, 44 percent had earned an advanced degree.

Three programs provided even more detailed data as shown in Table 3-3. For these programs, the percentage of all participants who had graduated ranged from 80 to 99 percent. Of those who graduated, between 71 and 96 percent had been accepted into graduate school, between 16 and 39 percent were either in graduate or medical school, and 37 to 55 percent had earned advanced degrees.

This sketch appears to confirm the overall success of students in the T34 COR program. At the workshop in October 1999, T34 COR training directors commented on this level of student success as summarized in an NIMH staff report:

> PIs and other participants in the October Workshop expressed the opinion that it is probably not reasonable to expect undergraduate students to commit to long-range plans for a research career. In fact, they believe the kind of outcomes witnessed in the T34 COR are outstanding, especially in the absence of more clearly defined and communicated vertical and horizontal career development support options. At this level, the incentives for pursuing a research career are not clear to students. The NIMH/NIH need to work with training institutions to help educate young people about the positive and exciting aspects of scientific pursuit.
>
> The T34 COR programs graduating high percentages of students also enter and complete further research training tend to have enthusiastic and highly motivated faculty, usually multi-ethnic who themselves are engaged in some form of research. These programs offer expanded curricula (involving multiple departments), supplemented with on- and off-campus research and didactic experiences that create a climate of scientific enquiry [that] also embraces non-T34 COR students. These programs require trainee attendance and presentations at local, regional, and national scientific meetings, independent research projects, and they also offer intense career and academic counseling and communications skills development. A sizeable number [of trainees] co-author publications with their mentors in reputable scientific journals. Hence, they are already contributing scientifically to mental health related science at this stage of their training.[35]

---

[35] National Institute of Mental Health, National Institutes of Health. Undated. NIMH Training Programs for Underrepresented Racial/Ethnic Minorities (NIMH interim staff report). Bethesda, Md.: U.S. Department of Health and Human Services.

TABLE 3-2 Indicators of Degree Progress for Ten (T34) COR Institutional Programs

Institution	Program Age (Years)	Entrants (No.)	Graduates (No.)	Graduates (%)	Advanced Degree (No.)	Advanced Degree (%)	Ph.D. (%)	M.D. (%)	M.A. or M.S. (%)	Other (%)
1	20	98	97	99	36	37	16	0	21	0
2	20	117	112	96	62	56	30	3	20	3
3	20	134	118	88	54	46	13	9	24	0
4	18	74	59	80	27	46	5	7	29	5
5	18	86	77	90	23	30				
6	17	78	67	86	13	19	9	10	0	0
7	15	62	62	100	45	72	27	18	27	0
8	14	64	44	69	22	49	27	11	9	2
9	10	53	39	74	15	38	23	0	0	15
10	10	52	36	69	16	45	3	3	33	6
Total		818	711	87	313	46	18	7	19	2

SOURCE: National Institute of Mental Health (NIMH), National Institutes of Health. Undated. NIMH Training Programs for Underrepresented Racial/Ethnic Minorities (NIMH interim staff report). Bethesda, Md.: U.S. Department of Health and Human Services.

TABLE 3-3 Detailed Indicators of Degree Progress for Three (T34) COR Institutional Programs

Institution	Program Age (Years)	Entrants (No.)	Graduate (No.)	Graduate (%)	Accepted into Graduate School (%)	Currently in Graduate or Medical School (%)	Advanced Degree (%)	Ph.D. (%)
1	20	98	97	99	71	21	37	16
2	20	117	112	96	96	39	55	30
4	18	74	59	80	81	16	46	5

SOURCE: National Institute of Mental Health (NIMH), National Institutes of Health. Undated. NIMH Training Programs for Underrepresented Racial/Ethnic Minorities (NIMH interim staff report). Bethesda, Md.: U.S. Department of Health and Human Services.

There appears to be variability in the success with which institutions are successful in moving students to program completion and on to matriculation in graduate school. Again, the comments of T34 COR training directors on this variability as summarized in an NIMH staff report is instructive:

> The T34 COR training directors caution that judging success of a program can and should be done at many levels using many criteria. They emphasize this because T34 COR programs at different institutions are unique, and should be evaluated for their unique contributions and not compared with each other or judged against mainstream programs.[36]

Conclusion

Overall, the T34 U*STAR and T34 COR programs appear to work for most program participants. Both programs appear to have substantial success in moving students through to program completion and the baccalaureate. Estimates of program completion range from 85 to 99 percent, depending on the program. Eighty-nine percent of T34 U*STAR trainees interviewed have completed the program. This is similar to the 87 percent of T34 COR respondents who eventually graduate. The many important and useful features of the program include the opportunity to engage in a hands-on research experience, the availability of mentoring, and the financial support provided by these programs. All are central to the programs and to their success. In the course of reviewing these programs, however, there are areas for further review that may lead to program enhancement. These areas are described briefly below.

Demographics and Recruitment. T34 U*STAR and T34 COR respondents were overwhelmingly female. Program administrators reported a need for greater outreach to African-American males.

Financial Support. There are differences of opinion about whether trainees should work for wages or salaries while in the program. One T34 U*STAR program administrator said that because the stipend of $10,500 was not enough for some students, trainees work on the side. Also, a sizable minority of T34 U*STAR and T34 COR trainees reported earning wages or salaries while in the program. Another administrator, however, screens students to make sure that they do not work outside the program, saying that such work distracts students from their studies and is a "recipe for failure."

Research. The research experience is a central feature of the T34 U*STAR and T34 COR programs. The adequacy of the research infrastructure available to trainees, however, appears to be an issue for at least some of the recipient institutions. Recipient

---

[36] National Institutes of Health, National Institute of Mental Health. Undated. NIMH Training Programs for Underrepresented Racial/Ethnic Minorities, NIMH interim staff report. Bethesda, Md.: U.S. Department of Health and Human Services.

institutions tend to focus on providing access to higher education for lower-income and minority students. Because of this they tend to be institutions that focus on teaching rather than research and tend to charge lower tuition. One consequence is that they do not have the kind of research infrastructure that a more research-intensive institution could provide. This creates a certain tension because the research experience is critical to the success of the T34 U*STAR program and developing an interest among students in scientific research. NIGMS recognizes this problem and has, since the inception of the T34 U*STAR program, required recipient institutions to develop opportunities for extramural research projects for their trainees. This is mandatory for the summer research experience and may also be developed as necessary for research projects during the academic year. Whether recipient institutions are providing a high-quality research experience under these arrangements should be investigated further by NIGMS.

Student Career Goals. A perennial issue, more pertinent to T34 U*STAR than to T34 COR, is whether a student who goes on to earn an M.D. degree should be considered a success for the program. One T34 U*STAR administrator indicated that they screen out students who plan to go to medical school. Another has each trainee sign an agreement to drop out of the program if he or she decided to go to medical school. However, although no T34 U*STAR respondents had yet earned a M.D., more than one-fifth said they planned to. This percentage is similar to the nearly one-quarter of MARC Honors graduates who reported later earning the M.D. degree.

4

Graduate Fellowships and Traineeship Programs

Graduate education and research training differs significantly from undergraduate education and research training. The undergraduate years are generally exploratory in nature, and the coursework is usually broad and inclusive of a variety of disciplines. A successful undergraduate education is designed to produce an intellectually "well-rounded" individual. Undergraduate research training is similarly forgiving. An earnest effort in the laboratory is expected of all undergraduate research trainees, but novel research findings are not a requirement for graduation.

Graduate education and research training, on the other hand, are extremely focused and specific. "Broadness" in the biomedical sciences may mean that psychology trainees also study neuroscience and evolutionary biochemistry, or that immunology trainees also study botany and statistics. Graduate-level training in the biomedical sciences does not often stray into nonscience disciplines. Graduate research training is similarly focused and demanding. Not only is one expected to spend countless hours in the laboratory or office, but novel research findings are a prerequisite to graduation with one's Ph.D. degree.

Graduate training includes traditional learning through classes, seminars, and the like, but it also includes training for other skill sets, such as how to design definitive experiments, how to critically read published research literature, how to present one's research findings to a scientific audience, how to write a research paper suitable for publication in a peer-reviewed scientific journal, how to write a competitive grant proposal, and how to collaborate successfully with others.

Graduate trainees also experience their own unique brand of stress. Many are financially strapped. Many teach undergraduates in addition to doing their own research. Some have young families to attend to. Long hours in the laboratory or office may stress partner relationships or lead to divorce. In many cases, graduate training has no set end point. It could take four to ten full-time years to earn a Ph.D. At some point, trainees must identify, propose, and defend a suitable dissertation topic and hope that, in the meantime, their work is not preempted by another research group. Importantly, mentors have extraordinary influence over the lives and futures of their graduate trainees. Power struggles and disagreements are common among these long-lived training relationships. mentors usually have the final word on whether or not a trainee graduates at all.

Some graduate-level underrepresented minority trainees experience additional challenges. Some may not have had sufficient undergraduate preparation to withstand the rigors of graduate-level coursework. In these cases, remedial training may be necessary in addition to everything else. Graduate training often entails moving to another city or state. Distance from family and community brings with it a whole host of problems. For example, as the gap in educational achievement between minority trainees and their family members grows, previously shared interests may diminish and finding common ground may become more difficult. Family members who do not understand why graduate training takes so long may be critical of minority trainees. Familiar family refrains include, "Why didn't you go to medical school?" and "When are you going to graduate and get a job?" Some minority trainees are viewed by their own communities as having "sold out" or as being "too good for the rest of us" simply because they left the neighborhood or the reservation in pursuit of doctoral-level training. Such phenomena may also affect some nonminority trainees.

On campus, minority trainees may experience further isolation.[37] They have fewer peers with whom they share a common cultural background. Indeed, many learn not to discuss anything related to their cultural background because doing so may elicit ignorant and offensive remarks by nonminority lab mates, whether intended or not. Some faculty view minority trainees as inherently less-qualified than nonminority trainees. This negatively impacts minority trainee morale. Minority trainees have difficulty finding prospective relationship partners with whom they share a common background, simply because there are comparatively fewer minorities on campus. When minority trainees seek to become involved in minority scientific professional societies, they are sometimes discouraged or even prohibited from doing so by faculty mentors who do not value such organizations. Regardless of these challenges, some minority trainees do ultimately graduate with their Ph.D. and go on to become successful biomedical researchers and allied professionals.

The National Institutes of Health (NIH) has a critical role in training future generations of biomedical researchers. First, graduate training is an extension of the support NIH provides our nation's scientists as they advance the forefront of biomedical knowledge. In other words, graduate trainees do much of the work funded by NIH research grants. Thus, they are integral to the NIH mission. Second, the costs associated with graduate-level training in the biomedical sciences far exceed those of other graduate or professional training programs, both because the training itself takes longer and because research supplies are particularly expensive. Third, as a condition of their fiscal relationship with NIH, many graduate trainees in the biomedical sciences are not permitted to take an outside job. They are, in essence, wedded to the laboratory bench or office until such time as they graduate. Thus, if graduate trainees were required to pay for even a

---

[37] The statements in this paragraph reflect graduate trainee responses to open-ended survey questions.

portion of their training, this would undoubtedly exclude some trainees from participation. Since scientific aptitude is a unique commodity in limited supply across the human population, it does not make sense to endorse policies that further limit the pool of scientific talent available for development. Graduate training in the biomedical sciences is difficult enough, and the prohibition on outside work ensures that trainees are contributing all they can to the research enterprise. Thus, it seems fair and reasonable that NIH continue to support our nation's best graduate programs in the biomedical sciences, as well as requiring that trainees devote 100 percent effort to them.

Graduate Programs for Underrepresented Minorities

Increasing the number of qualified underrepresented minorities who can contribute meaningfully to the national research enterprise is a challenge on many different levels. The training pipeline between the undergraduate and graduate career stages is a metaphorical constriction that limits the number of individuals who may advance to the next step. The constriction is sustained, in part, by the high academic standards required for entry into graduate training programs. It is also sustained by a limit of scientific aptitude across the human population. Indeed, this is why so many foreigners are invited to train within our system. Given recent world events, fewer foreigners are coming to the United States to train, and this is impacting our research capacity on a national scale.

Minority-targeted training programs are not an attempt to lower academic standards for entry into graduate training programs; rather, they are an attempt to increase the available supply of qualified underrepresented minority applicants to these programs. One way to increase supply is to support research training at minority-serving institutions. To this end, NIH supports a variety of capacity-building mechanisms that are intended to bolster the research infrastructure of minority-serving institutions. These capacity-building mechanisms provide for laboratory renovations, equipment costs, research supplies, and trainee support. Unfortunately, this study does not examine minority-serving institution capacity-building awards because electronic trainee data were unavailable to the study committee.

(R25) Bridges to the Doctorate

The R25 Bridges to the Doctorate program is administered by the National Institute of General Medical Sciences (NIGMS) and supported by a cluster of NIH Institutes and Centers (ICs). It is designed to improve the preparation and increase the number of underrepresented minorities at master's degree-awarding institutions who will continue on to doctoral programs in biomedical research at doctorate-granting institutions. "Many underrepresented minority students enter terminal master's degree programs and have the potential to become independent research scientists," according to the program announcement. "That potential may be developed by improving the skills they need to be successful research scientists and by providing challenging curricula, outstanding mentoring, active research experiences, guidance, advice, and financial support."

The R25 Bridges to the Doctorate awards are made to partnerships between master's institutions and doctoral institutions, with the goal of providing a seamless transition between these institutions for underrepresented minority students in biomedical research. The master's institution must have a significant enrollment of underrepresented minority students. Further, the partnership may involve a consortium of several institutions or several institutions within a single state system. Collaborative agreements between the institutions involved in a particular grant are designed to fit local needs and meet local goals. As discussed in the 2002 Request for Application (RFA) for the program,[38] institutions may include, but are not limited to, the following kinds of program elements:

- Establishing a mentoring program for master's students with faculty at the doctoral institution.
- Enhancing the curriculum of the master's institution.
- Enabling and encouraging students from either institution to take classes at the other institution.
- Offering academic counseling for master's students.
- Providing research opportunities for master's students at the doctoral institution or in private industrial laboratories (students may receive compensation for these activities).
- Strengthening the research capability of the master's institution (e.g., by fostering research collaborations among faculty and joint seminar programs).

Since the R25 Bridges to the Doctorate program does not provide doctoral-level training support, partner institutions must specify how institutional support will be provided to students once they transfer to a Ph.D. program.

(T32) NRSA Minority Institutional Research Training Program

The Ruth L. Kirchstein National Research Service Award (NRSA) program for minorities provides predoctoral support through T32 institutional training grants. During the period covered by this retrospective study (1970-1999), two NIH institutes offered minority-targeted versions of the NRSA Institutional Training Grants program. Since 1984, the National Heart, Lung, and Blood Institute (NHLBI) has awarded Minority Institutional Research Training Grants to minority-serving institutions. The program provides training to graduate and health professional students enrolled at minority schools that have the potential to develop a meritorious program in cardiovascular, pulmonary, hematologic, or sleep disorders research. These individuals should be in the developmental stages of their career. The minority institution collaborates with a research center that has

---

[38] National Institutes of General Medical Sciences (NIGMS), National Institutes of Health. Initiative for Minority Students: Bridges to the Baccalaureate, Program Announcement (PAR-02-084). See http://grants2.nih.gov/grants/guide/pa-files/PAR-02-084.

strong, well-established programs of research in these areas. The partnering institution opens its facilities to the minority individual and provides a mentor to work with the individual's adviser at the minority institution.

Since 1978, NIMH has employed the minority-targeted T32 grant mechanism. These awards are designed to provide training programs that significantly increase the number of underrepresented minority scientists trained to conduct research in mental health, mental illness, drug abuse, and neurological sciences. The programs do so by training future scientists with state-of-the-art research skills in cutting-edge science and a commitment to research in their chosen field.

(T35) NRSA Short-Term Institutional Training Grants

The Ruth L. Kirchstein National Research Service Award (NRSA) program for minorities provides predoctoral support through T35 institutional training grants. These awards support intensive, short-term research training experiences (usually during the summer) for students in health professional schools, and in the case of the National Institute of Environmental Health Sciences (NIEHS), they are also used for undergraduate research training. NHLBI supports T35 Short-Term Research Training for underrepresented minority undergraduate and graduate students and for students in health professional schools to expose them to biomedical and behavioral research and career options in these fields. The proposed training must be in either basic or clinical aspects of the health-related science and should be of sufficient depth to enable the trainees, upon completion of the program, to have a thorough exposure to principles underlying the conduct of research. Awards are made to eligible institutions to develop or enhance research training opportunities specifically in cardiovascular, pulmonary, hematological, and sleep disorders research. NHLBI has utilized the T35 minority-targeted Short-Term Institutional Training Grant funding vehicle since 1990.

(F31) NRSA Minority Institutional Research Training Program

The Ruth L. Kirchstein NRSA program for minorities also provides predoctoral support through F31 individual predoctoral fellowships. During the period covered by this study (1970-1999), 17 of the 27 NIH institutes have utilized the NRSA F31 Predoctoral Fellowship Award for Minority Students. These awards provide up to five years of support for research training leading to a Ph.D., M.D.-Ph.D., or other professional degree combined with a Ph.D. in the biomedical or behavioral sciences. The intent of this fellowship program is to encourage students from underrepresented minority groups to seek graduate degrees and, thus, further the goal of increasing the number of minority scientists who are prepared to pursue careers in biomedical and behavioral research. The F31 fellowship provides an annual stipend, tuition, and fee allowance as well as an annual institutional allowance that may be used for travel to scientific meetings and for laboratory and other training expenses.

(F31) MARC NRSA Predoctoral Fellowship Program

The NIGMS awards F31 Minority Access to Research Careers (MARC) predoctoral fellowships to outstanding graduates of the R25 MARC Undergraduate Student Training in Academic Research (U*STAR) program to help them pursue a graduate degree in the biomedical sciences. The F31 fellowships are individual NRSAs that provide up to five years of support. These awards provide an annual stipend, tuition and fees, and an allowance to the predoctoral fellow's sponsoring institution to help defray such trainee expenses as research supplies and equipment. Support is not available for individuals enrolled in medical or other professional schools unless they are enrolled in a combined-degree (e.g., M.D.-Ph.D., D.D.S.-Ph.D., or D.V.M.-Ph.D.) program.

(R03) Minority Dissertation Research Grant

The National Institute on Aging (NIA) and the National Institute of Mental Health (NIMH) have utilized this funding vehicle since 1991 and 1994, respectively. It provides R03 Minority Dissertation Research Grants to doctoral candidates from racial and ethnic groups that are underrepresented in the biomedical and behavioral sciences to pursue research careers in any area relevant to the supporting institute. Eligible doctoral candidates are minorities enrolled in accredited doctoral degree program in the behavioral, biomedical, or social science s and must have approval of the dissertation proposal by a named committee. The award provides support to the candidate to facilitate completion of the doctoral research and dissertation.

Focus of the Assessment

Information on these programs was gathered and assessed through the following steps:

1. Key documents related to the programs were reviewed, including any previous evaluations that were conducted by NIH institutes and centers.
2. Trainees previously supported by these graduate research training awards were interviewed by the NIH-approved contractor using a computer-assisted telephone interview (CATI) protocol. These interviews were about 30 minutes in length and utilized both structured response and open-ended questions.
3. Information was collected through formal interviews with program administrators at recipient institutions (PARIs). These telephone interviews were conducted by the NIH data contractor. The interviews were open-ended and administered in an ethnographic style.[39]

---

[39] Ethnographic interviewing uses techniques from anthropology to collect concrete information from individuals in their context of use. Thus, rather than studying individuals per se, ethnography entails learning from them. This nuance has implications with regard to the kind of information that is collected.

Previous Program Evaluations Conducted by NIH

Evaluation of the (R25) Bridges to the Doctorate

In 1999, NIGMS convened a working group to examine the current status of the two R25 Bridges programs (undergraduate and graduate) and to review and revise program goals for the future.[40] As part of its work, this group reviewed data from NIGMS staff and found that, as of September 1999, NIGMS could assert some success with the R25 Bridges to the Doctorate program and urged the program to improve further. However, recent data show decreases in the rate of student success over time.

1. Indicator: Transfer Rate

- In 1999, NIGMS reported that after five years, 57 percent of all R25 Bridges to the Doctorate program trainees had transferred to a doctoral program.
- The 1999 working group recommended an increase in the number and percentage of underrepresented minority students in R25 Bridges institutions who successfully transfer from master's to doctoral programs by achieving a 90 percent transfer rate by 2005.
- However, in the most recent year (FY 2003) for which data are available, the percentage of trainees who were transferring had declined to just 30 percent.

2. Indicator: Completion of the Ph.D.

- In 1999, NIGMS reported that of the R25 Bridges to the Doctorate trainees who transfer, 60 percent had obtained a Ph.D. or were seeking the advanced degree.
- The working group recommended an increase in the number and percentage of underrepresented minority students in R25 Bridges institutions who successfully complete the doctorate by achieving a completion rate of 70 percent of all students who transfer by 2005.

---

[40] National Institute of General Medical Sciences and Office of Research on Minority Health, National Institutes of Health. Undated. Planning and Priorities of the Bridges to the Future Program. Bethesda, Md.: U.S. Department of Health and Human Services. See http://nigms.nih.gov/news/reports/bridges.html.

Evaluation of the (F31) MARC Predoctoral Fellowship Program

Published by NIGMS in May 2000,[41] this study was designed to assess the success of F31 MARC predoctoral fellows in establishing research careers and the types of research careers and research activities engaged in by these individuals. The data were drawn from existing NIH databases as well as from curricula vitae (CVs) provided by individuals supported as MARC predoctoral fellows. The study group population included all individuals with initial support under the F31 MARC Predoctoral Fellowship Program from 1981 to 1993. It is unlikely that individuals receiving initial support after 1993 would have had adequate time for completion of postdoctoral training and establishment of a research career. A total of 191 individuals were supported under this program during 1981-1993. The study population was stratified into three cohorts based on initial year of fellowship support: 1981-1985, 1986-1990, and 1991-1993.

Overall, the results of this study show a favorable achievement pattern for former F31 MARC predoctoral fellows consistent over the three cohorts. Furthermore, the data presented in this study parallel results obtained in previous evaluations of NRSA trainees and fellows.

The level of application for NIH grants and the number of publications by former F31 MARC predoctoral fellows are comparable to those of other NIH trainees and fellows. Moreover, even though these results should not be generalized because of the small sample size, they do suggest that the potential for individuals supported by F31 MARC predoctoral fellowships to pursue active careers in research is good. Summary data on the postgraduate training and career involvement in research for recipients of F31 MARC predoctoral fellowship support are displayed in Tables 4-1 and 4-2. Note that some individuals were unresponsive to NIGMS requests for their CVs; thus, the percentages may appear somewhat "off" because the tables do not resolve how many respondents with Ph.D.s actually submitted their CVs.

As shown in Table 4-1, the completion rate of 63 percent for F31 MARC predoctoral fellows from 1981 to1990[42] compares favorably to the 69 percent completion rate for NRSA F31 predoctoral fellows and trainees from 1967 to 1975 documented in a 1984 study by the National Academy of Sciences.[43] A more recent study of predoctoral trainees supported by NIH from 1980 to 1986 found a higher completion rate of 76 percent.[44]

---

[41] National Institute of General Medical Sciences, National Institutes of Health. 2000. The Careers and Professional Activities of Former NIGMS Minority Access to Research Careers Predoctoral Fellows. Bethesda, Md.: U.S. Department of Health and Human Services. See http://www.nigms.nih.gov/news/reports/marcstudy.html.

[42] *Ibid.*

[43] Coggeshall, P.E., and P. W. Brown. 1984. The Career Achievements of NIH Predoctoral Trainees ands Fellows. Washington, D.C.: National Academy Press.

[44] Pion, G. M. 2001, The Early Career Progress of NRSA Predoctoral Trainees and Fellows. Bethesda, Md.: National Institutes of Health.

TABLE 4-1 Postgraduate Training of F31 MARC Predoctoral Scholars, 1981-1993

		Completed Ph.D. (all fellows)		Postdoctoral Training Support Received (respondents only)		Research Support Received (respondents only)	
Cohort	Total No. of Fellows	Number	Percentage of Total	Number	Percentage of Ph.D.s	Number	Percentage of Ph.D.s
1981-1985	49	31	63	14	66	14	67
1986-1990	78	49	63	27	61	11	25
1991-1993	64	30	47	18	62	1	3

TABLE 4-2 Research Involvement of F31 MARC Predoctoral Fellows, 1981-1993

		Applied for NIH Grant (all fellows)		Received NIH Grant (applicants only)		
Cohort	Total No. of Fellows	Number	Percentage of Ph.D.s	Number	Percentage of Applicants	Median Number of Articles (respondents only)
1981-1985	49	11	35	5	45	7
1986-1990	78	10	20	9	90	5
1991-1993	64	n.a.	n.a.	n.a.	n.a.	4

NOTE: n.a. = data not available

The average time lapse for completion of the Ph.D. degree by former F31 MARC predoctoral fellows was 7.3 years, slightly less time than comparable life sciences Ph.D. degrees as seen in a 1999 study sponsored by the National Science Foundation.[45] The average lapsed time for completion of the M.D.-Ph.D. by F31 MARC predoctoral fellows was 7.7 years.

The greatest percentage of F31 MARC predoctoral fellows obtained doctorates in biochemistry-chemistry, with the next largest discipline being physiology-biophysics.[46]

---

[45] National Science Foundation, Division of Science Resources Statistics. 2002. Doctoral Scientists and Engineers: 1999 Profile (NSF 03-302). Arlington, Va.: National Science Foundation.

[46] National Institute of General Medical Sciences (NIGMS), National Institutes of Health. 1998. Careers and Professional Activities of Former NIGMS Minority Access to Research Careers Predoctoral Fellows. Bethesda, Md.: U.S. Department of Health and Human Services.

Of former F31 MARC predoctoral fellows with Ph.D. degrees, 63 percent received postdoctoral training, similar to graduates of the NIGMS Medical Scientist Training Program[47] but lower than F31 NRSA predoctoral fellows and trainees (78 percent).[48]

As shown in Table 4-2, of the 127 F31 MARC predoctoral fellows supported between 1981 and 1990, 17 percent have applied for NIH grants. The success rate for the 21 individuals who did apply for NIH support was 67 percent.

The majority of former F31 MARC predoctoral fellows are or have been employed in academia. The number employed by industry increased threefold from the 1981-1985 cohort to the 1986-1990 cohort and remained stable at approximately 25 percent for the 1991-1993 cohort. The percentage of former F31 MARC predoctoral fellows employed by the government was extremely small.[49]

Trainee Interview Data

As shown in Table 4-3, NIH supported 16,480 graduate trainees in the study's universe of targeted and nontargeted comparison programs between 1970 and 1999.[50] The NIH-approved data contractor utilized for this study interviewed a total of 328 trainees who were supported by these programs during the time frame of the study.

In the absence of NIH-wide electronic trainee tracking data, the NIH data contractor was not successful in its efforts to locate and interview trainees. Of the 2,464 graduate trainees in the sample, the contractor was able to obtain contact data on only 759 trainees, or 31 percent of the eligible trainees. This was the case despite its use of two commercial and proprietary credit card databases that together maintain credit card-related contact information for millions of Americans, and the query of the U.S. Postal Service address-forwarding database. There is, consequently, a high likelihood of sample bias among the trainee survey results. The committee believes that the external validity of the data is compromised and that this caveat should be considered when making inferences based on these data.

---

[47] National Institute of General Medical Sciences (NIGMS), National Institutes of Health. 1998. The Careers and Professional Activities of Graduates of the NIGMS Medical Scientist Training Program. Bethesda, Md.: U.S. Department of Health and Human Services.

[48] National Institute of General Medical Sciences (NIGMS), National Institutes of Health. 2000. Careers and Professional Activities of Former NIGMS Minority Access to Research Careers Predoctoral Fellows. Bethesda, Md.: U.S. Department of Health and Human Services.

[49] *Ibid.*

[50] Nontargeted comparison program parameters were matched as closely as possible to targeted program parameters. Thus, both categories of program derive from the same institutes and were administered during the same temporal window.

TABLE 4-3 Graduate Fellows and Trainees by Program, Race/Ethnicity in the Universe and Sample, and Race/Ethnicity as Self-Identified in Interviews

			No. of Trainees		No. Interviewed		
Type	Title	Categories	Universe	Sample	Total	URM	Non-URM
Targeted	(R-25) Bridges to the Doctorate	URM	300	200	23	22	1[a]
Targeted	(T-32) NRSA Institutional Training Grant	URM	999	200	22	16	6[b]
Nontargeted	(T-32) NRSA Institutional Training Grant	URM	492	330	28	27	1[c]
		Non-URM	3,948	290	46	0	46
		Unknown	3,594	290	56	7	49
		Total	8,034	910	130	34	96
Targeted	Short-Term Institutional Training Grant (T-35)	URM	2,646	200	19	15	4[d]
Nontargeted	(T-35) Short-Term Institutional Training Grant	URM	300	300	28	25	3[e]
		Non-URM	1,725	150	25	0	25
		Unknown	1,348	150	16	2	14
		Total	3,373	600	69	27	42
Targeted	(F-31) NRSA Predoctoral Fellowship and MARC Predoctoral Fellowship	URM	126	126	19	10	9[f]
Nontargeted	(F-31) NRSA Predoctoral Fellowship	URM	64	64	7	6	1[g]
		Non-URM	691	60	15	0	15
		Unknown	203	60	12	1	11
		Total	958	184	34	7	27
Targeted	(F-34) Predoctoral Faculty Training Grant	URM	10	10	0	0	0
Targeted	(R-03) NIMH Dissertation Grant	URM	34	34	12	11	1[h]
All	**All Programs**	**URM**	**4,971**	**1,464**	**158**	**132**	**26**
		Non-URM	**6,364**	**500**	**86**	**0**	**86**
		Unknown	**5,145**	**500**	**84**	**10**	**74**
		Total	**16,480**	**2,464**	**328**	**142**	**186**

NOTE:

URM = underrepresented minority. For the universe and sample, under-represented minorities are defined as African American, Hispanic American, Native American, or Alaskan Native. For purposes of defining the universe and the sample, it was assumed that all participants in targeted programs were underrepresented minorities. Among those interviewed, the number of URMs also includes individuals who self-identified as Pacific Islander and the number of non-URMs includes those who self-identified as Asian or white in the interview process. The footnotes below indicate in the "Interviewed" column the number of individuals by race/ethnicity who were indicated as URMs in the universe and sample, but self-identified as non-URM in the interview process.

Non-URM = white or Asian. The footnotes below indicate in the "Interviewed" column the number of individuals by race or ethnicity who were indicated as URMs in the universe and sample, but self-identified as non-URM in the interview process.

Unknown = for large fractions of the trainees in the universe and trainees selected for the sample, their race or ethnicity was unknown (i.e., not recorded in NIH data sets). Their race or ethnicity was later resolved in the interview process as noted in the "Interviewed" column.

[a] Among the 23 targeted R-25 trainees interviewed, one self-identified as Asian.
[b] Among the 22 targeted T-32 trainees interviewed, six self-identified as Asian.
[c] Among the 28 URM trainees in the nontargeted T-32 program who were interviewed, one self-identified as white.
[d] Among the 19 targeted T-35 trainees interviewed, three self-identified as Asian and one self-identified as white. For analytical purposes, the one white trainee was re-classified as a nonminority in the nontargeted program.
[e] Among the 28 URM trainees in the nontargeted T-35 program who were interviewed, two self-identified as Asian and one self-identified as white.
[f] Among the 19 targeted F-31 trainees interviewed, two self-identified as Asian and seven self-identified as white. For analytical purposes, the seven white trainees were re-classified as non-minorities in the nontargeted program.
[g] Among the 7 URM trainees in the nontargeted F-31 program who were interviewed, one self-identified as white.
[h] Among the 12 targeted R-03 trainees interviewed, one self-identified as Asian.

In addition, the NIH data contractor was not able to interview all those trainees for whom it had contact data. Of the 759 eligible graduate trainees, 344 were never contacted, 9 failed the screener, 60 refused the interview, and 18 failed to complete the interview, resulting in 328 completed interviews. Some evidence suggests the trainees interviewed for our survey were more likely to be among the more "successful" program participants. For example, among those who participated in the R25 Bridges to the Baccalaureate program, survey respondents were more likely to have transferred to a four-year institution and completed a bachelor's degree than program participants in general. The study committee was similarly skeptical of the large numbers of respondents who had at least one family member with a bachelor's or graduate degree. The committee believes the data from these interviews may not reflect the responses that would have been obtained had the respondents been more representative of the larger universe of program participants. Nevertheless, the data are instructive in a general way and are described in this report qualitatively. For example, respondent data are reported using a variety of nonspecific phrases such as: "nearly all reported," "a majority of respondents said", "a minority of respondents said," "more likely," and "less likely." Such phrases should not be equated with statistical significance.

Trainee Characteristics

The gender distribution of trainees shows some differences by program and minority group. The majority of minority trainees for each of the graduate-level programs were female. This finding is consistent with demographic characteristics of trainees in NIH minority undergraduate research training programs.

Nearly all nonminority respondents in the F31 fellows and T32 trainees programs were white. Among all targeted graduate-level programs, African Americans and Hispanics prevail, and this is consistent with the demographics of targeted programs at the undergraduate level. By contrast, there were more Hispanics than African Americans among minority trainees in nontargeted programs. Finally, R25 Bridges to the Doctorate trainees reflected the highest percentage of Native Americans (12 percent) relative to other graduate-level programs. There is no cognate nontargeted program for comparison with the R25 Bridges to the Doctorate.

Roughly one-quarter of the minority trainees in targeted programs said that English was not their first language. About one-half of all graduate-level trainees were married or living in a long-term relationship. The F31 fellows and T32 trainees, regardless of minority status, were more likely to have dependents than those who participated in T35 short-term training grants. About one-fifth of the R25 Bridges to the Doctorate respondents reported having had dependents while they were in the program. Among minorities in the nontargeted F31 fellows and T32 trainees programs, roughly one-third report having had dependents while they were in the program.

A majority of respondents across programs and minority groups reported that a parent or sibling had earned a graduate degree. The proportion of minority trainees having family members with graduate degrees may be high relative to the general population, but lower than that for nonminority trainees.

Recruitment

Respondents reported differences in the way they learned about the program in which they participated. R25 Bridges to the Doctorate respondents reported learning about the program primarily from an undergraduate professor or a graduate adviser. The F31 fellows and T32 trainees usually learned about their program from their graduate adviser. Nonminority respondents reported this more often than did minority respondents. The second most cited sources of information about the programs were departmental staff and colleagues. Nonminority respondents were more likely to cite these sources than minority respondents. The latter reported learning about the program from a bulletin board or some "other" source more often than did their nonminority peers. For the T35 short-term training grant respondents, sources of information about the program varied widely. This likely reflects the heterogeneity of this trainee population, but the numbers of respondents were too small and had too great a chance of bias for comparisons among programs.

Funding

Respondents were asked two questions about funding support: (1) their sources of support during graduate school, and (2) additional sources of support while they were in the program. A majority of F31 fellows and T32 trainees and T35 short-term institutional training grant respondents reported holding scholarships while in graduate school. This was not true for R25 Bridges to the Doctorate respondents whose graduate school support came from a variety of sources, including spouse or family. A large fraction of respondents across all graduate-level programs reported having taken out loans while in graduate school. Nonminority respondents, in general, were more likely to cite personal, family, or spousal support while in the program. Numerous respondents across the graduate-level programs said that the financial support offered by the program was necessary and helpful but should be increased.

Mentoring

Respondents were asked if they had a mentor while in the program, specifically "someone who took a personal interest in and was supportive of the trainee's research career." The vast majority of respondents regardless of program and race or ethnic group indicated that they had a mentor. Mentors for R25 Bridges to the Doctorate respondents were evenly split between male and female and reflect diverse racial and ethnic backgrounds. Mentors for respondents from the F31 fellows and T32 trainees programs and the T35 short-term institutional training program were overwhelmingly white and male.

Respondents were asked a series of questions about their laboratory heads or principal investigators (PIs), including whether they encouraged the trainee in his or her research, whether they were good to work with, if they were active in the scientific community, whether they provided good career advice, if the career advice was good, and whether they helped the trainee obtain funding for research. There was little variation in the response patterns to these questions across programs and racial or ethnic groups. The majority of respondents reported that their PIs provided some or abundant encouragement to participate in research and that their PIs were either good or very good to work with. Respondents also reported that their PIs were mostly active or very active in the scientific community. A majority of respondents indicated that their PIs provided good or very good career advice. The majority of respondents across programs and racial or ethnic groups interacted with their PIs at least weekly.

The majority of respondents across programs and racial or ethnic groups reported being close to or familiar with their PIs. Nearly one-half of F31 fellows or T32 trainees remained in contact with their PIs for more than six years. This was not the case for trainees on T35 short-term training grants perhaps because of the transient nature of the short-term training experience. R25 Bridges to the Doctorate respondents demonstrate an even spread across the response variables. One-third of these did not remain in touch with their PIs.

A modest majority of respondents indicated that their PIs had some or abundant influence on their careers. R25 Bridges to the Doctorate and T35 short-term training grant respondents were more likely than F31 fellows and T32 trainees to report a "neutral" influence. One-quarter of the R25 Bridges to the Doctorate respondents and one-third of the targeted short-term training program respondents stated their PIs had no influence on their careers.

The majority of respondents across programs and racial or ethnic groups reported that the program influenced their education and their careers. Respondents who were F31 fellows and T32 trainees were somewhat more likely to report that their program influenced their careers than were respondents on T35 short-term training grants. In the case of R25 Bridges to the Doctorate, some PIs helped students conclude that a research career was not for them. Interestingly, one-half of all R25 Bridges respondents commented that mentoring within the program could be improved. One PARI touched upon the issue by saying, ". . . one of the things with all of these training grants is that basically the faculty time . . . is all pro bono."

Trainee Experience with Laboratory or Research Group

The majority of respondents across programs and racial or ethnic groups interacted with their laboratory or research group on at least a weekly, if not a daily, basis. Respondents reported less frequent interaction with other colleagues, but there were also differences in this interaction. Minority respondents supported by T35 short-term training grants were more likely to report interaction with other colleagues than did nonminority respondents. Conversely, F31 fellows and T32 trainees in nontargeted programs were more likely to report interactions with other colleagues than were respondents in targeted programs.

Nonminority respondents in general reported higher levels of social integration (familiar or close) than did minority respondents. Minorities in nontargeted programs were least as likely to report feeling familiar or close to their groups or colleagues. Not surprisingly, respondents who were F31 fellows or T32 trainees were more likely to stay in touch with their groups and other colleagues and for a longer period of time after leaving the program than were respondents on T35 short-term training grants. Similarly, respondents who were F31 fellows and T32 trainees reported that their groups influenced their careers more so than did R25 Bridges or T35 short-term training program respondents.

Trainee Expectations about the Program

Among respondents who were F31 fellows and T32 trainees, most expected their programs to provide financial support. Among those with this expectation, nearly all said that it was met. Among respondents who were in T35 short-term training grant programs, only a fraction expected their program to provide financial support, but most of those who had this expectation said it was met.

Nearly all respondents across programs and racial or ethnic groups expected the program to improve their research skills and to provide an opportunity to establish a relationship with a mentor. Among those who had these expectations, nearly all said that they were met.

Only a fraction of F31 fellows and T32 trainees expected the program to improve their teaching skills, and of those who had this expectation most said it was met. Whether respondents who received T35 short-term training grants expected the program to improve teaching skills depended on whether the respondent was in a targeted or nontargeted program. Only a fraction of respondents in nontargeted programs had this expectation, but most of those in targeted programs did. This likely reflects the heterogeneity of the targeted T35 short-term trainee population, which was comprised chiefly of undergraduate and graduate trainees. In either case, most respondents had their expectations met.

Trainee Outcomes with Regard to Program Completion

A modest majority of R25 Bridges to the Doctorate respondents said the Ph.D. was the highest degree they expected to earn. Almost one-half of R25 Bridges to the Doctorate respondents had successfully completed their master's degrees, and one-tenth had earned Ph.D.s. One-quarter left the program without earning any degrees. A decline in transfer rates from master's to doctoral-level institutions has been observed for this program in recent years. The vast majority of trainee respondents from the F31 Fellow and T32 Trainee programs said a Ph.D. was the highest degree they sought. A substantial majority of these successfully obtained the degree. The majority of respondents who participated in the T35 short-term training grant program said the M.D. was the highest degree they sought. Only a smaller fraction stated that the Ph.D. was their goal. Of those who said the M.D. was their goal, most attained it, with the exception of the minority trainees in targeted T35 short-term training programs, many of whom were undergraduates. Only a small fraction of these trainees attained an M.D. degree.

Trainee Expectations and Outcomes about Career after Program

Most F31 fellows and T32 Trainee respondents expected the program to increase their chances of obtaining postdoctoral positions after graduate training, or to improve their chances of obtaining research and/or faculty positions or assist in securing grants. Among these respondents, most reported that their expectations were met. Medical school and practicing medicine were far more on the minds of participants in T35 short-term training grant programs than for F31 fellows and T32 trainees.

Most F31 fellows and T32 trainee respondents said that their next career step would be postdoctoral work or a job in academe, private industry, or government. The frequency with which trainees did what they expected they would do was striking. Slightly more trainees undertook postdoctoral training than said they had expected to do so. The following factors are even more dramatic: Among nonminority trainees, only a fraction expected academe to be their next step, yet roughly one-half of this cohort reported taking work in academe. These may be mostly teaching positions, given that full-time research faculty positions are nearly impossible to obtain, at least in the biological sciences, without first doing postdoctoral work. Additionally, a tiny fraction of respondents expected to move to the private sector, yet fully one-fifth did. These trends may reflect the uncertainty and small size of the post-Ph.D. job market in academe, or they could simply be an artifact of trainee recall about expectations they may have had in the past. Since the same trend appears among the T35 short-term training grant respondents, a "recall artifact" may be more likely. Nonetheless, minority trainees were less likely than nonminority trainees to report that their expectations were met with regard to securing employment.

Among F31 fellows and T32 Trainee respondents the most recent employer for more than one-half of them is a U.S. university, U.S. community college, or U.S. medical school. A smaller fraction reported working in the private sector. For T35 short-term training grant respondents, most recent employer responses were highly variable.

Just over one-half of all F31 fellows and T32 Trainee respondents in these programs reported being a senior author on one or more published research papers subsequent to earning their Ph.D.; this proportion was higher for nonminority trainees than for minority trainees. Roughly one-half of all F31 fellows and T32 trainees reported obtaining one or more research grants after graduation. This does not hold for T35 short-term training grant respondents, perhaps because of this population's focus on clinical service delivery and its overall heterogeneity.

Comments of Trainees and Fellows about the Program

Trainees interviewed for this study were asked several open-ended questions including, What were the best features of the program? What were the worst features of the program? What improvements for the program would you recommend? and Do you have anything else you would like to say to NIH? Their answers provide a picture of the program features that were important to them and the concerns they had about the program and their experience in it.

Program Quality

In response to the question, Do you have anything else you would like to say to NIH? the overwhelming majority of respondents who were in these programs commented on the quality of and/or their appreciation for the program. There were some variations in the response by program and race or ethnicity as listed below.

(T32) NRSA Institutional Training Grants

- Among underrepresented minorities who were supported on minority T32 NRSA Institutional Training Grants, a high number of responses commented on the importance of the program for minority students. One respondent argued, "It's a fantastic program and it's trained a number of prominent minorities that are sociologists today. I'm proud to be a part of it." Another said, "Without the award, young researchers of color would not get the experience they need."
- Trainees who were supported on nontargeted T32 NRSA Institutional Training Grants emphasized the importance of the program to their education and training. One respondent called the program "wildly successful".
- There were respondents who indicated that, although the program was successful educationally, their job prospects after completion of the program were limited. When asked in what ways the program did not meet their expectations, the response offered most frequently was that career opportunities after the program did not meet the respondent's expectation. However, when asked in what way the program influenced their careers, one of the most cited responses across programs and racial/ethnic groups was the career opportunities that the award afforded them. The prestige of their awards featured prominently among their responses, especially for those respondents who were F31 NRSA predoctoral fellows.
- A handful of trainees who were supported under nontargeted T32 NRSA Institutional Training Grants also noted that there was a need for more trainees from underrepresented minority groups.

(F31) Fellowships and (R03) Dissertation Grants

- Respondents who were funded either through the F31 fellowship or R03 dissertation grant programs agreed that the program was very positive for them, and they were more likely than T32 NRSA Institutional Training Grant respondents to say that the funding either "came at the right time for" or "played a key role in" their research.
- Respondents, especially F31 NRSA predoctoral fellows, also noted that the fellowship was instrumental to their success in graduate school. One minority respondent on a nontargeted grant said, "I'm thankful for it. It came at the right time. It was very prestigious. It was a good opportunity." Another nonminority

respondent replied, "It's important to be funded so that one can focus one's attention on accomplishing a long-term goal."

Taken together, these comments indicate a high-level of satisfaction among survey respondents with their experiences with the program. Of note, when asked what the worst features of the program were? a frequent response was "none," but for almost all programs and racial or ethnic groups the majority of respondents raised important issues for consideration, which are described below.

Program Features

Financial Support. When asked what the best features of the program were, the feature cited more than any other was the financial support offered to students so that they could focus on their studies or dissertation research. This was true across all graduate-level programs and racial or ethnic groups. This differs from undergraduate programs whose respondents were less likely to cite the financial support as a best feature.

In addition to noting the importance of financial support, many respondents praised the flexibility that funding afforded. Rather than working at an outside job, predoctoral trainees said that the funding allowed them to focus exclusively on their research projects. A small handful of F31 fellows—in both targeted and nontargeted programs—noted the importance of the prestige attached to the award.

While financial support was most frequently cited as the best feature of these programs, when asked what improvements to the program they would suggest, the response offered most frequently among those who answered the question was to increase the stipend and other financial support.

A disturbing and somewhat ironic observation was offered by three F31 NRSA predoctoral fellows who said that when they received the fellowship, they lost the health insurance that had been provided to them as part of their institutional training grant support.

Educational Preparation. When asked what the best features of the program were one- third of the R25 Bridges to the Doctorate respondents cited activities leading to further intellectual development. These included laboratory research experience, classes, special seminars, and workshops. The skills cited by respondents included research skills, laboratory techniques, critical thinking, teaching skills, making presentations, organizational skills, and database management. A program feature cited as a best feature by several R25 Bridges to the Doctorate respondents was the opportunity to travel to conferences or to undertake research at another campus or at NIH. One respondent, however, indicated that traveling to another school to do research was a worst feature saying "that school lacked the technologies to do the research."

When asked how the program influenced their education, respondents who were on training grants frequently noted how it allowed them either to complete their education and acquire skills or to participate in research. They also frequently noted how the program shaped their career goals or was influential in determining their research focus.

Among those respondents who were on F31 fellowships or R03 dissertation grants, the most frequently cited response was the opportunity to conduct research or complete their dissertation.

Networking. Networking appears to be a key feature and key area of concern for respondents who were in targeted and nontargeted trainee programs. Networking was highly cited as a best feature by respondents in both targeted and nontargeted trainee programs. When asked in what ways the program influenced their education, minorities in targeted programs frequently answered that the program provided networking opportunities they otherwise would not have had. Networking was also mentioned by some respondents as an area in need of improvement.

Mentoring. Mentoring also appears to be a key feature and a key area of concern for respondents in targeted and nontargeted trainee programs. Although not highly cited, mentoring was an important best feature for some respondents, predominantly those in nontargeted trainee programs. It was also the third most often cited area in need of improvement. Indeed, in response to a question about ways in which the program did not meet the respondent's expectations, the second largest response focused on deficiencies in the mentoring offered.

When asked how their PIs influenced their education or career path, R25 Bridges to the Doctorate respondents reflected that they were either encouraged or discouraged to continue on to a doctoral program in biomedical research. Those who were encouraged received help in establishing the academic connections needed for a smooth transition to a Ph.D. program. Those who were discouraged reported experiencing varying degrees of benign neglect.

Program Outreach. A large number of respondents who were trained on targeted or nontargeted training grants indicated that they believed their program could improve outreach to new trainees.

Grant Writing and Application Process. When asked how the program influenced their education and careers, the most frequently cited response among those who had F31 fellowships or R03 dissertation grants, along with the importance of the research experience, was the acquisition of grant writing skills. The application process was often cited as one of the worst features of the program by F31 fellows or those in R03 dissertation grant programs and was an area in need of improvement. However, two respondents said they learned a lot from the feedback they received on their research proposals.

Payback. There were complaints about the payback provisions, especially among nonminorities on training grants.

Other Features. Other worst features or suggestions for NIH noted by only a few respondents included long hours, departmental politics, favoritism, and the use of trainees as "cheap labor." Several respondents said that NIH should demand greater accountability from recipient institutions, and two respondents suggested cutting funds for trainees or fellows who are not making sufficient progress.

On Being a Minority. When asked how being a minority affected their experience in the program, three types of answers were offered. First, almost exclusively among minorities on T32 NRSA institutional training grants—targeted or nontargeted—respondents indicated that being a minority focused their research interests on issues related to minority communities or populations. Second, a substantial number of respondents, chiefly those on NIMH R03 dissertation research grants, said it helped them secure the grant in the first place, and another substantial number of minority respondents in nontargeted training programs indicated that being a minority created opportunities for them.

However, an equally large number of respondents across all three programs reported negative experiences associated with being a minority. They expressed such concerns as feeling isolated or having inadequate support because of their race or ethnicity. Several noted that others appeared to perceive them negatively because they had targeted awards or simply because of their race or ethnicity.

Interviews with Program Administrators at Recipient Institutions (PARIs)

(R25) Bridges to the Doctorate Program Interviews

History and Evolution of the Program

The two R25 Bridges to the Doctorate program administrators interviewed for this study described very different origins for their programs. In one case, the program evolved out of a summer research training program that the institution had been running across a number of scientific disciplines. The program administrator related that the two partner master's degree institutions identified "students in their master's programs that the faculty at those institutions felt would be potential . . . candidates for pursuing the Ph.D. and [who] had interests that matched the kind of research that the faculty at [our] department was engaged in." These students, then, were invited to attend the doctoral institution for the summer, "and we basically had a variety of activities aimed at . . . orienting them to the research that was being done here and linking them up with one or more . . . mentors, with the initial goal being that these students would then select—when they returned to their home institution—the thesis option for the master's degree. In a lot of these clinical training master's programs, including ours, students have an option of doing a master's with or without a thesis." The goal is to interest the students in the possibility of pursuing the Ph.D. and a career in research.

In the other case, the program was initiated when the program administrator saw the announcement from NIH and decided to respond to it in partnership with a master's degree institution at which the administrator had previously been a faculty member. The master's degree institution had a healthy pool of students and a track record of success in recruiting minority trainees into the biomedical sciences. The focus of the R25 Bridges to the Doctorate program was to motivate these students to pursue doctoral studies. Unfortunately, shortly after the program was funded the master's degree institution became ineligible to continue as a grantee because it had just begun to offer its first doctoral program. So the program had to be reconstituted using a different master's degree institution that similarly targeted the Native American population. This program articulated four goals:

1. Target enrollment goals for research assistantships to support a certain number of students each year at the master's level;
2. Enhance the research capacity of the master's institution;
3. Prepare faculty at the doctoral institution for optimal advisement of students when they enter the doctoral program; and
4. Integrate the local Native American community into the program, by working with elders, medicine people, and other spiritual leaders from the urban Indian area around the school as well as from nearby reservations.

Advertisement and Recruitment

Both PARIs stated that recruitment begins at the master's level institution and targets nursing and clinical master's students. Brochures and web sites assist in advertising the program to students. The recruitment role of the program administrator at the doctoral institution involves discussing the doctoral program with prospective trainees. One PARI said that the master's institution works with the Indian Health Service in an effort to identify prospective trainees. Another PARI stated that recruitment relies primarily on faculty at master's institutions who identify and then recommend individual trainees to the department chair.

Criteria for Trainee Selection into the Program

The R25 Bridges to the Doctorate program administrators who were interviewed are faculty at doctoral institutions. They described the selection of trainees as follows:

- "We are interested in people who have an interest in a scientific career or careers as a nurse researcher. We want people who have some evidence of having the aptitude and the prior education that will allow them to be successful. We have a more holistic view of what their application is, rather than one that's sort of more . . . formulaic."
- "The typical student sort of coming into [our institution] is . . . primarily . . . looking at the clinical training as a sort of career path."
- "In nursing science, people who come to doctoral level training tend to be quite a bit older than your average doctoral student. It is not unusual to have people well into their 40s."

Trainee Experience in the Program

The two R25 Bridges to the Doctorate program administrators were asked to discuss the kinds of challenges that trainees in the program face. They provided frank insights about academic and personal issues, as summarized below.

The chief academic challenge that R25 Bridges to the Doctorate trainees face is that the requirements of the programs tend to be additions to their regular academic load, making participation and success a somewhat daunting task. "The problem that we and our partner institutions face is that the second year of the master's program is very heavily clinically oriented. And there just aren't as many hours in the day as students could possibly need in order to do everything plus take on the added responsibility of doing a master's thesis." The other administrator interviewed remarked, "I think one challenge for many of them has been the need to carry a full course load."

The combination of increased academic load and the fact that many of the trainees are in clinical programs further reduces the opportunity for success. As one program administrator related, "Our big challenge is to basically convince them that a research and teaching career is one that they should consider over simply going the route of . . . the typical undergraduate who might major in biochem but is really interested in going into medicine."

A key issue for many students is that they need to move away from family, community, and/or tribe to participate in these programs and this makes adjustment difficult. One administrator related that the willingness to make a long-distance move for their education was difficult, saying "I think moving away from family and from their tribes is a challenge." Their program tries to overcome this through several mechanisms:

> ***General sociability***. "I think one big factor is just personal acquaintance with all the people in the project. So we are a pretty, I think, . . . friendly and personable group, and we engage the students right from the start in the larger group of people involved in the project."
>
> ***Annual retreat***. "We have an annual project retreat that brings everyone involved in the project together, students and faculty from all the institutions, medicine people and spiritual leaders, elders, and some of our . . . staff. And we have this retreat off-site at one of the reservation communities, and that serves as a gathering for the whole group. It gives us a chance to do [a] kind of team building. It is an opportunity for everybody to get kind of a dose of culture, to carry everyone through to the next year's meeting. And for those people who are involved who aren't Indians, it serves as an immersion experience to acquaint them with the background of our students. So I think that is probably the highlight of our year in terms of their own success."

The other administrator interviewed also brought up this set of issues, noting that "the thought of going away from the family is sort of very difficult. Going to college, then doing a two- or three-year clinical training program, and then continuing on for more education is both from . . . the personal development and [from the] financial standpoint, a real difficulty."

The program elements that appeared to be the key to success for these students were oversight and mentoring. One of the administrators interviewed said, "There is support in two ways. One is through the Indian support programs at each school that are already in place, not part of our program funding, but the [Indian Health Service] funding. And the second is just the regular academic support services that are available at each school, people's academic advisers [and] student services. And we . . . recommend to the students to work with both of those. At [the master's institution], their Indian support program works with a model they call Intrusive Monitoring of all their students, and the students sign release forms so that the staff can check in with their teachers and get information about a student's progress as they go along. The people who have been to school up there will laugh and say, 'Well, you know, the . . . program knows we are going bad before we do.' So they have a very close, kind of, monitoring of progress. So that is one approach, and it seems to work for them. At [the other master's institution], what I have seen is really quite a different approach where the Indian program is very focused on helping students be ready to learn, and so it is more preventive. They work with biofeedback and the students are pretty engaged in doing this kind of thing. They stop by the American Indian focus room, and the programs are all set up on the computer. It is very much kind of a stop and take stock of the day and prepare yourself to move along and learn the best you can. And it is just a different approach, but it also seems to work really well."

One of the two administrators added that mentoring is critical as well. "One of the things about all of these programs is if you have at least a couple of faculty at each institution that are really committed to the mentoring of these individuals, you make significant progress. And . . . if for one reason or another, those individuals are not available or they're overworked so that the amount of time that they can commit to these programs is limited, you are not as successful."

Ways to Improve the Administration of the Program

One of the two administrators noted that a key area for improvement in going forward was the need to improve communication between the doctoral institution and the two master's institutions. They have begun this process by having regular videoconferences that both improve the efficiency of communication and allow the campuses to draw more on the partnership. The administrator seeks to establish a "day-to-day" presence on the master's institution campuses that will allow the programs to communicate regularly about recruitment, program activities, and trainee follow-up. The administrator related, "Our goal is to basically have it so that there's at the very least a weekly seminar that links students at the partner institutions with students here and with faculty here. So that if we have this infrastructural seamless connection between the institutions, the task of keeping people on-task and moving toward a goal, I think, would be a lot easier."

(T32) NRSA Institutional Training Grant Interviews

Five PARIs were interviewed about the T32 NRSA Institutional Training Grants that they administer. All of those interviewed were PIs on the grants.

History and Evolution of the Program

Collectively, these programs have been around for 22 to 30 years. Generally speaking, the grant is used to train pre- and postdoctoral trainees in interdisciplinary research across a number of departments.

Advertisement and Recruitment

One PARI described the use of a targeted campaign of writing letters to faculty and deans across the country to advertise the program and solicit trainee interest. Some institutions conduct outreach to nearby minority-serving institutions. "We have specific targeting to predominantly black enrollment universities. And we have local efforts within the city to seek out minority candidates." Another PARI lamented that the problem is that so many universities are competing for such a small pool of minority talent. Yet another PARI complained that the definition of minority is too restrictive. "[There] was a first-generation Vietnamese kid whose parents spent time on boats in the South China Sea. He was brilliant as all get-out. I could not get him any minority help."

Some PARIs advertise the availability of training grant slots by using the web or purchasing advertisements in minority trade magazines. Within the institution, one PARI described an announcement that was circulated to faculty with the invitation to nominate their best predoctoral student. According to one PARI, "The frustrating thing I have found over the years is we could recruit to our heart's content, but the young smart African Americans are much more interested in the professions for advanced training than they are in basic research." This same PARI recommended, "Increase stipend levels to be competitive with professional training programs." Another PARI argued for a more proactive outreach strategy, "We need to go to junior high schools and high schools and begin there. Since ours is a graduate program, we clearly need to do a better job in the undergraduate years to even announce the fact that there is [a discipline called] public health."

Criteria for Trainee Selection into the Program

For predoctoral trainees, one PARI described a fairly traditional set of criteria, "They have to meet the criteria of the graduate training program that they are admitted to, and those criteria include a certain set of prerequisite courses that they need to have taken. Since biochemistry is typically a last year course at the undergraduate level, it means that they had to take organic and inorganic [chemistry]. They also need to have had at least a year of calculus. There isn't a GPA [grade point average] cutoff, but the higher the GPA, the happier we are. And similarly, there isn't a GRE [Graduate record Examination] cutoff, but the higher . . . [the scores] are, the happier we are. Probably, the most critical thing in the entry process is having letters from faculty at other institutions, or this institution, depending upon where they did their undergraduate work, that indicate that they have been exposed, in some fashion, to research, because, in my experience, that's a big predictor of success. They know what a Ph.D. program is all about when they apply."

Another PARI described a different set of criteria, "We're looking for bright people. I mean, we take people—in public health we have people that range in skills from basic laboratory biology all the way to geography and demography and social sciences, and everything in between. So, the training, discipline, and interests really don't matter, because we need everybody. We look for bright, creative, imaginative people. And if you give me somebody bright and creative, we'll work it out." One more PARI stated, "We deal with a pretty good cut of intellectual quality. So it turns out, the most important factor is interest and dedication. It's not accomplishment. It's not prior research. It is interest and commitment. That's the most important predictor of success."

Trainee Experience in the Program

In terms of the challenges faced by minority trainees, one PARI shared, "I've had a number of minority students over the years, and the general problem that I've seen over the years is [their lack of a] good earlier education. For example, one of the super bright students I'm working with now is working on her Ph.D., but she can't write. We're not talking about intelligence or energy or creativity; we're talking about basic skills. I think a lot of the minority students are not getting a good basic education." Another PARI said, "Getting a job after the program is the biggest challenge. We've had people come to us and say 'I can't get a job. Can you find the funding for me for another year?'" One of the biggest challenges faced by trainees at another institution was described as follows: "My institution funnels all of the training grant stipends through the Financial Aid Office. They are paid in three installments, one at the beginning of each semester and one at the beginning of summer, rather than getting a monthly check. [Furthermore] Financial Aid people deny these students other forms of financial aid because they regard the training grant as a source of financial aid. And so the students who are on the training grant are at a disadvantage, compared to other students who are paid the same amount of money, but from a different source. And, when you give them their checks a month late, it creates hardship for them. I've written checks from my own bank account to cover these kids who don't get their paychecks on time because, you know, they have to pay the rent, they have to eat, regardless of whether the Financial Aid Office thinks it's worth their time to pay them on time. So that's the biggest problem."

Mechanisms for keeping up on trainee progress are important to maintaining a high training standard and ensuring that trainees are on the right track. One PARI said, "We have different levels of feedback. Coursework is one. Formal candidate reviews is a second. Review by the mentor is third. There is little opportunity at these graduate levels for remediation. I think that we see people who fall off the ladder because they're just not able to keep up and aren't given reinforcement of what skills sets are required and what the expectations are." Another PARI said, "We're part of a large medical school. I don't know every candidate because there are hundreds and hundreds of graduate students and postdocs here. Sometimes a person will come to us and say, 'This lab isn't working out for me.' We either give them advice about what to do, or if it looks like it's a real serious problem, we talk to their preceptor. Our view is, first of all, it's the right thing to do to try and help this person. But also, it isn't good for our training program if people are unhappy and unsuccessful." Yet another PARI adds, "Graduate students interact with trainers on a daily basis. They submit reports twice yearly to the principal investigator. They meet with their committee at least twice a year. They attend weekly conferences designed specifically for the group of trainees on the training grant.

Share a Trainee Success Story

One PARI related, "We have a number of candidates from 15 to 20 years ago who completed their degree, went on to postdoctoral work, and from there went on to academic positions at various institutions across the country. [They] are now full professors. We also have candidates who have gone into the pharmaceutical industry."

Describe a Trainee Who Was Not Successful in the Program

One PARI explained, "I'm working with a doctoral student now who's having trouble with writing. Her problem is that when you ask her a question, she thinks of 15 things that are important to put in the answer, and then she answers with all the 15 things. You can't do it that way. That's something you learn in grade 10. So, this has been a problem." Another PARI added, "You do get some people without a good work ethic, and they aren't productive. If they're not productive at this stage of their career, they cannot get a job. We've had several of those."

Comments on Relationships of PARIs to NIH

One PARI was asked to describe his or her interactions with NIH about the training program. "Basically, none. If the occasional financial question comes up, then I talk with the financial administrator, but I don't have a great deal of interaction with the program administrator." Another PARI related, "Hardly ever. We've had this training program over 25 years. I know a fair amount about training grants and how to do them, what's expected. So if I had a problem, I wouldn't hesitate to call them and talk with them. You know, occasionally around renewal time, I may call them and talk to them to make sure that I'm on target and I do a good renewal. I've done these five or six times and they've always been funded. So I don't talk to them a lot because things seem to be going well." In contrast, another PARI remarked, "They're my life blood, of course. When I wrote to the director's office recently for help with a small crisis, they were fabulous. I was really amazed at how terrific they were."

Ways to Improve the Administration of Training Programs

"More money for administration!" argued one PARI. Another had a few suggestions for improving administration of these programs: "I would say one frustration that we have relates to the demography of who is coming to the United States. What we're seeing is an increasing number of people from Thailand or China or India, and they're really good. But they don't qualify for the training grant because under NRSA policies you've got to be a permanent resident or a citizen. When the act was written 30 years ago this probably made sense. There is a certain irony in that you can be on an NIH grant if you're not a citizen, but you can't be on any training grants. There are places right now where they can't even fill their training grants, because they don't have enough qualified applicants. I wish we had more flexibility and could pick the best people, and not the best people who have a green card or are American citizens."

According to one PARI, "I think most people will tell you that putting together the application for a training grant renewal is probably the least pleasant experience you'll ever have. People would rather have a root canal without anesthesia than put one of these grants together, because the documentation and requirements of what you have to present are just enormous. If there was some simplified process for applying and the grant wasn't so complicated that would help a lot." Also, "I guess there are two things I would say about the money part, which NIH ought to think about. One of them is when a graduate student goes to work in your lab the school charges the preceptor of the graduate student for the tuition. I think if you're really interested in training pre-docs NIH should help the preceptors by paying a larger fraction of that cost." Then, "For grants where there's more clinical research, I think sometimes preceptors have a hard time being a good preceptor, because they're often earning their living seeing patients and the student sometimes doesn't get the amount of attention they deserve. I think the NIH in general is concerned about this, and they're starting to ease up on allowing funds for faculty to be part of packages for grants."

Another PARI said, "I think the whole class of training grants ought to be reviewed as career development efforts. What's missing is a sense of national commitment amongst the successful awardees in promoting and developing. It's the opportunity and, I would argue, responsibility of the government, in the process of funding training activities, to promote training as a career development effort. What does a trainee get out of participating in NIH-sponsored training programs? The answer is a stipend. And it could be a whole lot more. The NIH could very cheaply offer a whole lot of added value such as career development, contacts, networking, access to specific NIH programs, invitations to come to NIH for conferences. NIH could take advantage of these future leaders and give them value added, but it fails to do so."

NIH Policies That Hinder Administration of the Programs

"We need more money above the line. It's always been a problem. I mean, NIH basically said it is going to invest money in the fellow. Who could argue with that? But it does take institutional resources to keep a program going. And so, I admire the fact of putting the money where it counts, but NIH has gone too far." Also, "It's clear that NIH's intent is that a trainee be awarded for a minimum of a year. But there's a requirement that you can't reuse dollars if somebody doesn't complete their year. That's a waste for everybody. Changes happen in peoples' lives. You can't even go on maternity leave. What sort of nuttiness is that?" Another PARI said, "The obligation, without any sort of advice or support or national coordinating effort, to follow candidates for 20 years is a burden on universities. This is a national issue. For all training grants, why isn't there some effort to coordinate 'tracking' efforts nationally?"

Program Evaluation

PARIs were asked whether they engage in any program evaluation activities in relation to the T32 NRSA Institutional Training Grant. One PARI remarked, "We appointed a steering committee of fairly distinguished senior scientists in [the field]. They're like a board of trustees, and they give us advice. They look over who we're training. They go over the progress reports. They review our application when we do renewals." As another PARI described it, "We have a steering committee that evaluates the program at least annually, and usually, they are involved in all appointments to the training grants. So they review all trainees on an annual basis prior to reappointment." A number of PARIs stated that they view the five-year competitive renewal process as an evaluation of sorts. One PARI provided a bottom line, "To me what really counts is, have they gone out and achieved significant positions? If they're in the research field, are they being productive?"

(T35) Short-Term Institutional Training Grant Interviews

Twelve PARIs were interviewed. All were either current or recent PIs of the programs. Some were founders and others began running the program within the last five years.

History and Evolution of the Program

All programs have been well established for ten years or more. Some T35 programs were started in response to a specific NIH RFA (Request for Proposals), and others evolved as a part of larger institutional efforts to recruit and train underrepresented minority (URM) students into research science, especially environmental health and toxicology.

Programs Stated Goals

All programs have the goal of attracting minority students to research science, and this goal has not changed over the years for any of the programs.

Percentage of PARI Time Working on Program

PARIs report that time spent working on the program is variable, depending on immediate program needs. Activities that require PARI time include setting up the program for the following summer, recruitment of students, review of student applications to the program, and conducting the program itself. One PARI said that asking what percentage of time he or she spends on running the program is a "nonsense question." Another said, "The NIH says that I spend no time on the program . . . . At certain times of the year I spend 50 percent of my time." Others gave generalized percentages ranging from less than 10 percent to 35 percent of their time.

Advertisement and Recruitment

A variety of methods are used to advertise the T35 NRSA Short-Term Institutional Training programs and recruit students to them. Some programs send minority faculty and students to nearby minority-serving institutions or other colleges to deliver a brief talk explaining the program and encouraging students to apply. Another institution is part of a consortium of schools that includes the Big Ten. Given its extensive connectivity with regional institutions, word of mouth has been sufficient advertisement for this T35 program, in particular. Yet another institution uses a top-down approach, and its T35 advertising and recruitment activities rely on the institution's already comprehensive minority recruitment infrastructure. Still other institutions use a web site or booth at the annual MARC undergraduate conferences to advertise and recruit future applicants to their programs. Some PARIs remarked that female applicants both outnumber and outcompete male applicants. One institution is challenged to identify Hispanic and Native American applicants, given its geographic locale. Yet another institution is challenged to identify African-American applicants, given a different locale.

Criteria for Trainee Selection into the Program

Trainee selection criteria vary across the T35 Short-Term Institutional Training programs and institutions, in part because this funding vehicle may be utilized to support the training of undergraduate, graduate, or postdoctoral students. Some institutions accept students anywhere between their second year of college and the first few years of graduate school. Others accept only junior or senior undergraduates. One institution is academically traditional and accepts only those trainees whose GPA is 3.6 or better as long as the student has stellar letters of recommendation and comes from a high-caliber undergraduate school. Others have a lower GPA requirement but scrutinize each application for evidence of a research orientation, such as previous lab research experience or a well-written personal statement that explains the student's curiosity for scientific research. In the words of one PARI, "I look for that spark, that genuine interest in research, as opposed to those that just thought it might be a good way to help their resume for medical school, which, really [is] the vast majority of the applicants." Yet another PARI explains what he or she looks for when reviewing student applications, is "... a student [who has] a high energy level, intellectually curious, good work ethic ...." Some institutions accept only applicants whose stated research interest is in the environmental health sciences. Another institution looks for students expressing an interest in clinical research, specifically public health and community medicine. Yet another institution focuses on "growing talent" as opposed to "harvesting" talent that is already apparent. This PARI explains, "I take a lot of students with borderline grades, ... students who might well think they want to go to med school, but may simply not have the performance to get into medical school, and who may be open to looking for an alternative career." Another PARI concurs, "I think there's a tendency to want to get the best numbers, but I think you miss the sort of middle group that is really a rich target for research careers."

Trainee Experience in the Program

A few PARIs commented that students' science and writing skills may be deficient. One PARI said, "Our program is academically challenging. The students who are not well prepared, . . . it was tough going. Our program is rigorous and we don't compromise. That was a challenge for some students." Another says, "Sometimes we wind up with students who probably are not as well prepared as the bulk of the students. And so, we try to have a variety of special programs to help them deal with the academic material."

Another challenge facing students in the T35 short-term training programs is, as one PARI put it, "the vast difference between here and home." Some PARIs said that students may be challenged by the drastic change in their living situation. Some institutions put students in dormitories; others house them off-campus in private student homes. One PARI believes that cultural issues are at play when T35 trainees come to the campus. He generalized by saying that African-American students can at times come across as aggressive, and Hispanic students may at times come across as passive. Nonminority persons in the labs in which these students work for the summer do not always know how to negotiate cultural norms different from their own.

Trainee Success Stories

PARIs offered many stories of students who succeeded in the T35 Short-Term Institutional Training program and then went on to graduate from Ph.D., M.D., or MD-Ph.D. programs. In some cases, the students were academically stellar to begin with. In other cases students were "rough around the edges" at the start of T35 short-term training, yet quite polished by the end of it. One PARI said, "the other kind of student that we consider a real success is the kind of student who comes in not really aware of what research really is, or the opportunities it provides, and then finds that they're really excited by research and that they really love doing it."

Yet another PARI said, "Typically in the first two or three weeks, I hear, 'I don't understand my project. I don't know what we're doing . . . I just don't get it.' But, invariably by the end of the summer and, I guarantee, 90 percent of the time—the students are able to give a very eloquent discussion of what they did during the research experience. And the quality of the posters they present is analogous to what I see when I go to scientific meetings. By the end of the summer, the kids know they've made the transition. The sense of empowerment that the students get is incredible."

Unsuccessful Trainees

PARIs were asked to describe situations in which an individual trainee was not successful in the T35 Short-Term Institutional Training program. The reasons given for "failing the program" vary widely. Here are some representative quotes: "We have maybe one or two students drop out every other year, . . . because of [either] personal problems or health problems or family problems." Also, "A student with a serious substance abuse problem who refused offers of help. He was dismissed from the program." Then, "I'm not sure that someone does not succeed. I think what happens is that a student may realize that this is an endeavor that they don't wish to pursue any further." In addition, "Occasionally we have a student who seems virtually abandoned by their lab and so we intervene and try to fix that. That's pretty rare, but that lab doesn't get called upon after that." And, "Early on, we had some students that took advantage of the program. They felt getting in was all they needed to do. So, they didn't show up, or they didn't work very hard." All PARIs agreed that diligent oversight of students' progress is critical to facilitating trainee success in the program. Oversight in this regard includes regular meetings and interactions with both students and mentors.

Comments on PARI Relationship to NIH

Most PARIs reported low-frequency, albeit positive, contacts with NIH. Other than filing annual progress reports and a five-year competitive renewal, little interaction takes place between the institution and NIH. One PARI reported a strong relationship to NIH. Another PARI lamented the paperwork saying, "It's way too bureaucratic and way too much paperwork for what's involved, the amount of money, the amount of . . . I'm going to be honest with you because, they have just added another level of bureaucracy, another form this year, and it's so silly, for students who are here for ten to twelve weeks." Another PARI reported, "I contacted NIH about the issue of these reverse discrimination lawsuits."

Ways to Improve the Administration of These Programs

"More money for administrative support and funding for more social events for trainees." "More flexibility operating the program. Less bureaucratic interference."

NIH Policies That Hinder Administration of the Program

One PARI replied, "[There is] no administrative support on grants. Everything depends on the goodwill of a few." Another PARI said, "NIH prohibits faculty from receiving salary support from these grants. Yet doing so would be an incentive for faculty to run these programs." Yet another PARI said, "There is no salary support for me as the PI and minimal salary support for my assistant, who helps me administer the program." Another said, "There's no reward [for running these kinds of programs] other than a personal and internal award. In fact, by putting time into this program you penalize your career." "Finally, [we need a better way to] reward people for throwing away their time on an altruistic activity that doesn't pay."

Several PARIs reported that their institution allows nonminority students who are economically disadvantaged to participate in the programs. One PARI said, "I think NIH needs to address and offer some support to program directors about the issue of reverse discrimination. My feeling is that the NIH approach is, Well, you figure it out. Then they kind of bury their heads in the sand."

Another PARI comments that the funding cycle is off-kilter with the administration of a summer program, "It's possible that I would have five students who have signed on to come here [in the summer], then all of a sudden I find out in April that the program hasn't been re-funded. There's a bit of time discrepancy there." Another PARI commented, "The overhead allowed is only 8 percent. Thus, it's better to pursue other types of grants, as they offer more overhead." Another PARI laments, "The [research] supply monies that are offered are about $125 per student per month. Those monies aren't enough to cover anything, to tell you the truth. I mean, you could burn that in a morning." Yet another said that "[students] frequently request more socializing activities, but the NIH policies will not allow it." Finally, "NIH requires you to describe a plan for minority recruiting, but it prohibits the consideration of results. They used to want to know what the outcome of your plan was. Did you manage to bring in minority students? Did they succeed and so forth? Now they don't want you to do that. It seems nuts to me. That is the best measure of success!"

Program Evaluation

All PARIs said that there is an evaluation component to the program they administer, usually on an annual basis. The evaluation includes some form of input from students and mentors whether by survey or in-person interviews conducted by a third party. A few PARIs mentioned ongoing efforts to track student outcomes. As for results, one PARI said, "I think the major change [that resulted from this program] has been the growth in the minority population in the medical school, which I believe is the desired outcome of this effort." Another said, "Whether these students [get a Ph.D.], whether they end up in environmental health. Even if they went on to medical school and so forth, we think that's okay. We still believe they benefited from the program and that will eventually be to everyone's benefit." Another PARI remarked, "The numbers of minority applicants that have applied to the medical school and graduate school here have skyrocketed. And it's a result of this program."

Final Comments from PARIs

Final comments include the following: "Outreach and recruitment to science needs to start in K-12, " and "I think maybe getting undergraduate educators together with graduate educators and even high school educators looking at the whole process, you know, could be very helpful, very rewarding." "The lack of adequate preparation at minority-serving institutions is problematic for generating a competitive applicant pool." Finally, "I hope that NIH . . . keeps these programs running. They clearly serve a purpose and [fill] a huge need. This program has really impacted our school."

Conclusion

Minority respondents to our survey who participated in graduate-level NIH training programs were predominantly female across all of the programs sampled. This parallels what was observed among minority undergraduate respondents, yet it diverges from what was observed among minority postdoctoral and junior faculty respondents who were predominantly male. The reason for the demographic shift at higher career stages is unknown and worthy of further study. The majority of graduate-level respondents across programs and without regard to minority status reported that a parent or sibling had earned a graduate degree. Thus, individuals who become graduate trainees, regardless of minority status, tend to come from families with a history of high educational attainment.

With regard to trainee outcomes, almost one-half of R25 Bridges to the Doctorate respondents successfully completed a master's degree, and one-tenth had earned a Ph.D. One-quarter left the program without a degree. Among F31 NRSA fellows and T32 trainees, a majority were successful in obtaining their Ph.D. Further, slightly more than one-half of the graduate respondents reported being a senior author on one or more published research papers after obtaining their Ph.D. In addition, about one-half report successfully obtaining one or more research grants post-Ph.D. These data are consistent with the committee's impression that the sample of survey respondents who could be located was biased toward more successful NIH trainees. This tells us little about the majority of graduate-level trainees who could not be located using commercial credit card databases and a U.S. Postal service database, and it does raise questions as to why such individuals do not appear to be participating in today's credit economy.

Responses from F31 NRSA fellows and R03 dissertation award recipients indicate a high-level of satisfaction with their experiences in the training programs, although minority respondents in nontargeted training programs were least likely to report feeling familiar or close to their research groups and colleagues. The T32 NRSA Institutional Training Grant trainees frequently noted the difficult job prospects they faced after completion of their training program. When trainees were asked to report the best feature of the training programs in which they participated, financial support was cited most frequently. When asked if there was anything else they wished to tell NIH, the most common response among this cohort was that stipend support needs to be increased. Mentoring was cited by all graduate trainees as a key feature of the programs, although there was consensus among trainees that mentoring is an area in need of improvement. This sentiment was particularly prevalent among R25 Bridges to the Doctorate trainees.

Nineteen program administrators were interviewed regarding graduate-level training programs. All of those interviewed are associated with programs that are well established. When asked to comment on the challenges faced by minority trainees, the following themes figured prominently among program administrator responses: the lack of adequate academic preparation among minority trainees, the pervasiveness of financial hardship, frequent "culture shock" when transitioning to higher-caliber institutions, personal or family problems, and problems integrating or being accepted into one's research group. In light of these problems, program administrators emphasized that outreach for these programs should begin during the K-12 years and that graduate trainee stipends should be increased so that trainees are not set up for failure.

When asked about the criteria that are used to select trainees for entrance into various programs, administrators emphasized two modes of screening. The first applies traditional graduate school criteria such as high grades, excellent letters of recommendation, and a record of scientific accomplishment at the undergraduate level. The committee refers to this approach to trainee selection as *harvesting* talent. The second applies nontraditional selection criteria that emphasize a student's potential, rather than past accomplishments. For example, some programs will accept minority trainees with borderline grades and limited undergraduate scientific achievements as long as the student demonstrates a sincere interest in pursuing biomedical research as a possible career path. The committee refers to this approach to trainee selection as *growing* talent.

Most program administrators reported that a critical program element is oversight and monitoring of trainee progress, in order to catch problems before they become intractable for trainees and faculty alike. When asked how NIH could improve these programs, the following suggestions were offered: simplify the grant application process, provide greater local flexibility, increase the allowable budget for administrative support, compensate faculty for the time they spend mentoring trainees, provide more legal guidance on affirmative action policies, and finally, implement a trainee tracking system in order to better monitor trainee outcomes.

5

Postdoctoral Training Opportunities: Postdoctorate Fellows and Junior Faculty

The postdoctoral position in the United States was started by Johns Hopkins University in 1876. That year, Johns Hopkins offered 20 postdoctoral traineeships out of a pool of 152 applicants. In 1919, the Rockefeller Foundation donated $500,000.00 for the support of a fellowship program; in 1922, the Rockefeller Foundation and the Rockefeller-endowed General Education Board pledged $500,000 for postdoctoral traineeships in the medical sciences; and in 1923, the Biological Sciences received $325,000 from the Foundation.[51]

By 1979, it was estimated that there were more than 10,000 postdoctoral trainees in science and engineering in United States universities. As the value of postdoctoral training increased, the number of postdoctoral trainees at institutions throughout the United States also increased. By 2001, the number of science and engineering postdoctoral trainees had increased to nearly 22,000 and the number in the biological sciences had increased to over 12,000.[52]

Despite the growth in the number of postdoctoral trainees, minorities remain underrepresented in postdoctoral positions in science and engineering in general and in the biological sciences in particular. In 2001, less than 7 percent of science and engineering postdocs were underrepresented minorities; within the biological sciences, only 6 percent of postdocs were underrepresented minorities. One major factor that impacts the number of minority postdocs is the equally low number of doctoral degrees granted to underrepresented minorities. For example, in the 2003 academic year, out of 5,492 U.S. citizen doctoral recipients in the life sciences, only 190 were African American, 213 were Hispanic, and 17 were Native American.[53]

The postdoctoral experience in the United States has been the subject of studies designed to assess the success, or lack thereof, of postdoctoral programs. It has been

---

[51] National Research Council. 1981. Postdoctoral Appointments and Disappointments. Washington, D.C.: National Academy Press.
[52] National Science Foundation, 2001 Survey of Doctorate Recipients.
[53] National Opinion Research Center. 2005. Doctorate Recipients form Untied States Universities: Summary Report 2003. Chicago, Ill.: NORC.

clear for sometime that postdoctoral trainees are valuable resources to the institutions and senior faculty who employ them, but their status is often ambiguous. On some campuses, postdocs are viewed as students, even though they do not take classes and are not working toward a degree. On other campuses, they are viewed as employees, but they are not provided employee benefits such as medical coverage, holiday leave, and maternity leave. Nor are they provided other protections afforded to employees by law, such as the Family Medical Leave Act or whistleblower protection. Postdocs are not represented by labor unions either. When medical and other benefits are provided to postdocs, there is no regulatory oversight or guidance to ensure that these benefits are applied consistently. The National Institutes of Health (NIH) has a role in this situation. Postdocs on NIH training grants have one set of benefits, while those on NIH research grants have another. According to one program administrator, "The health benefits available from my institution, if one is on a research grant, are vastly better than what the government makes possible through a training grant. Family leave is vastly better if you are on a research grant than if you are on a training grant. When NIH institutes hire postdocs, they get full government benefits, whereas those who are supported on training grants, which are supposedly equivalent positions, are not treated anywhere near as well."

Further, there are no standards or benchmarks of achievement for postdoctoral training as there are in the medical or legal professions, for example. The lack of achievement standards leaves postdocs vulnerable to abuse by mentors, who have a vested interest in keeping their labs fully staffed for indeterminate amounts of time. Prolonged postdoctoral training is interpreted by some potential employers as an indicator that the individual is not productive.

Underrepresented minorities face additional difficulties. Being the only minority in a lab, research group, or department is an isolating experience. Minority individuals may feel that they are under a microscope or that they are carrying the burden of an entire race of people. Because so few minority mentors and role models exist at the faculty level, some minority trainees report that they endure the "imposter syndrome," that is, a lingering feeling that they do not deserve their professional status or achievements. Such manifestations of lowered self-esteem have the potential to subvert minority trainees' desires to "aim high" professionally. Even mentors may project lower achievement standards onto their minority trainees. This and other expressions of ignorance or bias by mentors have the potential to sour mentor-mentee relationships, erode trust, and create social and professional distance. For those minority trainees who are unique within their families by virtue of their educational attainment, there is added stress. Lesser-educated family members may criticize the postdoc for "not getting a real job" or for their inability to shoulder family burdens proportionally, such as caring for a disabled or elder family member or child.

Postgraduate Programs for Underrepresented Minorities

(T32) NRSA Minority Institutional Research Training Program

The Ruth L. Kirchstein National Research Service Award (NRSA) program for minorities provides postdoctoral support through T32 institutional training grants. Trainees supported on these grants have already received a Ph.D., D.V.M., D.D.S., M.D., or comparable doctoral degree from an accredited domestic or foreign institution. (Faculty members are not eligible for support using this grant mechanism.) Research training at the postdoctoral level emphasizes specialized training in the biological, behavioral, or clinical sciences. These grants are a desirable mechanism for postdoctoral training of physicians and other health professionals who may have extensive clinical training but limited research experience. For such individuals, the training may be a part of a research degree program. In all cases, postdoctoral trainees should agree to engage in at least two years of research, research training, or comparable activities beginning at the time of appointment. Funding is for up to two years.

(T35) NRSA Short-Term Institutional Training Grants

The Ruth L. Kirchstein NRSA program for minorities provides short-term postdoctoral training support in biological, behavioral, and clinical sciences through T35 institutional training grants. Many of the NIH institutes and centers use this grant mechanism to support intensive, short-term research training experiences for students in health professional schools during the summer. In addition, these grants can be used to support other types of postdoctoral training in focused, often emerging, scientific areas relevant to the mission of the funding NIH institute or center. Postdoctoral trainees must have received, as of the beginning date of the appointment, a Ph.D., M.D., or comparable doctoral degree from an accredited domestic or foreign institution.

(K01) Mentored Research Scientist Development Awards

K01 Mentored Research Scientist Development Awards provide support for an intensive, supervised career development experience in one of the biological, behavioral, or clinical sciences leading to research independence. Candidates for this award must have a research or health professional doctorate and be senior postdoctoral trainees or junior faculty members at the time of application. In addition, the candidate must be able to demonstrate the need for three to five years of additional supervised research, as well as the capacity and/or the potential for highly productive independent research. The proposed career development experience must be in a research area new to the applicant and/or one in which an additional supervised research experience will substantially add to the research capabilities of the applicant. The award provides funding support for graduate students who conduct research under supervision by the K01 awardee. Finally, the candidate must provide a plan for achieving research independence by the end of the award period.

(K08) Mentored Clinical Scientist Development Awards

K08 Mentored Clinical Scientist Development Awards support the development of outstanding clinician research scientists. This mechanism provides specialized study for individuals with a health professional doctoral degree committed to a career in laboratory or field-based research. Candidates must have the potential to develop into independent investigators. The K08 supports three to five years of supervised research experience that may integrate didactic studies with laboratory or clinically based research. The proposed research must have intrinsic importance as well as serve as a suitable vehicle for learning the methodology, theories, and conceptualizations necessary for a well-trained independent researcher. Because of the focus on progression to independence, the prospective candidate should propose a period of study and development consistent with previous training and his or her career development needs. For example, a candidate with limited experience in a given field of research may find that the most efficient means of attaining independence is a phased developmental program lasting for five years that includes a designated period of didactic training and supervised research experience. A candidate with substantial previous research experience may require a shorter award period to facilitate the transition to independence.

Focus of the Assessment

Information on these programs was gathered and assessed through the following steps:

1. The committee reviewed key documents related to the programs such as program announcements and institute web sites. No previous program evaluations were evident and available.
2. Trainees and junior faculty previously supported on these research-training awards were interviewed by the NIH-approved contractor using a computer-assisted telephone interview (CATI) protocol. These interviews were about 30 minutes in length and utilized both structured response and open-ended questions.
3. Information was collected through formal interviews with program administrators at recipient institutions (PARIs). These interviews were conducted by the NIH data contractor over the telephone. They were open-ended and used an ethnographic interviewing style. There are no PARI interviews for the K01 or K08 awards, because they are awarded to individual investigators rather than institutions, as with institutional training grants.

Previous Program Evaluations Conducted by NIH

The committee identified no previous program evaluations for the support mechanisms addressed within this chapter.

Trainee Interview Data

The NIH data contractor identified a total of 1,901 postdoctoral trainees and junior faculty who met the requirements for the CATI survey. Potential respondents were selected so that one-half were underrepresented minorities and one-half were nonminorities. For each targeted program included in the study, two untargeted comparison groups were defined using similar parameters, such as awarding institute and time frame of the awards.

Nearly 80 percent (n = 1,514) of the potential respondents came from the T32 institutional training award pool. This was expected because the T32 mechanism is the largest of the mechanisms that met the committee's selection criteria. All of the 71 junior faculty trainees held K01 Career Development awards.

The NIH data contractor was able to obtain contact information for 736, or 39 percent, of the 1,901 eligible postdoctoral and junior faculty trainees. Of these, 8 trainees failed the screener (wrong person), 12 failed to complete the interview, and 66 refused to complete the interview. From the 728 eligible (736 in sample minus 8 who failed screener) postdoctoral and junior faculty trainees, the NIH contractor was able to obtain 328 completed interviews, of which 285 were with postdoctoral trainees and 43 were with junior faculty. Finally, the committee believes that data from these interviews may not reflect the responses that would have been obtained had the respondents been more representative of the larger universe of program participants. Nevertheless, the data are instructive in a general way and are described in this report qualitatively. For example, respondent data are reported using a variety of nonspecific phrases such as "nearly all reported," "a majority of respondents said," "a minority of respondents said," "more likely," and "less likely." Such phrases should not be equated with statistical significance.

Trainee Interviews

From one perspective, all persons—both postdoctoral trainees and junior faculty—engaged in these programs are successes. All program participants have received a doctoral degree in a scientific or clinical area. All program participants have successfully competed for the award. When the committee surveyed postdocs who received NIH funding, it found that nearly all program recipients stressed the importance of the award as a mechanism that enabled them to engage in independent research. In addition, the awardees said that the award allowed them to focus on and ultimately decide upon their particular career subspecialty. For many, the award hastened their mastery of new skills and techniques. One awardee stated, "I intended to go into academic medicine and the training grant allowed me to work in a research lab, which helped me understand how basic research and clinical practice interrelate." Another trainee stated, "It gave me time to accurately develop a line of research that I have been pursuing ever since; it allowed me to get an academic job." Finally, one respondent stated, "It taught me both technical skills, as well as the importance of healthy criticism. It introduced me to new areas of thought, as well as expanding my networking, both within my field of expertise and beyond it."

Characteristics of Postdoctorate Trainees

The majority of postdoctoral trainees interviewed were funded through the T32 Minority Institutional Research Training Program (see Table 5-1). Most postdoctoral respondents learned about the T32 postdoctoral programs through multiple sources, especially from colleagues, graduate advisers, or departmental staff. Trainees conducted research in laboratories with a median of five persons, although a few laboratories were quite large (up to 90 persons). However, the number of minorities working in the laboratories was small. One-fourth of the labs of all postdoctoral respondents contained no minorities; about a third had one minority; a small number had four or more minorities.

For most of the trainees, the Ph.D. was the only doctorate they earned; considerably fewer had M.D.s; and very few had M.D.-Ph.D.s. During their postdoctoral training, trainees had multiple career goals. Almost all trainees cited teaching as a career goal; other important goals included biological research, clinical research, and medicine. Nearly all respondents stated that their participation in the program had an influence on both their education and their careers.

At the time of the interview, nearly all of the postdoctoral respondents were employed. Most were working in academic positions; a smaller percentage was employed in industry; and a few were working in government or nonprofit organizations or were doing something else. For those in academia, about one-half were at medical schools. More than half obtained academic positions following the completion of their postdoctoral program, and a quarter sought additional postdoctoral training. At the time of interview, only a few postdoctoral respondents were still working in the program about which they were interviewed.

TABLE 5-1 Postdoctoral Trainees and Junior Faculty by Program, Race/Ethnicity in the Universe and Sample, and Race/Ethnicity as Self-Identified in Interviews

			No. of Trainees			No. Interviewed	
Type	Title	Categories	Universe	Sample	Total	URM	Non-URM
Targeted	(T-32) NRSA Institutional Training Grant	URM	166	166	38	12	26[a]
Non-Targeted	(T-32) NRSA Institutional Training Grant	URM	698	698	93	75	18[b]
		Non-URM	7,679	325	54	0	54
		Unknown	5,433	325	43	3	40
		Total	13,810	1,348	190	78	112
Targeted	(T-35) Short-Term Institutional Training Grant	URM	26	26	4	2	2[c]
Non-Targeted	(T-35) Short-Term Institutional Training Grant	URM	8	8	1	0	1
		Non-URM	23	23	1	0	1
		Unknown	20	20	5	0	5
		Total	51	51	7	0	7
Targeted	(K-01) Mentored Scientist Development Awards (Postdoctoral)	URM	17	17	0	0	0
Non-Targeted	(K-01) Mentored Scientist Development Awards (Postdoctoral)	URM	10	10	2	2	0
		Non-URM	13	13	24	0	24
		Unknown	13	13	1	0	1
		Total	36	36	27	2	25
Targeted	(K-08) Mentored Clinical Scientist Development Awards	URM	21[e]	21	8	5	3[f]
Non-Targeted	(K-08) Mentored Clinical Scientist Development Awards	URM	11	11	4	4	0
		Non-URM	154	140	5	0	5
		Unknown	14	14	2	0	2
		Total	179	165	11	4	7
Targeted	(K-01) Mentored Scientist Development Awards (Junior Faculty)	URM	17	17	10	7	3[g]
Non-Targeted	(K-01) Mentored Scientist Development Awards (Junior Faculty)	URM	11	11	5	5	0
		Non-URM	36	36	24	1[h]	23
		Unknown	7	7	4	3	1
		Total	54	54	33	9	24

All	**All Programs**	**URM**	**985**	**985**	**165**	**112**	**53**
		Non-URM	**7,905**	**537**	**108**	**1**	**107**
		Unknown	**5,487**	**379**	**55**	**6**	**49**
		TOTAL	**14,377**	**1,901**	**328**	**119**	**209**

NOTE:

URM = underrepresented minority. For the universe and sample, under-represented minorities are defined as African American, Hispanic American, Native American, or Alaskan Native. For purposes of defining the universe and the sample, it was assumed that all participants in targeted programs were underrepresented minorities. Among those interviewed, the number of URMs also includes individuals who self-identified as Pacific Islanders and the number of non-URMs includes those who self-identified as Asian or White in the interview process. The footnotes below indicate in the "Interviewed" column the number of individuals by race/ethnicity that were indicated as URMs in the universe and sample, but self-identified as non-URM in the interview process.

Non-URM = white or Asian. The footnotes below indicate in the "Interviewed" column the number of individuals by race/ethnicity that were indicated as URMs in the universe and sample, but self-identified as non-URM in the interview process.

Unknown = For large fractions of the trainees in the universe and trainees selected for the sample, their race/ethnicity was unknown (i.e., not recorded in NIH datasets). Their race/ethnicity was later resolved in the interview process as noted in the "Interviewed" column.

[a] Among the 38 targeted T-32 trainees interviewed, eight self-identified as Asian and 18 self-identified as white. For analytical purposes, the 18 white trainees were re-classified as nonminorities in the nontargeted program.
[b] Among the 93 URM trainees in the nontargeted T-32 program who were interviewed, 18 self-identified as white.
[c] Among the 4 targeted T-35 trainees interviewed, two self-identified as white. For analytical purposes, the two white trainees were re-classified as nonminorities in the nontargeted program.
[d] The 1 URM in the nontargeted T-35 program who was interviewed, self-identified as white
[e] The universe for the K-08 Mentored Clinical Scientist Development (targeted) program is estimated.
[f] Among the 8 targeted K-08 recipients interviewed, three self-identified as Asian.
[g] Among the 10 targeted K-01 junior faculty interviewed, two self-identified as Asian and one as white. For analytical purposes, the one white awardee was re-classified as a nonminority in the nontargeted program.
[h] Among the 24 non-URM in the nontargeted K01 junior faculty program who were interviewed, one self-identified as African-American.

Most trainees were married or in long-term relationships, although minority trainees were somewhat more likely to be so than nonminority trainees and trainees in targeted programs were more likely to have dependent children. The spouses of these married trainees were highly supportive of their education. In addition, almost all of the parents of trainees supported their education. This is not unexpected because the families of origin of all trainees themselves were, in general, well educated. Trainees were asked if their parents or siblings had baccalaureate or graduate degrees. Nearly all postdoctoral respondents indicated that their parents or siblings had a baccalaureate degree, and a majority of postdoctoral respondents indicated that their parents or siblings had a graduate degree.

Of the postdoctoral trainees interviewed, 103 were underrepresented minorities, but only 19 of these were funded through targeted programs (note that 11 persons funded through targeted programs were not underrepresented minorities). One-half of the minority postdoctoral respondents in targeted programs indicated that English was their primary language, compared to three-fourths of minorities in untargeted programs and nearly all nonminorities. Slightly more than one-half of all postdoctoral respondents were male.

Relative to undergraduate and graduate survey respondents, postdoctoral respondents demonstrated markedly reduced variability among their survey responses. This is interesting, because in terms of gender, minority undergraduate and graduate survey respondents were mostly female, whereas minority postdoctoral respondents were mostly male. Furthermore, the loss of females at this stage of the pipeline is also seen among nonminority females (see Appendix E). The shift in gender distribution suggests that a selection process has occurred, one that may relate to the reduced variability observed among postdoctoral respondents, in general Put another way, expressions of diversity diminish from the population as one ascends the career stage ladder. Thus, one indicator of future research success among trainees may be the extent to which each conforms to research community participant characteristics and norms.

Despite the many similarities among those who achieve postdoctoral trainee status, three issues stand out for minority trainees that may address the differences in achievement between minority and nonminority postdoctoral trainees. First is the fact that a large fraction of minority trainees reported that they did not have a mentor. This is highly unusual. Second is that more than one-half of the minority postdoctoral respondents felt that their race affected their training experience in some way. Third, minority postdoctoral trainees were more likely to report that the next step taken in their career path was to obtain another postdoctoral assignment. In contrast, nonminorities were more likely to report that the next step in their career path was attainment of an academic position. These intriguing differences may warrant further study by NIH.

Postdoctorates Receiving (T32) Training Awards

Nearly all postdoctoral respondents received outside funding at some point during their postdoctoral years. The most frequently cited funding sources were fellowships, grants, family support, savings, or a job. One-quarter of postdoctoral respondents received outside funding—funding beyond that provided directly by the program—while they were supported by the T32 training grant. The most frequently mentioned outside funding sources were a job, savings, or teaching assistantship.

Additionally, program participants stressed the financial rewards of the award. However roughly equal proportions thought the award amount was either too small or very good. When asked about the best features of the training program, respondents said: "Of course getting paid. It was very versatile in that you could choose a field that interested you"; "Not only were you paid, but you were paid to do something you enjoyed"; and "It provided financial support for people to engage in research without distractions and provided opportunity to be mentored by a scientist." A physician scientist stated, "It provided a salary so that I could spend time in the laboratory free of clinical duties."

On the other hand, some program participants were disappointed in the level of funding. They stated: "It would be nice if there was more money"; "The amount of the award could be better correlated with the cost of living in the area in which it was granted"; and "I think the salary was pretty low if I remember correctly."

For the remainder of this chapter, the term mentor will be used to describe the person who guided the trainee's research, whether that role was mentor or principal investigator (PI). More than half of the trainees who reported having had a mentor said that the PI of their lab was their mentor. For trainees in nontargeted programs, nearly all reported that their mentors or PIs were nonminorities. Minority trainees in targeted training programs were more likely than others to report having a mentor who was also a minority. This may be explained by the fact that targeted T32 awards are often awarded to minority-serving institutions (MSIs), which tend to have greater numbers of minority faculty than non-MSI institutions. Very few postdoctoral respondents reported having a female mentor or PI.

Nearly all postdoctoral respondents who reported having a mentor considered their mentor good to work with and supportive of their research. Many of the awardees stressed the importance of their mentor. One respondent described his or her mentor as follows: "She taught me how to do research and worked closely with me. She was also a role model." Mentors were also described as "very supportive. I found him also to be very bright and intelligent. I had a lot of respect for him. And he was willing to show that type of relationship with all the people in his lab." When asked what the most outstanding attributes of the mentor were, one awardee responded, "As a role model, the contributions he made to the scientific community, the intellectual stimulation that he brought, the quality of life that he led as a PI."

Most characterized their mentor or PI as active in the scientific community. Less than one-half of the postdoctoral respondents reported having received positive career guidance from their mentor or PI. About one-half of the postdoctoral respondents considered their mentor helpful in obtaining funding. Most postdoctoral respondents had frequent contact with their mentor or PI and discussed their research with the others in the lab. However, the social distance between the mentor and respondent was familiar or close for only one-half of the trainees. The social distance between others in the lab and the trainee was familiar or close for two-thirds of the trainees, but trainees were less likely to be familiar or close to other colleagues.

Only one-half of the postdoctoral respondents who reported having a mentor believed that their mentor had a strong influence on their career and fewer believed the same for others in the lab. However, among those who reported having a mentor, most remained in contact with their mentors, laboratory group, and colleagues for five or more years.

Other Training Programs for Postdoctoral Trainees

Interview data were obtained from a small number of postdoctoral trainees from three additional funding mechanisms. These include the (T35) Short-Term Institutional Training Grant, the (K08) Mentored Clinical Scientist Development Awards, and the (K01) Mentored Research Scientist Development Award. The numbers of persons included in this group of training programs is too small to analyze by program type and the programs are too disparate to commingle for analysis. There were 11 minority trainee interviews from all three programs combined.

Nevertheless, examination of the interview data leads to some interesting generalizations about participants in the three different programs. Participants in the T35 programs tend to be medical students or physicians who are using the program as an opportunity to get some specialized training in a technique or procedure, generally during a summer quarter. Consequently, the fellows do not establish the same types of relationships with PIs and colleagues in their labs as T32 postdoctoral trainees do. Nor is the experience directly linked to career goals and expectations; rather, it serves as one of many stepping stones in their career pathways.

Postdoctoral respondents who are awarded the K01 Mentored Research Scientist Development Awards responded similarly to their junior faculty counterparts, with one obvious exception: they viewed a faculty position as the important next step in their career paths.

Finally, the K08 Mentored Clinical Scientists Development Award is dedicated to providing research opportunities for persons with clinical backgrounds. Nevertheless, most of the trainees interviewed held the Ph.D. as their only doctorate and a much smaller percentage held some sort of clinical degree. Their career goals focused on teaching, clinical research, biological research, and behavioral research. Most sought academic appointments as the next step in their career paths.

The career development awards were important because they gave the recipient the experience of supervising staff and conducting independent research with the safety net of a mentor. When asked to assess the impact of the mentor, one respondent replied, "He enabled me to develop needed skills for my research and guided me into independent research." Another recipient responded, "[the mentor] made it possible for me to become a faculty member and helped me to continue to become independent investigator."

One awardee described the impact of the award, "It put me on steep trajectory on an independent research career. It formed the basis for clinical research later in my career." The importance for career development was stressed by a respondent who stated, "The award gave me the opportunity for protected time and research support. It allowed me to obtain independent R01 funding and to be promoted." Another respondent stated that the award "gave me a chance to really launch an independent research career." Finally, one award recipient described the award thusly, "The K01 was the most important thing in my career at a difficult time."

Characteristics of Junior Faculty

Forty-three interviews were conducted with junior faculty who were awarded a K01 Mentored Research Scientist Development Award. Most of the awardees had Ph.D.s; just a few of the postdoctoral faculty had M.D.-Ph.D.s or M.D.s. The primary function of the award is to give the awardee an opportunity to conduct independent research while at the same time receiving guidance from a mentor. Awardee after awardee stressed the importance of gaining independence, securing protected time, and the ability to define a new research agenda. For example: "It put me on track to be an independent investigator on a steep trajectory"; "It provided me five years of protected time to develop an independent research career"; or "It helped me to launch my lab. It allowed me to get other funding as a principal investigator."

As was the case for T32 postdoctoral trainees, there was considerable homogeneity among the responses of K01 faculty awardees. All K01 faculty respondents had a mentor and nearly all the mentors were white males. Mentors encouraged the respondents' research; were good to work with; were active in the scientific community; and gave good career advice. The K01 faculty respondents met with their mentors regularly, at least once a month, but slightly less than one-half reported feeling familiar or close to their mentors. About one-half of all the K01 faculty respondents believed that their mentor had some or a great deal of influence on their career, although all of the minority-targeted K01 faculty felt this way. The K01 faculty respondents received feedback on their research from their mentors and other colleagues. Nearly all discussed their research with other colleagues at least two to three times per month.

Nearly all of the K01 faculty respondents were married during the time of the award and most had families; however, minority-targeted junior faculty were more likely to have children than nontargeted awardees. English was the primary language for most of the K01 faculty respondents, but a small number of minority respondents reported that English was their second language. Similar to the T32 postdoctoral trainees, K01 faculty respondents had exceptionally well-educated families of origin. Nearly all of the K01 faculty respondents had parents or siblings with baccalaureate degrees and most had parents or siblings with graduate degrees. Parents and spouses of K01 faculty respondents were supportive of their chosen career path.

With one exception, all of the awardees were working at the time of the interview and nearly all were working in academia—primarily in medical schools. Their career goals, as a group, focused on biological research, allied health professions, and clinical research. The most frequently cited expectations from (K01) awardees included, in rank order: getting tenure, getting grants, setting their research agenda, publishing research results, and increasing the size of their lab. A little more than one-half of the (K01) faculty respondents had supplementary sources of income at the time of the award; these sources included other grants, employment, savings, family support, and fellowships.

Interviews with PARIs about the (T32) NRSA Institutional Training Grant

Two PARIs were interviewed about the (T32) NRSA Institutional Training Grants they administer. Each is a PI on the grant.

Recruitment into the Program

The T32 Institutional training programs actively recruit predoctoral and postdoctoral trainees and graduate students. According to the program administrators interviewed for this study, the recruiting efforts of the training programs vary according to the nature of the host institution. The committee obtained interviews with representatives of two training programs that were concerned principally with identifying and recruiting postdoctoral trainees.

In one institution, a university, most candidates are identified and recruited internally based on their research track record. However, some effort is made to recruit from outside, especially when trying to identify qualified minority candidates. The ideal recruit has great intellectual potential but not necessarily outstanding accomplishments or prior research experience. According to one program administrator, interest and commitment are the best predictors of success in the program.

Another institution is an academic medical center with a National Heart, Lung, and Blood Institute (NHLBI) program in hematology. The program supports about 40 scientists, of which 8 or 9 are minority M.D.s or Ph.D.s. The program actively tries to recruit minority candidates, but the number of inquiries is small, possibly because hematology is not an area of interest to minority postdoctoral trainees or physicians, compared to other fields.

Experience with the Program

For each program, admission is highly selective; therefore, trainees whether minority or not, tend to be successful in their research efforts. One program administrator explained that one of the most important factors that impacts trainee success is the fit between the trainee and the lab—an issue of community. Every once in a while there is a mismatch whereby the lab does not serve the needs of the trainee. In these cases the program administrator talks at length with the PI of the lab. Sometimes this intervention remedies the problem. In a few cases, however, the best solution is to relocate the postdoctoral fellow into a new lab. One program administrator said, "Our professors are smarter than our students—that's not the case at Harvard where the students are as smart as or smarter than the professors. We have a different type of student." Consequently, the program works hard to create mentoring environments; thus, trainees have multiple mentors and multiple committees so that they have the opportunity to get advice from different levels.

Conclusion

One of the hallmarks of postgraduate research training is the striking homogeneity observed among its participants who tend to come from highly-educated families that are supportive of the participants' chosen career paths. These data reflect the programs' overall failure to train minorities from more modest backgrounds. Postdoctoral training awards and career development awards serve as important, even essential, mechanisms that enable recipients to successfully bridge the world of graduate school and that of a professor. The training awards were important for four reasons. First, they offered the opportunity to engage in independent research. Second, for many of the recipients, the awards enabled them to work with a mentor or principal investigator who guided their research. Third, the awards placed the recipients in laboratories that enhanced networking with other scientists. Fourth, for some postdocs the awards led directly to faculty positions. The career development awards provided advanced mentoring opportunities for awardees and helped senior postdoctoral trainees and junior faculty members make the critical transition to research independence.

6

Perspectives of NIH Program Administrators

The successes of National Institutes of Health (NIH) training programs are influenced, in part, by the attitudes, expectations, and support of the program administrators. This chapter offers a perspective on the views and practices of 22 program administrators across the NIH institutes and centers (PAICs), in response to their training responsibilities, including training of underrepresented minorities. The interviews draw attention to the absence of inter-IC (institutes and centers) coordination of minority research training programs across the NIH campus as a whole and underscore the widely perceived need for an NIH-wide trainee outcomes tracking system. In addition, the interviews elicited numerous strategies for improving the success of minority training programs and reveal a prevalence of mixed attitudes among PAICs, regarding minority-targeted programs, in general.

Methods

The committee developed two interview instruments that were designed to clarify the perspectives of PAICs and identify their views on the strengths, barriers, and strategies associated with the management of training programs, in general, and minority training programs, in particular. One instrument addressed programs that are awarded to individuals (e.g., F31, R03, K01), and a second addressed programs awarded to institutions, such as the T-series training grants (a sample instrument is located in Appendix D). Three pilot interviews were conducted in the course of developing the interview protocol. The pilot interviews were not included in the analysis of PAIC input because of varying protocols, the purposeful selection of particularly supportive participants, and the presence of observers.

The interviews were designed to be ethnographic (e.g., open-ended and exploratory), but unfortunately, in many cases, interviewers allowed the discussions to stray considerably from the interview questions in ways that the committee had not anticipated. As a result, the interview contents are highly variable with regard to topic and relevance to the questions originally identified by the committee.

The format of the interviews was further complicated by the lack of consistent structure in the management of training programs across the NIH ICs. Some have a centralized training officer who coordinates all training (minority targeted and nontargeted); others have a separate minority training officer; still others assign training to individual health scientist administrators depending on the specific research area being funded. In some cases, when training program management was ostensibly centralized, the contractor was told to speak with someone else regarding minority programs. Thus, it appears there is no uniform utilization of minority training programs or training program management policies across the ICs. The inclusion of minority-targeted programs, minority status of participants, career stages served, or whether the program is awarded to an individual or an institution varies considerably across the ICs. For this reason, it was not possible to analyze the response data strictly in terms of career stage. This degree of program management decentralization and heterogeneity made it challenging at times to identify the best respondents for each of the programs. Because some PAIC respondents were responsible for several training programs, it was challenging for the contractor to manage the interviews and ensure that all relevant programs were discussed. Unfortunately, in actual operations, some of the interviews focused on one or more programs that were not even included in the scope of the study.

A total of 22 PAIC interviews were conducted and analyzed for this study. The interviews were administered to a group of rationally selected respondents who administer programs assessed by the study. For reasons of confidentiality, respondent identities and institute affiliations were concealed to anyone other than the contractors who conducted the interviews. The contractor began the interview by introducing the study and explaining how respondents' comments would be integrated into the study.

The qualitative data analytic program Nu*dist version 6.0 was used to classify response data. Comments were grouped into 347 different clusters of related statements and then subjected to additional analyses by the study committee. The data were organized into four "layers" (or node levels) based on career stage served by the program, whether the program was awarded to individuals or institutions, whether the program was targeted or nontargeted, and the specific topics of discussion.

Common themes are identified and an example quote is provided for each. Rather than duplicating quotations, the prevalence of the response is indicated whenever possible. Unique responses are identified as such. Every effort was taken to ensure accuracy among the quotes reflected in this chapter. Extraneous and irrelevant comments were replaced by ellipses. Words were added to a quotation in cases where missing words could be reasonably discerned from the interview context; added words are included in brackets.

Results

The data are grouped into four major content areas: (1) recruitment strategies; (2) funding application process; (3) definition of program goals; and (4) reliable methods of outcome monitoring.

Recruitment Strategies

In general, program administrators expressed one of two views about the adequacy of trainee recruitment to the programs: a modest majority was content with current trainee recruitment strategies, whereas a substantial minority was less so. With regard to the former, respondents said that underrepresented minorities who wish to pursue a career in biomedical research are welcome to locate specific program information on IC web sites or from printed matter such as program brochures or trade journal announcements. Respondents in this group emphasized that it is up to the minority trainee to identify the appropriate training program for him- or herself: "I think the programs are [fine], if any one is at all interested in doing research they know to look at NIH [web sites], and when they get to the NIH, the programs are, I think . . . easy to find." Another respondent said, "Because the people come to the web site, they'll see the 'diversity page' that they can click on. They'll see there are opportunities." Other respondents in this group mentioned that NIH staff regularly attends professional conferences and other meetings where they give presentations about IC training opportunities. Some respondents added that sometimes NIH staff make contact with key individuals in the community just to let them know about a pending announcement. A few respondents in this group noted that there may not always be an adequate number of eligible minorities in certain geographic regions of the country. "we encourage . . . investigators to . . . enroll underrepresented minorities, . . . we don't have quotas but we have a firm expectation. There are some realities when you get out of [major urban areas] there aren't very many minorities enrolled in the school in [less populated areas], . . . " and thus their expectation is that NIH must accept their limited ability to recruit underrepresented minorities. An unexpected comment came at the end of one interview: "We are not in a position here, as a funding institution, to really have a hands-on meaningful effect on young individuals, convincing them to come into science and stay in science, . . . that is a reality, . . . we just aren't close enough to the individuals."

The second group felt that current trainee recruitment strategies are largely insufficient and that ICs should conduct a more proactive and targeted outreach to prospective minority trainees. Such targeted outreach may include dissemination of minority trainee success stories, training opportunity advertisements, and program announcements infused into popular media that serve minority audiences. This group of respondent also placed great value in outreach targeted to minority students at the primary and secondary school levels. They noted that in low-income areas, where access to computers is limited, the web and other literature may not be available to potential applicants. In addition, the information provided does not always address the issues that concern underrepresented minorities in the first place. For example, many minorities want to know how to survive economically and support their families while participating in NIH-supported programs.

Several respondents with this viewpoint suggested that NIH policy and procedures become more flexible in announcing and marketing their research programs. One respondent said, "It would be nice to have the flexibility of being able to structure grants a little bit more . . . in fact, we can't pay recruitment costs. Recruitment is a non-allowable cost at NIH, so some kind of [support for] recruitment for our local programs would be nice."

A small number of these respondents suggested that a broader and more creative approach to recruiting minorities may be needed. "We need people that are actually anthropologists, psychologists . . . not just geneticists to look at the bigger picture. To . . . question the assumptions. One of the basic assumptions . . . [in] most of our programs is that if you get kids involved in a lab, they're going to get excited and good things will happen. It's going to turn them on. They're going to become better students. It's a gratuitous assumption." They also suggested studying the process: "[study] the career tracks of successful minority students who have turned into postdocs and funded investigators, [those] who have impacted a given area of science . . . . That could teach us what the critical components are."

Another positive approach suggested by multiple respondents focused on broader public outreach. "I think we need to continue to not only just present [approaches], but make sure that we write information that can be published in different venues, . . . Everybody I know reads *Ebony* magazine. Why can't we do an article looking at minority investigators, . . . on what minority investigators are doing and then the opportunity for research . . . " This approach could be implemented in several public venues such as popular magazines and public service announcements in Native American, Hispanic, and African-American popular media publications.

One of the most aggressive approaches to minority recruitment included a plan to follow promising minority and economically disadvantaged students from the undergraduate career through the professional career. " . . . We carry some . . . postdocs all the way through career development. The program is designed the same way so individuals have support all the way through the career development, but the key thing is for them to know about this." Another respondent indicated, "We want to follow them. We do have all the mechanisms here to . . . go with them up to they get an R01. The comprehensive follow-through approach is not yet implemented . . . " In another perspective on outreach, it has been noted that the Bridges programs seem to draw more Native Americans than does any other program "because there aren't any other programs that reach out to community colleges specifically."

Recruiting programs intended for minority junior faculty appeared to have some unique issues. The individual faculty applicants seeking targeted support for mentoring need to have a well-developed research plan. "We do like to see that in the first year that the research plan is fairly detailed and specifically laid out." In addition to the research plan, the applicant needs to have a career plan laid out as well. However, it was noted by several respondents that the minority faculty are often located in schools that emphasize teaching and that teaching loads sometimes reach four courses per semester. The minority-serving institutions are focused on teaching to the extent that it may be difficult for supported minority faculty to do the required research or even build the necessary research record to apply for career support. One particularly clear expression of this point was raised at the end of an interview. "I've talked to a few minority [faculty] applicants who want to do research but there's so much heavy emphasis on teaching . . . they can't get the time to devote to research. And so I don't know if there are any more creative ways to do that. Not everyone can take advantage of minority K01 awards, which require a certain amount of hours in research time." In order to obtain funding, the faculty has to have an active research program. This seems to be a "catch-22." One individual proposed that minority junior faculty could be encouraged to engage in research if given an opportunity to do so, perhaps using a mechanism that would essentially "buy" one year of teaching credit.

Some of the PAIC interview respondents provided particularly insightful thoughts on common barriers to enrolling targeted minorities into graduate school: " . . . Some of them . . . don't have very good undergraduate records, . . . sometimes they have very bad grades. Application reviewers and the special emphasis [program administrators need] to realize that some of these students have different realities than other students." In addition they have added responsibilities. "A lot of them have to work a full-time job while they're students. A lot of them . . . have two to three children . . . those are the things that explain why [they] get Cs or ... failed this [course] but I passed [it] later with an A." It might simply be cultural differences between the applicant and the reviewers. "Sometimes you don't understand where a person's coming from. . . . You're not familiar with people from that culture. And its one of the things we're trying to bridge in a rewrite of the program announcements."

One respondent was clear that recruitment had to happen much earlier than in college: "We try to go out to elementary schools, if possible. I've not done that in a number of years, but we have participated in science fairs. And, in terms of educating the community, because in elementary school, while they are still very young, it's really at this level oftentimes that it's piqued their interest." A few respondents discussed science fairs and other activities that engaged students at all levels of training.

There may be some confusion among the various training management staff about targeted mechanisms. For example, some program administrators believed that their nontargeted programs are exclusive to nonminority applicants: "In fact, minorities can't apply for any of our grants."

As a separate issue, several respondents suggested that minority recruitment requirements be tied more closely to funding of training grants "when someone comes up on a competing renewal grant and they don't show any progress. You can hold up the award on their grant until they submit a revised application to make sure that they are approaching the situation more effectively."

Funding Application Process

A few training officers felt that minority applicants must meet the same requirements that nonminority applicants do and that essentially nothing can be done, from an NIH perspective, to develop more underrepresented minority biomedical researchers. A second perspective offered by a large number of program administrators was that many more of the applicants from underrepresented communities could succeed in obtaining support for their training if they were given some technical assistance in grant proposal preparation. A third perspective is that NIH itself should make the necessary adjustments to reduce barriers to science participation among members of underrepresented groups.

Several respondents suggested ways in which NIH staff could enhance the likelihood that minority applicants and their institutions are awarded training and research support. One individual explained, "[When the applicant] asks about the review, they'll have their summary statement, . . . but also any other thing that didn't quite make the summary statement we can provide . . . and, in general, just input about the overall sense [of the review committee at] the time of review." Another respondent has a specific routine for addressing promising minority grantees who didn't get funded the first time: "I normally . . . send my letter with the summary statement. I ask the applicant to share the summary statement with their mentor and contact me if they have any questions. Normally they will contact me because sometimes they don't know what [the summary statement] really means, ..." Another NIH staffer actually goes beyond this simple approach and takes the time to increase the likelihood that a second effort is successful. "I normally . . . offer them [the mentor and mentee] a conference call, if they want to amend the application and resubmit it . . . . I read the summary statement . . . and give my recommendations [to them]. Most of the . . . recommendations . . . are constructive criticisms." This appears to be a successful approach. The same respondent reported that he works with "the students that . . . have 10 points or 20 points out of the pay line, . . . I had about six amended applications. Five of them are likely to get funded" after they are resubmitted.

A different way in which NIH staff can improve the number of minority applicants who win grants is to modify the standard granting procedure. "We've had training grants that have done exceptionally well. In review of . . . one [grant cycle] . . . we gave [grantees] limited funding. And we gave them limited funding with milestones as to how they were going to achieve this. So, instead of them getting the full five years they were given three years, which meant they had to . . . apply for the grant after two years. And they were given milestones basically of what they could do to encourage people . . . ."

Some program administrators offered insights about the problems associated with research capacity-building awards to minority-serving institutions. These awards are granted to institutions that demonstrate a commitment to research and have a clear research plan. In those circumstances, reviewers are instructed "to look at how well the faculty [are] prepared in terms of being able to do research—the kinds of research that they are proposing—whether the project is well thought out. If there's a need for the kind of research being proposed—the experimental details . . . are there . . . ." If all of those things and more are present, then the capacity-building award is more likely.

One exception to this rule may be the Bridges to the Doctorate program. The criteria for the Bridges program may be more moderate because of the relationship between the two involved institutions. "For Bridges, I'm looking for institutions that have a real interest in educational reform. Institutions that have pools of minority students with potential [and] who really care about developing that potential, . . . who have a real interest in scientific research as opposed to technical capacity . . . . I'm interested in research training."

Some respondents commented that the criteria for minority training grants may include too many barriers for even the most qualified minority institutions. It may be that some institutional applicants are schools that do not already have the infrastructure to sustain an effective and ongoing research program. Faculty at these schools often have a full teaching load with as many as four courses a semester. Further, there is reason to believe that it may be particularly difficult to enlist the caliber of researchers needed to serve as mentors. One respondent said, "People that are just really good. And the real good people . . . [have heavy] workloads . . . so how do we . . . collaborate [with these good] mentors? The really good investigators are too busy to give the kind of time required to be good mentors, too."

In fact, a couple of respondents suggested that NIH consider revising its grant review policy to include a more culturally sensitive approach that does not pit the minority schools against the rest of the research community using mainstream research community standards. "But in general, minority students, . . . some of them are being educated in very good schools. They come from Harvard or MIT [Massachusetts Institute of Technology]. They have a different demeanor than a person who comes from a . . . very small minority school." This may influence the way minority participants are viewed and may hinder their progress in working toward successful research careers.

With some NIH institutes, the minority graduate student seeking fellowship funding will have a better chance of success if the application reflects an early interest in the proposed research area or science in general. "Even some of them, as a high school student, they have demonstrated some kind of interest in science." An undergraduate science major is also a boost to likely funding as a graduate student: "The other thing though I would look for is what they have done during their undergrad education. If some of them . . . don't choose a major until sophomore year and beyond the sophomore year . . . the ones that are interested in science, they really would like to start pursuing science the first year. They are loaded with academic requirements for science programs."

Beyond issues that involve improvements in the applicants and programs, several NIH respondents suggested that changes in NIH policies and procedures could be made that would also help improve the effectiveness of grant training programs. For example, staff expressed a number of concerns about their work environment and its effect on their performance. For example, the impact of outsourcing within the government is reflected in morale problems. "Also, all of the federal government is going through something called A-76. This is outsourcing. We've worked real hard to build a really good working team that likes to work together . . . does a good job. We know each other, . . . [we] may lose all . . . [staff] support, . . . it is exquisitely demoralizing for everybody." A related NIH staff complaint is the workload: "The real problem that we have is . . . that we would need more people to really have [an effect on training] . . . the workload [is increasing] because some of the programs have been growing enormously. That means . . . more work for the same number of people. So, we are really stretched very thin." The time pressures, as perceived by NIH staff, have made it difficult to be effective at managing their training programs.

A few respondents commented that mentors need to be trained in mentoring. "Well, I don't know if this is really NIH's job, but mentors need training on how to be a mentor. There are those who are natural at it, and there are those who really don't know how to do it, and so . . . NIH might have a role in providing mentoring to the mentors."

Several respondents commented on grants management in general: "One is if institutions we work with have better training in how to manage grants. And the other is if our mechanisms were managed and these clusters of grants were streamlined considerably. I think our grant management practices for these grants are very cumbersome."

When talking about outreach barriers to minority trainees, some respondents raised the issue of communication challenges. "I think a lot of the efficiency in the process . . . depends on me. I see myself more as a facilitator . . . for the applicants than anything else. Sometimes we complain that the grants administration branch takes too long to award the grants that have been recommended for funding . . . . They really sometimes take a long time." There have also been complaints about difficulties in accessing administrative offices within the Department of Health and Human Services Administration.

Definition of Program Goals

NIH program administrators reflect diverse perceptions about the goals of research training programs, particularly as they pertain to underrepresented minorities. A majority indicated that programs are geared toward the goal of producing Ph.D.-level researchers. Others indicated that interim vocational outcomes, such as entering the science field at different levels of training, are just as important for generating science role models. Most respondents indicated that the primary goal of the training programs is to produce more researchers in the sciences NIH supports. "With the training grants and career awards, our only interest is the training and we want to push them along until they . . . become researchers." Or at least the goal is to produce researchers with promise. They will produce "publications, scientific presentations and so forth. Keep in mind that R01 grants will come. We're just not there yet." The ideal outcome expressed by several NIH respondents was "We have some people that come from K01 awards, that go right into the R01 . . . . That's the big grant. . . . that's the one we want to see."

The same point made by both statements above is also expressed in terms of institutional award programs. In this case, the goals are "increasing research capacity at minority and minority-serving institutions, addressing the underrepresentation of . . . minorities and other groups, disabled individuals, and so forth in the scientific workforce." Another goal has a broader impact on the country: "And then the other . . . goal of this office is to . . . address health disparities."

There are some variations on the theme of producing minority scientists. For example, one institute "introduced [minority support] at the dissertation stage because we believe that underrepresented minority students had a particular . . . difficulty in finding funds. . . . So that program was meant to address that particular transition. And I suppose it was the easiest program to measure success because every single one of the people we looked at had completed their dissertation and got their doctorate." In the final analysis, "a success for us is anybody who actually completes the Ph.D."

At the undergraduate level, the expressed goals are clearly focused on continuing along the education pipeline: "This student with some supplement [will] . . . go on to get the F31 [or] . . . go on to graduate school."

A few respondents identified a different criterion for success, in lieu of formal evaluation, in terms of the number of applications and even number of successful applications. "The target is the number of applications that we would like to get funded. For example, we would like to have a portfolio of let's say 60 F31 applications."

There seems to be agreement among many respondents that the details of outcomes are not yet well established. It is possible that academic settings are not the only places in which successful scientists can work. "I think we're just starting to take a look at it now from all of the programs, but I think there's enough where . . . outcomes of all of these career awards [might be evaluated]. How many of these [funded students and faculty] are getting there? And also, . . . individuals can go into research and industry and still be doing what they were trained to do."

Although most respondents gave the same goal of recruiting scientists into various fields and producing scientists who win NIH R01 grants, a few respondents agreed that not all participants should be expected to end up in that situation. These few PAIC respondents who differ from the norm, seemed to feel that progress may be multigenerational: "[undergraduates] are a little bit less successful than pre- and postdocs. ... it would be unrealistic to expect every trainee to continue to the next stage. [But] we would like to see that happen." In discussing predoctoral training programs, one respondent recognized the possibility that phasing science into underrepresented minority communities may be a positive outcome. "What's the benefit to NIH? ... as a whole for . . . training scientists who are going to go into academia . . . that's where the next generation of scientists are going to come from. . . . 40 percent of them, maybe more in the future, will be minorities, so they'll also be role models." Short-term goals may be more realistic than expecting minority Ph.D.s at the first effort. One person characterized this perspective as holistic. "First of all, science is a broad domain. There are 27 institute centers and divisions at the NIH, so perhaps if they choose not to continue within our scientific mission area, they may elect another mission area, related to us or unrelated to us. We don't consider that a failure. We do view this enterprise, you know, a bit more holistically."

A second divergent point of view among the respondents is the unique and interesting perspective on the criteria for success among targeted programs: "Another marker of success would be once those people [in targeted programs] are off and running, . . . are they going back and reaching back for somebody else with the kind of help to . . . bring them along. I can say that I'm seeing that now."

More often than not, respondents assured the interviewers that the institute is genuinely interested in increasing the number of minority scientists in the field. "And we really would like to see more minority individuals [participating] because we [dominate science] in the [majority] populations." This quote was from an individual managing only nontargeted mechanisms. Individuals managing a minority project also strongly supported the idea of programs targeting underrepresented minorities to get them into science: "to integrate these folks into the mainstream. And I think . . . that kind of philosophy and attitude and way of thinking will come back and help the . . . next generation. But I think that without these kinds of programs and these kinds of support mechanisms . . . this underrepresentation and isolation . . . will continue at the detriment . . . of increasing the diversity that is absolutely critical."

One NIH staff member suggested that recruiting minorities is a way of increasing the labor pool in fields with extensive shortages of scientists. "There's a shortage in many areas of research and science in general in the country. And you've asked the premier health organization in the country and I think we're really in a position where we should be reaching out and trying to target . . . underrepresented minorities and bring them into the loop." Others see that the need to pursue more minority researchers is based on rectifying historical deficits: "If you take a look at the people who consistently have been getting grants . . . from NIH in general . . . they tend not to be people of color. For historical reasons, obviously . . . educational opportunities for kids . . . for persons of color stink. . . . And so there was a real attempt to get . . . them involved in . . . a bachelor's degree and then on into professional degrees." However, another individual suggested that the minority population was a special needs group: "It's been a continuing interest from the top . . . recognition of the health disparities that exist . . . and recognition of the underrepresented minority investigators in the field."

In some cases the institutes use available mechanisms to help build careers of all promising researchers. For example, a person who is awarded a K01 could end up with a subsequent series of awards. "Then the K22 is our transitional award and that award is made to dovetail from the K01, or either K08 or K23, and is tailored to provide protected time for individuals who are pretty much ready to be independent or have been independent for two years or less . . . they just need a little protected time to get themselves ready to go into the big grant arena. The R01 arena . . . ". In this case the goal is to sustain support until the individual reaches as far as possible along the training pipeline.

An interesting digression from the usual perspective on clinical research support was raised by one respondent, who suggested the possibility that K01 awards could be used to support minority clinical research faculty. It is a particularly interesting approach because of the health disparity problem in this country. "The clinical arena many times helps to shape where the research questions are coming from. So we need to target that population. I think there are a lot of people there that would benefit from this."

A few program administrators view underrepresented minorities as just another group and they do not view the issue of increased minority participation in science as important. "The postdocs themselves need not be minority. I would say that the current appointees are probably at least 40 percent minority, which is higher than typical, average . . . ". This respondent manages a mixed array of targeted and nontargeted programs at both the individual and the institutional levels. "So we discontinued the R03 program for minority students and allowed it to be supplanted by the generic individual fellowship program under the F31 mechanism. And that transition has worked out well. So those applicants who would have previously perhaps come in through the minority R03 mechanism . . . would be coming in for the F31 on a faster review cycle."

A number of NIH program administrators mentioned moving away from targeted programs: "We did not see an advantage to the targeted approach in the case of predoctoral fellows as opposed to the generic approach . . . . And NIH central went along with us. We did try another targeted program, and that is a career award . . . ." A few respondents admittedly took exception to the practice of minority-targeted programs, saying that such programs should target disadvantaged individuals, rather than racial or ethnic minorities. In one case, an administrator of a minority-targeted program admitted to steering prospective minority applicants away the minority-focused program and into a nontargeted program because of a belief that "minority-targeted programs are unconstitutional and cannot be defended in court."

In debating the merits of targeted programs, one respondent said that no program is truly targeted; rather, they are open to any group. "There are none that are exclusive. One that comes closest is a Bridges program. And its authorization and its language says that recipients must be underrepresented minorities as defined by the institution." Thus, any individual representing a minority, in the eyes of the awardee institution, is eligible.

A few program administrators expressed frustration with members of underrepresented minority groups who participated in their programs. One respondent explained, "Just do[ing a program just] for underrepresented minorities. We [have had] countless problems . . . . You know they're bound to leave and don't tell us so we [don't] know how to handle [it]." The respondent, in this case, manages a targeted program for junior faculty. "If an institution is a small institution—private, public, you know, mostly a teaching institution with very few grants, they don't have these sophisticated means to know everything about the grant so that they need a lot of help and they call us." The staff member went on to say that extensive technical assistance is part of the support needed to foster more targeted minorities' participation in these programs.

Reliable Methods of Outcomes Monitoring

The greatest agreement among the NIH program administrators was the near-universal concern about the lack of consistent and reliable tracking information on the subsequent careers of individuals whose training was supported by NIH.

As noted in Chapter 2 of this report, there are major shortcomings in the NIH trainee data collection system. Although a new automated tracking system is a possibility in future NIH plans, the paucity of good reliable data remains a major barrier to the evaluation of targeted programs, as noted by one respondent: "The biggest issue that we have is how to collect data to demonstrate that these programs do or don't work. . . . [A lack of organized] data is our biggest snafu. We've got tons of data sitting [in] files, paper files. There's data sitting in our program director's file about how many hundreds of institutions out there that would be useful to have. But collecting that data is one thing and knowing what to compare it to is something else. And one reason we never had . . . to collect it effectively is we never knew what to compare it to. We never knew, we have never resolved the issue of how you analyze that data. And without some sense of . . . analysis, how do you use it so it can tell you something? . . . we've never been able to make the case . . . . " Others mentioned the need for a decent participant tracking system for analyses. "Well, I think the tracking system would be a big one . . . , if I can just get some systematic information . . . and do some real analysis."

Perhaps the NIH team needs to differentiate the functions of research and evaluation. "The people in evaluation speak, talk a different language than geneticists and cell biologists and so, consequently, if our leadership is geneticists and cell biologists, . . . we sometimes have a difficulty appreciating [the evaluation methodology]." Another evaluation activity suggested by PAIC respondents is the development of a long-term follow-up study that will require an effective tracking system.

The majority of responses indicated that little to no program evaluation has occurred yet. Most respondents said that they wanted to have an evaluation and/or that a plan to evaluate is in the works. "A formal evaluation . . . . We are thinking of doing that as soon as we get some free time because there is evaluation money and this is something that has to be done." Alternatively, it is not seen as the respondent's job: "This evaluation stuff is just not my area."

Monitoring success in targeted programs is greatly hampered by the lack of data on race or ethnicity. In many cases, there are no race or ethnicity data about the individuals applying for support. "We are hoping that there are minority individuals being included in the right programs, but we have no idea." One respondent noted that "it's just unfortunate that [racial or ethnic] data isn't really asked because we don't have the measure of, really, who . . . ." Without a clear picture of how many minorities enter science, it will be difficult to mobilize institute interest in growing the number of minority researchers.

One respondent described the situation with targeted programs and their effectiveness as a question yet to be answered. "We often struggle with that because we are trying to see where all the programs are going. I think that what the NIH needs to do is . . . really beginning to look up all the minority programs because I know that there are all kinds of minority programs throughout the NIH. . . . I think that the big question is, are we really meeting our goals? How are the numbers [of minority scientists] increasing . . . ? But you need to have a good evaluation strategy with people being willing to invest the money that it takes . . . ."

Some groups conduct local evaluations of their programs. "For the research supplement program, I just completed an evaluation for the director. So I do have the information on that . . . ." The nature of the evaluation was not made clear, and the results were expressed in qualitative terms such as patience, technical assistance support, and visibility.

Some of the barriers to evaluation include the cost, clearances, changing priorities, and data infrastructure. "Our hope was that in having this underlying database we would be able to at least go back and get data on the performance of students . . . . And it was built with the idea of being able to do program evaluation. As it turns out, it hasn't been successful in doing that and there are a couple of reasons. One is that we cannot get institutional baseline data. It's just not there. So there's no way to say, based on what's in the database, this institution has improved its transfer rate. . . . The other problem is that grants plug along, then they may get six years of support and then they don't get supported . . . . Once they lose their support they stop tracking students." Perhaps the burden of evaluating NIH programs might be more effectively applied as an NIH activity with appropriate infrastructure and administrative support.

According to some NIH staff, attrition, defined as those not entering research careers, is hard to document "because they require tremendous amount of data. They require information on the training pool, they require information on the mentors and on the trainees, what they've done, and they also record information on where the trainees are going after they've left the training program."

Conclusion

Because of the qualitative approach taken with the NIH program administrator interviews, the results are obliquely tied to the committee charge. An additional consequence is the fact that the interviews often fail to differentiate the specific program, the career stage, or even whether or not the program under discussion was targeted. As a result, the interview data provide an overall context in which NIH training programs are supported, rather than the detailed mechanics of program operations. Viewed from this perspective, the interviews provided useful information relative to the committee charge. In general, NIH program administrators were supportive of the interview process and its purpose.

There seems to be a strong opinion among a large number of NIH program administrators that NIH should do more to recruit and retain underrepresented minorities in science. Although, a slight majority of respondents view current NIH recruitment efforts (postings on the web, announcements in professional journals, and speaking engagements at professional meetings) as adequate, a sizable fraction believes that current efforts are inadequate. The underrepresentation of minorities in science, according to many of the respondents, results in inadequate scientific input from divergent social or cultural perspectives and detracts from our nation's ability to resolve health disparities.

Several respondents recommended that the NIH training community review its recruitment and retention practices to find new ways to include more minorities in science training programs. Some respondents recommended an aggressive trainee tracking effort. Others recommended that program administrators provide more technical assistance to minority applicants, in order improve their chances of being funded on a second round.

Minority junior faculty may also require specialized support to enhance their ability to conduct scientific research. For example, faculty serving at smaller schools need more support than is currently offered, because of their heavy teaching load and other academic responsibilities. New mechanisms, such as funding for "teaching release time," may have to be developed in order to impact the numbers of minority faculty engaged in research. The NIH program administrators indicated a need for more mentor training as a way to improve outcomes.

Another approach to increasing the number of underrepresented minorities in science requires that the NIH community review its own policies and procedures. Issues to be addressed include the following: What is being done to sustain NIH staff investment in the minority trainee development process? What steps have been taken to maintain a high level of staff competence and morale? NIH administrators need to delineate more clearly the goals of minority-focused programs, and they must provide strong evidence of support for those goals.

There is a clear consensus among the NIH program administrators participating in these interviews that NIH needs to establish a systematic and effective trainee tracking system. Such a system should be able to track the career outcomes of any person supported with NIH funds. An ancillary concern expressed by several other respondents is the need for ongoing internal and external evaluations of the NIH training programs. At this juncture, there is no way to evaluate whether the training programs are effective for underrepresented minorities. A successful effort at tracking requires that NIH provide specific financial and logistical support to ongoing data management and evaluation of all of its training programs, including those for underrepresented minorities.

7

Findings and Recommendations

The National Institutes of Health (NIH) is the world's foremost medical research center. Its web site states, "The goal of NIH is to acquire new knowledge to help prevent, detect, diagnose, and treat disease and disability, from the rarest genetic disorder to the common cold. The NIH mission is to uncover new knowledge that will lead to better health for everyone. NIH works toward that mission by conducting research in its own laboratories; supporting the research of non-Federal scientists in universities, medical schools, hospitals, and research institutions throughout the country and abroad; helping in the training of research investigators; and fostering communication of medical and health sciences information."[54]

The training of research investigators is a critical component in the attainment of NIH research goals. Efforts by NIH and the research community to increase the participation of underrepresented groups in these training activities are important for maximizing the potential of individuals from underrepresented groups and the biomedical research enterprise. Recent data on graduate enrollments in science and engineering have shown a long-term decline in the number of white males enrolling in NIH research training programs over the last decade. Moreover, the number of international trainees participating in U.S. science and engineering graduate and postdoctoral training programs is also in danger of sharp decline given recent world events. Minority groups therefore, are largely untapped populations that can help to remedy a significant and growing problem.

For this study, the committee was charged with (1) assessing how well these NIH minority research training programs work; (2) identifying characteristics of successful programs, trainees and institutions; (3) recommending strategies to render future assessments feasible; and (4) providing recommendations for a coordinated trainee tracking information system. This chapter synthesizes findings from across the career stage levels and concludes with specific policy recommendations for NIH. These recommendations suggest ways to enhance NIH's minority research training programs and provide guidance to NIH for future data collection efforts that will enhance the ability of evaluators to assess the success of these programs at regular intervals. This report does not address whether or how ineffectual programs should be dealt with. The

---

[54] See http://www.nih.gov/about/Faqs.htm#NIH.

committee believes this is a matter of policy that is best addressed by NIH once legitimate program evaluation becomes feasible.

Findings

Data Collection and Accountability

In the course of assessing NIH's minority research training programs, the study committee engaged in a lengthy and detailed information-gathering process. This effort to collect information quickly became a diagnostic test of the NIH trainee data systems. The test found these data systems and the information available to be uncoordinated and inadequate for the task the committee was assigned. The committee identified the following concerns:

- Numerous NIH trainee data sets are distributed across NIH institutes and centers (ICs) in both hard-copy (i.e., annual progress reports, grant supplements) and digital formats (i.e., in-house Excel spreadsheets). Furthermore, archival trainee data sets are housed in off-site storage facilities. The committee determined that some essential trainee tracking data are already being collected on a regular basis by the ICs, but since these data are not stored centrally and electronically, and since the data do not use common definitions, are in different formats, and include quite different forms of information, the task of assessing trainee outcomes across all NIH research training programs is not currently feasible.[55]
- Although NIH-wide trainee data sets such as the Trainee Fellow File (TFF) and the Information for Management, Planning, Analysis, and Coordination (IMPAC) system are centralized and electronic, they do not contain adequate trainee tracking data. The data sets are similarly inadequate to identify minority trainees who participated in targeted programs, because no data element contained within these data sets specifically denotes a program as targeted to minorities. NIH may wish to consider incorporating such a data element into these systems in the future. To that end, NIH-wide consensus on trainee data collection practices in general will ultimately enhance the ability of future evaluators to assess these programs.

---

[55] Pursuant to a Congressional mandate requiring federal agencies to migrate from paper-based to electronic systems, NIH has undertaken the "electronic Research Administration" (eRA) project to lower costs and administrative effort, expedite extramural grants processing, and provide better-quality information to NIH and the external grantee community. A functional component of eRA is the electronic Streamlined Non-competing Award Process (eSNAP). When fully implemented, eSNAP will allow researchers and grantee institutions to submit progress reports electronically for their noncompeting awards. The pilot phase for eSNAP began in 2003 and ended in 2004. Currently, grantees are required to submit all hard-copy progress reports to a central NIH mailing address, so that they may be electronically scanned into the eSNAP database. Scanning of progress reports is an interim measure that will eventually be phased out, as full-scale electronic functionality of eSNAP is achieved.

In part because of the absence of NIH-wide electronic trainee tracking data, the NIH data contractor achieved a very low response rate from its efforts to locate and interview trainees. This was the case despite its use of two commercial and proprietary credit card databases that together maintain credit card-related contact information for millions of Americans and the query of the U.S. Postal Service address-forwarding database. The committee was disappointed, but not entirely surprised, by the low response rate. Establishing an NIH-wide, centralized, electronic data collection system for trainee tracking is necessary to assess program efficacy on an ongoing basis. Current plans for an electronic system—the electronic Streamlined Noncompeting Award Process (eSNAP)—that would capture trainee tracking data supplied to NIH by recipient institutions in the context of annual progress reports include collection of the following data elements for all trainees: trainee's first, middle, and last name; date of birth; Social Security number; degrees earned; and role on the project. It is important to note that these data are insufficient for tracking trainee outcomes, as evidenced by the trainee survey discussed in this report. NIH may wish to consider asking trainees to provide parents' contact information and/or contact information for three individuals who will always know how to locate the trainee. Doing so will render the task of locating trainees after they move on from the program much easier.

The committee experienced additional difficulty at the outset of the study, because it was unable to obtain a comprehensive listing of minority research training programs, current or past, supported by NIH. Perhaps due to the distributed nature of the NIH campus, the independence of the ICs, and the dynamic nature with which programming is offered or retired, no one at NIH maintains such a list. The committee believes that having a ready means for maintaining such an inventory of active programs will greatly assist future accountability practices.

Another difficulty faced by the committee at the study's outset was the prohibition against accessing or viewing individual trainee race and gender data. Given the necessity of distinguishing minority from nonminority trainees for purposes of carrying out this study, the committee had to rely on an intermediary NIH-approved contractor that was allowed access to individual trainee race and gender data. Since the National Academies had no direct contractual relationship with the NIH-approved contractor, it had little leverage in terms of the deliverables produced.

The committee is cognizant of the sensitivity of race and gender data and the degree to which the NIH Office of the Director strives to protect the privacy of its trainees and grantees, but in this case it made the very task the committee was contracted by NIH to conduct, very difficult. Thus, NIH may wish to revisit its policy regarding access to individual trainee race and gender data for circumstances in which an outside evaluator is used to conduct research training programs assessment. It may also want to revisit the value of having more than one contractor approved for access to individual trainee data.

The committee observed a lack of coordination among NIH minority research training IC representatives. Many of these IC representatives agreed that this lack of coordination works to the detriment of the programs' overall ability to be effective. At the study's outset in 2001, the committee convened a meeting of minority training IC representatives on the NIH campus to discuss the administration of these minority research training programs. The IC representatives commented that it was the *first time* they had ever met in the same room with their programmatic colleagues. The committee believes that discussion of these programs among IC representatives is critical to the overall health and evolution of the programs and will improve the larger effort of collecting coordinated trainee tracking information in the future. NIH may wish to consider establishing a vehicle for bringing minority training IC representatives together on a regular basis. A series of "best-practices" discussions among IC representatives should be part of the ongoing dialogue within this group.

The aforementioned observations provided the committee with a rich appreciation of the complexity inherent to supporting, managing, and accounting for NIH research training program expenditures, whether targeted or not. It is the committee's view that, at this time, NIH is not adequately equipped for full accountability of its research training programs, targeted or untargeted. The ability to document trainee outcomes is so central to the task of training program evaluation that no remedy short of that goal may suffice.

In addition, the committee believes it is important for NIH to engage trainees actively in the tracking process in order to document trainee outcomes. Throughout the trainee interviews, respondents expressed positive regard for both the programs and NIH's first effort to contact them directly for feedback. The committee believes that trainee tracking participation should be mandatory (i.e., as a condition of support) and continue annually for five years following the trainees' participation in the program. Five years will allow sufficient time for most trainees to advance to the next educational or career stage. NIH may wish to consider establishing a system by which trainees can log-on to an NIH web site annually, in order to update their contact information and educational or vocational activities. Given the financial costs of trying to locate trainees after they leave the training program and the very low probability of actually finding them, investment in a tracking protocol that engages trainees directly will conserve future resources and render future assessments feasible. Another reason to engage trainees in future evaluations is simply because they are the programs' primary informants. When a trainee chooses to leave science, for example, NIH needs to know why. Such data are critical to informing the optimization of program features such as recruitment activities, trainee selection criteria, and mentoring practices. In this way, evaluation becomes an iterative process and programs may continue to evolve to greater and greater specificity and success.

Policy and Program Observations

In the following paragraphs, the committee offers some ideas and suggestions based on its efforts to assess whether NIH minority research training programs work.

A thorough analysis of historic NIH program announcements for minority research training programs showed that the stated goal of these programs is, and always has been, to increase the number of Ph.D.-level minority biomedical researchers. Earlier phases of this study recommend that evaluation of minority research training programs should employ "advancement to the next step" in the science, technology, engineering and mathematics (STEM) pipeline as a metric for assessing program success.[56,57] For reasons described in this report, the study committee could not reliably document trainee educational and career outcomes. Thus, it was unable to apply either metric of program success reliably and, as a result, decided to address the issue on philosophical grounds using qualitative descriptors. For example, respondent data are reported using nonspecific terms such as "a majority of respondents said" or "a minority of respondents said". Such phrases should not be equated with statistical significance.

Furthermore, it is the committee's view that NIH minority research training programs have intrinsic value both to individual trainees and society as a whole, even when a Ph.D. is not conferred, by virtue of their "value added."

Given the stated mission of NIH, increasing the number of minority doctoral-level biomedical researchers is an appropriate benchmark for program success, although it must be acknowledged that, in reality, only a subset of trainees will achieve this, as is true for nonminority trainees. In other words, some measure of trainee loss from the programs (and therefore the STEM pipeline) should be expected and tolerated, as it is for nontargeted programs. The committee, therefore, asks, "Should those trainees who do not go on to earn a doctoral-level degree be viewed as program failures?" The committee does not support this view on the grounds that when minority trainees leave a training program to become lab managers or employees in the biotech or pharmaceutical industries, they are persisting in science and are visible as such. This is value added.

It is not realistic to expect that every minority program trainee who participates in the NIH targeted programs will successfully complete doctoral-level research training. If that were the case, it would suggest that the program was merely harvesting talent rather than growing talent. Harvesting talent in this context means supporting trainees who probably would have, for a variety of reasons, "made it" regardless of support from targeted programs. Growing talent, on the other hand, refers to the promotion of science

[56] Office of Research on Minority Health, National Institutes of Health. 1993. Assessment of NIH Minority Research/Training Programs: Phase 1. Bethesda, Md.: U.S. Department of Health and Human Services

[57] Office of Research on Minority Health, National Institutes of Health. 1997. Assessment of NIH Minority Research/Training Programs: Phase 2. Bethesda, Md.: U.S. Department of Health and Human Services.

and science careers to individuals and communities that may not otherwise have entered science. Growing nascent talent implies that some program participants will indeed say, "No, thank you" to science, but still others will become turned on to science for the first time. The latter group is an important target audience for these programs. An excellent training program will, therefore, harvest and grow talent to appreciable degrees.

The committee goes so far as to recommend that one as-yet-untapped sector for growing nascent talent is the pool of high achieving non-science majors. Many bright undergraduates major in nonscientific fields not because they do not enjoy or excel at science but because they appreciate that college may be the only time in their life when they are free to explore a discipline without regard for its vocational implications. Thus, a music or philosophy major who successfully masters core science courses, such as calculus, chemistry, and physics, may make an excellent graduate student in the biomedical sciences, by virtue of his or her broad-based education. Such students have the potential to infuse science with uncommon creativity and synthesis.[58] Furthermore, because biomedical research training has clear and direct vocational applications, such students may be highly motivated to persist in biomedical research through a full career.

Minority Training Programs: What Works and What Doesn't?

The committee concludes that underrepresented minorities are entering the biomedical workforce as a direct result of the NIH minority research training programs. Further, among trainees at all career stages, there is profound appreciation for what these programs offer and recognition of the prestige associated with being an NIH research trainee. The number-one "best feature" cited by trainee respondents across all career stages is the research experience itself. For undergraduate trainees, the acquisition of laboratory skills was a key factor. For graduate trainees, laboratory experience was important but so were graduate-level coursework, research seminars and workshops, learning how to think critically, learning to make cogent research presentations, and learning to teach science to undergraduates. Among postdoctoral and junior faculty

---

[58] Medical Schools across the nation have dealt effectively with this issue. Numerous studies demonstrate that an undergraduate major in the sciences is not required for medical students to excel in medical school science courses. See: M.L. Hall and M.T. Stocks. 1995. Relationship between quantity of undergraduate science preparation and preclinical performance in medical school. Academic Medicine 70(3):230-235; Dickman, R. L., and R. E. Sarnacki, F. T. Schimpfhauser, and L. A. Katz. 1980. Medical students from natural science and nonscience undergraduate backgrounds. JAMA: The Journal of the American Medical Association 243(24):2506-2509; Bruer, J. T., and K. S. Warren. 1981. Liberal arts and the premedical curriculum. JAMA: The Journal of the American Medical Association 245(4):364-366; Smith, S. R. 1998. Effect of undergraduate college major on performance in medical school. Academic Medicine 73(9): 1006-1008; Doblin, B., and S. Korenman. 1992. The role of national science in the premedical curriculum. Academic Medicine 67(8):539-541; Brieger, G. H. 1999. The plight of premedical education: Myths and misperceptions—Part I: The 'premedical syndrome'. Academic Medicine 74(8): 901-904; Brieger, G. H. 1999. The plight of premedical education: Myths and misperceptions—Part II: Science 'versus' the liberal arts. Academic Medicine 74(11):1217-1221.

trainees, the opportunity to choose a subspecialty and develop research independence was the most valuable aspect of the training programs.

Among undergraduate trainees, mentoring support was cited as the second most valuable feature of the training programs. Mentoring was most often provided in four key areas: (1) improving the trainee's research skills, (2) providing motivation and personal growth, (3) providing career guidance, and (4) promoting the trainee for scholarships and other development opportunities. Mentoring was also very important to graduate, postdoctoral, and junior faculty trainees, who reported many positive interactions and support from their mentors. Given the importance placed on mentoring by trainees across all career stage levels, NIH may wish to consider conducting a more in-depth best-practices examination of successful mentoring practices and associated behaviors. For that matter, NIH may also wish to examine best practices with regard to marketing a research career to prospective trainees. How do the best programs "close the sale"?

Financial support from the training programs was greatly appreciated by undergraduate trainees. Such support came in the form of stipends, summer research, and conference travel support. Funding was, for graduate trainees, frequently cited as a best feature. At the graduate level, a funding arrangement exists whereby NIH covers the cost of research training, including stipend and tuition support, research supplies, and benefits. In return, NIH requires that trainees refrain from taking outside jobs in order to devote 100 percent effort to the training experience. For postdoctoral and junior faculty trainees, funding was characterized as "critical and necessary." The "protected time" that funding provided trainees at this level allowed them to achieve research independence, which is the foremost goal of these programs.

Other positive program elements that trainees mentioned include the foundation of scientific knowledge that the program provided to undergraduate trainees; the opportunities to network and collaborate with other scientists was mentioned by trainees at all levels, especially graduate trainees. Undergraduate trainees underscored the ability of the programs to help them decide whether to attend graduate school or medical school. Graduate and postdoctoral trainees frequently cited the tremendous value of learning how to prepare a competitive grant proposal. Among junior faculty trainees, the K01 award, they said, allowed them to progress to the next step in their careers, namely to obtain an R01 research grant.

Administrators of these programs mentioned that there are many more applicants to undergraduate programs than there are available positions. Thus, recruitment appears to be highly effective and attrition from undergraduate programs is minimal. This is due in part to an effective system of oversight and monitoring of undergraduate trainees' progress. At the post-Ph.D. level, there appears to be a sharp drop-off among minority trainees. An indicator of this is the gender shift from predominantly female at the undergraduate and graduate career stages to predominantly male at the postdoctoral and junior faculty career stages (see Appendix E). Where do the minority female trainees go? This question warrants further study by NIH.

Across the board, trainees, while extremely grateful for the funding support afforded by the training programs, uniformly stated that the levels of funding support are not sufficient and need to be increased. Undergraduates who are greatly challenged by the addition of a demanding research program to a full load of coursework must often take on additional outside work, in order to make ends meet. Program administrators call this situation a "recipe for disaster," and it constitutes a barrier against participation in these programs for lower-income minority students. Graduate trainees have similar complaints. They are contractually prohibited from obtaining outside jobs, yet the stipend support is barely above the poverty line. In the context of the uneven health benefits afforded by these programs, this too seems like a "catch-22." Postdoctoral and junior faculty trainees are similarly disheartened by the low stipends afforded by the training programs. This is especially true when trainees have dependents and/or live in major metropolitan areas where the cost of living vastly exceeds what the stipend offers. All trainee respondents were clear and forceful in stating that trainee stipends have to be more in line with market trends; they need to be increased in order to sustain and build student interest in research careers. This sentiment was echoed by numerous program administrators, one of whom stated that the stiffest competition faced in attracting African-American trainees to a research career comes from the salary opportunities provided by advanced health professional programs.

Mentoring, although highly cited as a positive element of the training programs, was criticized as needing significant improvement. Too many trainees reported negative mentoring experiences in the lab. Some minority undergraduate trainees were given mundane administrative tasks to perform in lieu of experiments; others experienced "benign neglect" by their mentors or, at best, a lack of encouragement. Half of the T32 minority postdoctoral fellows reported having no mentor at all, and a trend that was not replicated by nonminority T32 postdoctoral trainees. This is a red flag to which NIH should pay attention especially in the context of the already low numbers of minority trainees at this relatively advanced career stage.

Training in the biomedical sciences historically assumes that if one is trained, one will therefore be a good trainer (mentor). This conclusion does not follow. Mentoring is a skill for which academic researchers rarely receive any formalized training. The old adage, "Do as I did" does not translate well in the context of today's diverse student populations. Such selective mentoring may indeed explain, at least in part, the homogeneity seen among this study's trainee respondents post-Ph.D. Those who are just like their mentor are promoted. Those who are different from their mentor are not. Program administrators emphasized that in addition to the lack of mentor training, mentors receive little credit or encouragement for the time taken to mentor trainees. Grants do not provide funds that cover mentoring activities and time. Academic departments do not view mentoring as a major activity that legitimately counts toward tenure. Yet mentoring is absolutely essential to the continued growth and sustenance of our biomedical workforce. NIH may want to take a look at this issue and consider changing the value it places on this essential activity in some concrete way.

Minority respondents to our survey provided additional clues that may bear upon their low numbers at higher career stages. Based on the survey data, which the committee believes are biased toward the most successful NIH trainees, minorities publish fewer papers than do nonminority trainees. They have greater difficulty securing post-Ph.D. employment. They report less social integration in their laboratories, and this was the case more so for minority trainees at institutions using nonminority training mechanisms. Finally, a large fraction of minority trainees believe that their minority status in some way affected their training experience. Given that one-half of the minority postdoctoral survey respondents reported having no mentor at all, one wonders what factors are at play in these training environments that affect minority trainee outcomes so profoundly.

In its efforts to train a new generation of minority research scientists, NIH is by definition effecting change, however small, in minority communities. The committee believes that increasing a community's interest in science requires more than a single generation. Achieving buy-in to the scientific enterprise requires not only that trainees become turned on to science, but also that families and community pillars demonstrate overt support for young persons' interests in science. The goal of producing more minority doctoral-level researchers may at first seem straightforward, but it is not. No single trainee outcome suffices for measuring program success. Interim outcome measures are germane and informative and should be taken into account when assessing the impact of these programs. The degree to which minority children can realistically envision themselves as future scientists, leaders of science, and biotech entrepreneurs is a reflection of how successful the intervention of bringing science to minority communities truly is.

Recommendations

The committee recommends that NIH articulate a clear and measurable training philosophy and implement change in data collection to better support rigorous evaluation and accountability efforts beyond the doctorate. In the meantime, the committee also strongly recommends that NIH commit to the continued funding of minority-targeted research training programs and implement measures to better coordinate them across the 27 institutes and centers. Finally, the committee recommends that NIH fund an independent follow-up to this assessment within five years. The committee's detailed recommendations follow.

By the end of 2005, the NIH director should articulate a set of clear and measurable training goals and objectives specific to minority training. The director should take into account the mission of NIH and the integral role of research training in attaining both societal goals (e.g., health and well-being, the ability to support oneself and one's family, community development) and research goals. Such a policy should be responsive to society's workforce needs in their broadest sense, with an understanding that contributions to society derive from all parts of the career stage pipeline.

NIH should commit to the continued funding of minority-targeted research training programs. Although the committee cannot substantiate this recommendation in quantitative terms for reasons described throughout this report, it does so in qualitative terms, using survey data that were collected from trainees and program administrators who are the programs' primary informants. The following reasons underlie this recommendation:

- These programs have added many minorities to our science workforce.
- The elimination of these programs would likely diminish the number of new minority scientists entering the scientific workforce.
- The trainees interviewed indicate overwhelmingly that these programs benefited them. These programs provided research experiences, financial support, and mentoring that were critical to their career success.
- Mentoring is a critical part of the career development of all scientists and is particularly important for minority trainees. Trainee survey data suggest that the diversity of mentors is greater in the minority-targeted programs than in the nontargeted programs. Atkinson et al,[59] found that when rating mentoring relationships, both mentors and mentees rated their relationships more positively when they were matched for race or ethnicity.

The committee recognizes two distinct and valid approaches to the development of minority research trainees. The training policy of the NIH institutes and centers in conducting these programs should emphasize the development of trainees who have already demonstrated promise in the sciences, so that they can overcome the barriers to becoming productive investigators. Two examples of minority training programs that emphasize talent harvesting include the National Institute of Mental Health Career Opportunities in Research Training and Education (COR) and the Minority Access to Research Careers (MARC) Undergraduate Student Training in Academic Research (U*STAR) programs. The NIH training policy should also emphasize the development of other trainees—those without demonstrated science promise—in order to add to the pipeline of trainees interested in pursuing science careers. An example of a minority training program that emphasizes growing talent is the Bridges to the Baccalaureate program.

The implementation of this training policy should also consider the following. NIH should more vigorously monitor the use of racial or ethnic eligibility criteria for these programs. Survey data from trainees and program administrators indicate that non-underrepresented minorities are participating in minority-targeted training programs.

[59] D. Atkinson, H. Neville, and A. Casas. 1991. The mentorship of ethnic minorities in professional psychology. Professional Psychology Research and Practice 22(4):336-338.

NIH should also examine gender differences among its trainee participants. For example, the minority trainee population at the undergraduate level is mostly female, but their proportion, in relationship to male trainees, declines at each successive career stage, suggesting the possibility of substantial attrition among women who could have continued on as investigators. This trend is particularly striking at the graduate-to-postdoctoral transition where men, conversely, outnumber women. This trend among women is independent of race.

Finally, given comments offered by both trainees and programs administrators on this issue, the committee recommends that NIH conduct a review to ensure that the research infrastructure (i.e., lab space, lab equipment, active faculty research programs) available to minority trainees at the institution level is adequate and, if not, seek ways to further address this programmatically.

The director of each institute should designate a single individual as minority research training programs coordinator for that institute by the third quarter of FY 2005. Some institutes have a centralized training coordinator; others do not. This recommendation would provide consistency and make coordinated efforts more feasible.

The NIH training director should convene a meeting of all minority training coordinators on at least a quarterly basis, beginning with the third quarter of 2005. The goal of these meetings is to coordinate the administration of NIH minority training programs and the collection of relevant program data. Currently, the programs and the accountability for them are so fragmented that external evaluation is not possible. Given the importance of the NIH training programs to the continuation of U.S. leadership in biomedical research, coordinated efforts to develop, manage, and rigorously evaluate research training programs are needed. The collective management of minority training programs, although not intended to supplant IC independence and expertise, requires ongoing communication and cooperation across disciplinary and institutional lines. It is expected that agendas for these meetings will change over time as the collaboration improves communication and advances meaningful planning. The meetings should at a minimum address the following issues:

- Clarification of NIH training policies regarding trainee recruitment and documentation of program activities and results;
- Discussion of the range of IC training program characteristics;
- Sharing of trainee recruitment strategies;
- Identification of effective elements of IC training programs;
- Review of IC evaluation results; and
- Development of long term objectives for addressing workforce needs and increasing the participation of underrepresented minorities in science.

The committee of minority training program coordinators should establish appropriate guidelines and measures for evaluating NIH minority research training programs. Training program administrators should participate in an ongoing and rigorous evaluation process. By defining program outcomes and monitoring their achievement, the ICs can better manage their programs. NIH should commit to making available all of the data needed to conduct internal or external evaluation of its training programs.

Further study of the relative effectiveness of minority-targeted versus nontargeted programs should be carried out by NIH institutes and centers under coordination from the Office of the Director. The reasons for this recommendation include the following:

- The ICs should establish outcome measures for each training mechanism in a coordinated fashion. To do this, the ICs should identify and document the range of trainee outcomes that result from participation in these programs. Then, the range of outcomes should be codified as either contributing or not contributing to the consensus definition of program success. The committee is cognizant that this recommendation reflects an interactive process.
- Continued integrated study of these programs can identify the best features of the programs and best practices among the recipient colleges and universities.

The director of NIH training should administer the funds for evaluation, data collection, and marketing by FY 2006. The centralized training activities should include a centralized and robust evaluation and planning activity. This approach will empower the director of NIH training to be able to coordinate accountability mandates (i.e., the U.S. Office of Management and Budget's Program Assessment Rating Tool and the Government Performance and Results Act) with organizational policies and procedures.

The general issues reviewed in this report should be revisited periodically at the NIH level with the next report submitted by 2009. The Office of the Director at NIH should take the lead on this. The numerous, weighty, and very public issues regarding affirmative action that are raised by targeted research training programs require continuing attention by a consortium of the National Center for Minority Health and Health Disparities, the Office of Extramural Programs, the institutes and centers that fund such training programs, and the NIH Office of the Director. NIH should conduct an independent public review and accounting that will help ensure that the programs remain focused and effective. Doing so will inform the affected groups and general public of the programs' success and ensure that funding is being used effectively, thus yielding a positive return on the nation's investment. The committee believes that five years is a good interval for external review of the program(s), although experience may show that more frequent review would be useful. The committee further believes that the breadth and depth of the issues, compounded by the present fragmentation of many components of NIH, require that the Office of the NIH Director take the lead on this.

NIH should develop a relational database that collects a minimum data set (MDS) for all persons who receive funding as trainees, fellows, research assistants, or postdoctorates, including those programs targeted to underrepresented minorities.

- The database should be maintained by the Office of the Director of Extramural Programs, headed by the deputy director and NIH research and training officer. The Office of the Director of Extramural Programs should have the overall responsibility for coordination of the database and its constituent parts.
- The MDS should be a service to all institutes and contain variables that enable rigorous evaluation and assessment of training programs; institutes may add variables at their discretion.
- The MDS should collect data for all trainees, including all those funded through the training mechanisms covered here, as well as for research assistants funded through R and K awards.
- The Office of the Director of Extramural Training, in coordination with institute representatives, should develop a data entry system accessible from multiple sources, including external data entry points, such as grant-specific progress reports. In addition, the Office of the Director of Extramural Training should develop a user-friendly data entry form for the MDS that is web-accessible. The database and data coordination in the deputy director's office will emulate that of a coordinated data center. Considerations of personal privacy and confidentiality must be high on the list of necessary attributes.
- The Office of the Deputy Director of Extramural Training should identify data elements that help in tracking persons who received training funds—both directly and indirectly. These tracking data should be obtained at the time of initial NIH funding and should be updated periodically.
- Development of the MDS, database, and data entry system should begin immediately and be completed no later that FY 2008.

Bibliography

Atkinson, D., H. Neville, and A. Casas. 1991. The mentorship of ethnic minorities in professional psychology. Professional Psychology Research and Practice 22(4):336-338.

Bowen, W. G., and D. C. Bok. 1998. The Shape of the River: Long-Term Consequences of Considering Race in College and University Admissions. Princeton, N.J.: Princeton University Press, p. 10.

Brieger, G. H. 1999. The plight of premedical education: Myths and misperceptions—Part I: The 'premedical syndrome.' Academic Medicine 74(8):901-904.

Brieger, G. H. 1999. The plight of premedical education: Myths and misperceptions—Part II: Science 'versus' the liberal arts. Academic Medicine 74(11):1217-1221.

Bruer, J. T., and K. S. Warren. 1981. Liberal arts and the premedical curriculum. The Journal of the American Medical Association 245(4):364-366.

Building Engineering and Science Talent (BEST). 2004. A Bridge for All: Higher Education Design Principles to Broaden Participation in Science, Technology, Engineering and Mathematics. San Diego, Calif.: BEST.

Coggeshall, P. E., and P. W. Brown. 1984. The Career Achievements of NIH Predoctoral Trainees and Fellows. Washington, D.C.: National Academy Press.

Congressional Commission on the Advancement of Women and Minorities in Science, Engineering and Technology Development. 2000. Land of Plenty: Diversity as America's Competitive Edge in Science, Engineering and Technology. Arlington, Va.: National Science Foundation.

Dickman, R. L., R. E. Sarnacki, F. T. Schimpfhauser, and L. A. Katz. 1980. Medical students from natural science and nonscience undergraduate backgrounds. The Journal of the American Medical Association 243(24, June 27):2506-2509.

Doblin, B., and S. Korenman. 1992. The role of national science in the premedical curriculum. Academic Medicine 67(8, August):539-541.

Fechter, A., and Michael S. Teitelbaum. Spring 1997. A fresh approach to immigration. Issues in Science and Technology 13(3):28-32.

Hall, M. L., and M. T. Stocks. 1995. Relationship between quantity of undergraduate science preparation and preclinical performance in medical school. Academic Medicine 70(3, March):230-235.

Jackson, S. A. September 2004. The perfect storm: A weather forecast. Speech given at American Association for the Advancement of Science Annual Meeting in Seattle, Wash.

Mervis, J. 2003. Down for the count. Science 300(5622):1070.

National Advisory Mental Health Council Working Group on Racial/Ethnic Diversity in Research Training and Health Disparities Research, National Institutes of Health. 2001. Investing in America's Future: Racial/Ethnic Diversity in Mental Health Research Careers. Washington, D.C.: U.S. Department of Health and Human Services.

National Institute of General Medical Sciences, National Institutes of Health. 1992. Initiative for Minority Students: Bridges to the Baccalaureate (Program announcement, PAR-02-084). Bethesda, Md.: U.S. Department of Health and Human Services. See http://www.nigms.nih.gov/news/reports/marcstudy.html.

National Institute of General Medical Sciences, National Institutes of Health. 1995. A Study of the Minority Access to Research Careers Honors Undergraduate Research Training Program. Bethesda, Md.: U.S. Department of Health and Human Services.

National Institute of General Medical Sciences (NIGMS), National Institutes of Health. 1998. The Careers and Professional Activities of Former NIGMS Medical Scientist Training Program. Bethesda, Md.: U.S. Department of Health and Human Services.

National Institute of General Medical Sciences, National Institutes of Health. 2000. The Careers and Professional Activities of Former NIGMS Minority Access to Research Careers Predoctoral Fellows. Bethesda, Md.: U.S. Department of Health and Human Services. See http://www.nigms.nih.gov/news/reports/marcstudy.html.

National Institute of General Medical Sciences and Office of Research on Minority Health, National Institutes of Health. Undated. Planning and Priorities of the Bridges to the Future Program. Bethesda, MD.: U.S. Department of Health and Human Services. See http://nigms.nih.gov/news/reports/bridges.html.

National Institute of Mental Health (NIMH), National Institutes of Health. Undated. NIMH Training Programs for Underrepresented Racial/Ethnic Minorities (NIMH interim staff report). Bethesda, MD.: U.S. Department of Health and Human Services.

National Opinion Research Center. 2005. Doctorate Recipients from United States Universities: Summary Report 2003. Chicago, Ill.: NORC.

National Research Council. 2000. Addressing the Nation's Changing Needs for Biomedical and Behavioral Scientists. Washington, D.C.: National Academy Press.

National Research Council. 1981. Postdoctoral Appointments and Disappointments. Washington, D.C.: National Academy Press.

National Research Council. 1999. Selecting Instructional Materials: A Guide for K-12 Science. Washington, D.C.: National Academy Press.

National Science and Technology Council. 2000. Ensuring a Strong U.S. Scientific, Technical, and Engineering Workforce in the 21st Century. Washington, D.C.: Executive Office of the President of the United States, p. 4.

National Science Board. 2003. The Science and Engineering Workforce: Realizing America's Potential. Arlington, Va.: National Science Foundation.

National Science Foundation, Division of Science Resources Statistics. 2002. Doctoral Scientists and Engineers: 1999 Profile (NSF 03-302). Arlington, Va.: National Science Foundation.

Office of Research on Minority Health, National Institutes of Health. 1993. Assessment of NIH Minority Research/Training Programs: Phase 1. Bethesda, Md.: U.S. Department of Health and Human Services.

Office of Research on Minority Health, National Institutes of Health. 1997. Assessment of NIH Minority Research/Training Programs: Phase 2. Bethesda, MD: U.S. Department of Health and Human Services.

Pearson, W., and A. Fechter, eds. 1994. Who will do Science? Educating the Next Generation. Baltimore, Md.: The Johns Hopkins University Press.

Prewitt, K. 2002. Higher education and the diversity agenda. Speech given at the Annual Meeting of the Council of Graduate Schools in San Diego, Calif., in December 2002.

Pion, G. M. 2001. The Early Career Progress of NRSA Predoctoral Trainees and Fellows. Bethesda, Md: National Institutes of Health.

Smith, S. R. 1998. Effect of undergraduate college major on performance in medical school. Academic Medicine 73(9):1006-1008.

Appendix A

Committee Biographical Sketches

John Christian Bailar III, Committee Co-chair, is Professor Emeritus at the University of Chicago. Over the course of his career, he has held positions at the National Cancer Institute of the National Institutes of Health, Department of Health and Human Services; McGill University; Harvard University; and the University of Chicago. Dr. Bailar is a member of the National Academy of Sciences' Institute of Medicine and has served on numerous National Academies committees, including the National Cancer Policy Board, the Commission on Life Sciences, and the Report Review Committee. His research interests have included the causes and prevention of cancer, the health effects of air pollution, and the general methods of research study in epidemiology. Dr. Bailar earned his B.A. in chemistry from the University of Colorado, his M.D. from Yale University, and his Ph.D. in statistics from American University. He brings to this project his general understanding of medical research and the statistical expertise needed to analyze large and complex data sets.

Willie Pearson, Jr., Committee Co-chair, is Professor and Chair of the School of History, Technology, and Society at the Georgia Institute of Technology. Previously, he was professor of sociology at Wake Forest. Most of Dr. Pearson's research has centered on the career patterns of Ph.D. scientists (especially minority scientists) and human resource issues in science and engineering. He is author and co-author of six books and monographs, including *Black Scientists, White Society and Colorless Science: A Study of Universalism in American Science* (Associated Faculty Press, 1985), *Blacks, Education and American Science* (Rutgers University Press, 1989), *Who Will Do Science?: Educating the Next Generation* (John Hopkins University Press, 1994), and *Diversity in Science and Technology Centers* (Association of Science-Technology Centers, Inc., 1996). He earned his Ph.D. in sociology from Southern Illinois University at Carbondale in 1981. Dr. Pearson brings to this committee his expertise in program evaluation and qualitative research.

David Gordon is Associate Dean for Diversity and Career Development, Professor of Pathology, and general cardiovascular pathology consultant with the Pathology Department at the University of Michigan School of Medicine. Previously, he was an associate professor at the University of Washington-Seattle, a research fellow at Parke-Davis Pharmaceutical Company (later Pfizer), a professor of pathology and Assistant Dean for Faculty Affairs at the University of Michigan, and preclinical researcher on gene therapy and therapeutic angiogenesis at Pfizer, before returning to the University of Michigan. He earned his B.A. in chemistry from Amherst College and his M.D. from Harvard Medical School. Dr. Gordon brings to this committee a first-person perspective on minority clinical research training and extensive experience in mentoring minority research scholars from high school through the faculty levels.

Marigold Linton divides her time between the roles of Director of Math and Science Initiatives for the University of Texas System and Director of American Indian Outreach at the University of Kansas. In the latter role, she works closely with Haskell Indian Nations University and has developed programs to facilitate the pursuit of research careers by Native American college students. Dr. Linton worked closely with Arizona Tribes on educational and evaluation issues during her tenure at Arizona State University. Previously, she was a professor of psychology at University of Utah and, prior to that, she was a professor of psychology at San Diego State University. Dr. Linton currently serves on the Board of Directors of the Society for the Advancement of Chicanos and Native Americans in Science (SACNAS). She previously served as a member of the NRC Committee on Education and Employment of Minority Group Members in Science. She has served on the Board of Directors for the Carnegie Foundation for the Advancement of Teaching and the National Advisory Resources Council of the National Institutes of General Medical Science at the National Institutes of Health. She earned her B.A. in psychology from the University of California, Riverside, and her Ph.D. in experimental psychology from the University of California, Los Angeles. Dr. Linton brings to this committee her extensive experience in program evaluation.

Craig Love is a Senior Project Leader at Westat, Inc., in Rockville, MD. He oversees a $10-million portfolio of health intervention and program evaluation projects. Previously, he was a research associate at the Center for Alcohol and Addiction Studies at Brown University, where he conducted research on substance abuse treatment and prevention for criminal justice and Native American populations, and developed a Native American studies program. Dr. Love was also a lecturer in psychiatry at Harvard University. He was President of Clove, Inc., a program planning and evaluation business, specializing in substance abuse and mental health treatment and prevention. Earlier in his career, he was also Director of Evaluation and Research at Spectrum Addiction Services, Inc., where he specialized in program evaluation. Dr. Love earned his B.S. and M.S. in psychology from the University of Kentucky and his Ph.D. in educational psychology from Temple University. He brings to this committee his extensive experience in program evaluation, measurement, diversity in education, statistical analyses, and qualitative research methodologies, including interviewing minority subjects.

Barbara Lovitts is a senior program officer in the Center for the Advancement of Scholarship on Engineering Education at the National Academy of Engineering. Previously, she was a senior research analyst at the American Institutes for Research, investigating national and international education policy issues; Deputy Project Director for the National Science Foundation's Evaluation of the Graduate Teaching Fellows in K-12 Education program; a program officer in the Education Directorate at the National Science Foundation; and a program associate in the Education Directorate at the American Association for the Advancement of Science. She is a member of the American Sociological Association. She earned a B.A. in behavioral sciences from the University of Chicago, an M.S. in experimental psychology from the University of Wisconsin, and a Ph.D. in sociology from the University of Maryland. She is the author of *Leaving the Ivory Tower: The Causes and Consequence of Departure from Doctoral Study* and a forthcoming book, *Making the Implicit Explicit: Creating Performance Expectations and Assessing the Outcomes of Doctoral Education.* Dr. Lovitts brings to this committee his expertise in graduate education and qualitative research methodologies, including survey research and program evaluation.

Catherine Miller is a senior associate at Hampshire Research Institute in Hamden, Connecticut, where she serves as chief data and policy analyst, and senior programmer on North American, U.S. federal, and state toxics release data and information systems. Previously Dr. Miller was a research associate at INFORM (New York City), working on hazardous/toxic waste issues; a senior associate with Meta Systems Inc. (Cambridge, MA), working on U.S. Environmental Protection Agency (E.P.A.) projects; a consultant with the Rockefeller Brothers Fund (New York City) and with the U.S.E.P.A. (Washington, D.C.); a teaching assistant at the Kennedy School of Government, Harvard University; an intern with the Congressional Budget Office (Washington, D.C.); a program and operations research analyst with the U.S.E.P.A.; and a senior technical aide with Bell Telephone Laboratories (Murray Hill, NJ). She earned her B.A. in mathematics from Smith College in 1968; her M.S. in applied mathematics from the Massachusetts Institute of Technology in 1971; and her M.P.P. and Ph.D. in public policy from Harvard University's Kennedy School of Government in 1977 and 1980, respectively. Dr. Miller brought to the committee her expertise in public policy but health reasons forced her to withdraw from the committee in September 2002.

Javier Rojo is Professor of Statistics at Rice University. Previously, he was Professor of Mathematics at the University of Texas, El Paso. His statistical expertise includes point estimation, tail orderings of probability distributions, nonparametrics and survival analysis under order constraints, including censored data. Dr. Rojo was the Program Director for Probability and Statistics at the National Science Foundation and is an elected Fellow of the Royal Statistical Society, the American Statistical Association, and the Institute of Mathematical Statistics. Dr. Rojo is committed to the education of minority scientists; he has trained and mentored over 50 minority undergraduates, graduates, and junior faculty. He earned his B.S. in mathematics is from University of Texas, El Paso; his M.S. in statistics from Stanford University; and his Ph.D. in statistics from University of California, Berkeley. Dr. Rojo brings to this committee his statistical expertise needed to carry out the analysis portion of the study.

Terrence R. Russell is Executive Director at the Association for Institutional Research, an international association devoted to management research, policy analysis, and planning in higher education. He teaches a graduate seminar on institutional research, program assessment, and policy research at Florida State University. Dr. Russell has held research and management positions at the Office of Professional Services at the American Chemical Society, addressing the ethical, professional and career concerns of chemists and other scientists and engineers. He earned his B.A. in psychology, M.S. in community organizing/evaluation research, and Ph.D. in the sociology of science/social theory from Southern Illinois University. Dr. Russell brings to this committee his critical expertise in program evaluation.

Charles E. Vela is President and Chief Scientist of Expertech Solutions, where he leads the R&D program and advises the IRS in the planning, acquisition, and deployment of large-scale and strategic information technology. Previously, he was a Senior Science Advisor for the Illinois Institute of Technology Research Institute; Lead Engineer at the MITRE Corporation; Executive Director of the Center for the Advancement of Hispanics in Science and Engineering (CAHSEE); an assistant study director of a project on the utilization of technologies in mapping the brain at the Institute of Medicine of the National Academy of Sciences; and professor and research fellow in electrical engineering at the National Autonomous University of Mexico. Dr. Vela holds advanced degrees in electrical engineering and operations research from the California State University and the National Autonomous University of Mexico, respectively. He brings to this committee his expertise in tracking-system development.

Appendix B

2001 Census of NIH Extramural Minority Research Training Programs

Please see acronym definitions at the end of the table.

Institute	Funding Mechanism	Type	Initial Year	Program Name
NCI	F31	Individual	1995	NRSA Predoctoral Fellowship Award for Minority Students
NCI	K01	Institutional	1997	Mentored Career Development Award
NCI	K08	Individual	1996	Minorities in Clinical Oncology
NCI	K22	Individual	2000	NCI Transitional Career Development Award
NCI	K23	Individual	2000	Mentored Patient Oriented Research
NCI	T32	Institutional	1999	CURE
NHLBI	n.a.	Institutional	n.a.	MARC Summer Research Training Program
NHLBI	F31	Individual	1992	NRSA Predoctoral Fellowship Award for Minority Students
NHLBI	K01	Institutional	1984	Minority Institution Research Scientist Development Award
NHLBI	K01	Individual	1994	Mentored Career Development Award (Junior Research Investigator Enhancement Award)
NHLBI	T32	Institutional	1984	NRSA Minority Institutional Research Training Program
NHLBI	T35M	Institutional	n.a.	Short-Term Institutional Research Training Grants
NIAID	n.a.	Institutional	n.a.	Research Centers Minority Institutions
NIAID	F31	Individual	1993	NRSA Predoctoral Fellowship Award for Minority Students
NIAID	T32	Institutional	n.a.	Minority Institutional Research Training Program
NIAID	T35	Institutional	n.a.	Short-Term Institutional Research Training Grants
NIDDK	T32	Institutional	n.a.	Research Training of Underrepresented Minorities on Institutional training Grants
NIDDK	T34	Institutional	n.a.	MARC
NIDDK	T36	Institutional	n.a.	MARC
NIDDK	R03	Individual	n.a.	Small Research Grants for Minority Researchers

NIDDK	n.a.	Institutional	n.a.	MBRS
NINDS	F31	Individual	n.a.	NRSA Predoctoral Fellowship Award for Minority Students
NINDS	K01	Individual	1997	Ernest Everett Just Faculty Career Development Award
NINDS	S11	Individual	1996	CNS, Individuals, NIDCD, NIDA
NIMH	R24	Institutional	1995	M-RISP
NIMH	T32	Institutional	1978	Original name: Minority Fellowship Program; re-named in 2001: Institutional Research Training Programs: Increasing Diversity
NIMH	T34	Institutional	1979	COR Honors Undergraduate Research Training Grant
NIMH	F31	Individual	1995	NRSA Predoctoral Fellowship Award for Minority Students
NIMH	K01	Individual	1996	Scientist Development Award for New Minority Faculty
NIMH	R03	Individual	1994	Minority Dissertation Research Grants
NICHD	F31	Individual	n.a.	NRSA Predoctoral Fellowship Award for Minority Students
NIA	F31	Individual	1991	NRSA Predoctoral Fellowship Award for Minority Students
NIA	R03	Individual	1991	Minority Dissertation Research Grants
NIA	P30	Institutional	1997	RCMAR collaboration with NINR
NIGMS	F31	Individual	1991	NRSA Predoctoral Fellowship Award for Minority Students
NIGMS	F31	Individual	1981	MARC Predoctoral Fellowships
NIGMS	F33	Individual		MARC Faculty Senior Fellowships
NIGMS	F34	Individual	1994	MARC Faculty Predoctoral Fellowships (previous name F34 Faculty Fellowships, 1972-1993)
NIGMS	F36	Individual	1978-82 1984-87 1990 1993-95	MARC Visiting Scientist Fellowships
NIGMS	K01	Individual	1997	MORE Faculty Development Awards
NIGMS	K12	Institutional	1999	IRACDA
NIGMS	R25 Bridges	Institutional	1992	NIGMS Special Initiative: Bridges to the Baccalaureate Degree
NIGMS	R25 Bridges	Institutional	1992	NIGMS Special Initiative: Bridges to the Doctoral Degree
NIGMS	R25 IMSD	Institutional	1997	MBRS IMSD
NIGMS	R25 PREP	Institutional	n.a.	MARC PREP
NIGMS	R25 RISE	Institutional	1998	MBRS RISE
NIGMS	S06	Individual	1998	MBRS SCORE
NIGMS	T34 U*Star	Institutional	1996	MARC U*STAR

NIGMS	T36	Institutional	1982	MARC Visiting Professors for Minority Institution Awards
NIGMS	T36 MARC	Institutional	1982	MARC Ancillary Training Activities
NIDDK	n.a.	Individual	n.a.	Initiatives for Underrepresented Minorities in Biomedical Research
NIDDK	F31	Individual	n.a.	NRSA Predoctoral Fellowship Award for Minority Students
NIDDK	F32	Individual	n.a.	NRSA Postdoctoral Fellowship Award for Minority Students
NIDDK	K23	Individual	2000	Mentored Patient Oriented Career Award
NIDDK	K24	Individual	2000	Mid-Career Investigator Award in Patient-Oriented Research
NIDDK	R03	Individual	n.a.	Small Grants for Underrepresented Minorities
NIDA	F31	Individual	n.a.	NRSA Predoctoral Fellowship Award for Minority Students
NIDA	F31	Individual	n.a.	NRSA Predoctoral Fellowship Award for Minority Students
NIDA	R24	Institutional	1996	MIDARP
NIDA	S11	Individual	1996	CNS collaboration with NIDCD
NIDA	T35M	Institutional	n.a.	Short-Term Institutional Research Training Grants
NEI	F31	Individual	n.a.	NRSA Predoctoral Fellowship Award for Minority Students
NIEHS	F31	Individual	1995	NRSA Predoctoral Fellowship Award for Minority Students
NIEHS	T35M	Institutional	1994	Short-Term Institutional Research Training Grants
NIAMS	F31	Individual	n.a.	NRSA Predoctoral Fellowship Award for Minority Students
NIAMS	R01	Individual	1999	CAMSSA
NIAAA	F31	Individual	1992	NRSA Predoctoral Fellowship Award for Minority Students
NIAAA	T35M	Institutional	n.a.	Short-Term Institutional Research Training Grants
NIAAA	U24	Institutional	1997	CMIARD
NIDCR	F31	Individual	n.a.	NRSA Predoctoral Fellowship Award for Minority Students
NIDCR	T35M	Institutional	1994	Short-Term Institutional Research Training Grants
NIDCD	n.a.	Institutional	n.a.	NIDCD Partnership Program
NIDCD	F31	Individua	n.a.	NRSA Predoctoral Fellowship Award for Minority Students
NIDCD	K01	Individual	1997	Research Scientist Development Award
NIDCD	R03	Individual	1996	Minority Dissertation Research Grants

NIDCD	S11	Individual	1996	CNS collaboration with NIDA
NINR	F31	Individual	n.a.	NRSA Predoctoral Fellowship Award for Minority Students
NINR	K01	Individual	1997	Mentored Research Scientist Development Award for Minority Investigators
NINR	P30	Institutional	1997	RCMAR collaboration with NIA
NLM	n.a.	Institutional	n.a.	Training in Medical Informatics and Bioinformatics
NLM	n.a.	Individual	n.a.	Associate Fellowship Program

NOTE:

Collaborations should not be double-counted when tallying up the total number of programs.

CAMSSA = Collaborative Arthritis Musculoskeletal and Skin Disease Sciences Award
CMIAARD = Collaborative Minority Institution Alcohol Research Development Programs
CNS = Collaborative Neurological Sciences
COR = Career Opportunities in Research
CURE = Continuing Umbrella of Research Experience
IRACDA = Institutional Research and Academic Career Development Awards
MARC = Minority Access to Research Careers
MBRS = Minority Biomedical Research Support
MIDARP = Minority Institutions' Drug Abuse Research Development Program
MORE = Minority Opportunities in Research
M-RISP = Minority-Research Infrastructure Support
n.a. = data not available
NCI = National Cancer Institute
NEI = National Eye Institute
NHLBI = National Heart, Lung, and Blood Institute
NIA = National Institute of Aging
NIAAA = National Institute of Alcohol Abuse and Alcoholism
NIAID = National Institute of Allergy and Infectious Diseases
NIAMS = National Institute of Arthritis and Musculoskeletal and Skin Diseases
NICHD = National Institute of Child Health and Human Development
NIDA = National Institute on Drug Abuse
NIDDK = National Institute of Diabetes and Digestive and Kidney Diseases
NIDCD = National Institute on Deafness and Other Communication Disorders
NIDCR = National Institute of Dental and Craniofacial Research
NIEHS = National Institute of Environmental Health Sciences
NIGMS = National Institute of General Medical Sciences
NIMH = National Institute of Mental Health
NINDS = National Institute of Neurological Disorders and Stroke
NINR = National Institute of Nursing Research
NLM = National Library of Medicine
PREP = Post-Baccalaureate Research Education Program
RCMAR = Resource Centers in Minority Aging Research
RISE = Research Initiative for Scientific Enhancement
SCORE = Support of Continuous Research Excellence
U*STAR = Undergraduate Student Training in Academic Research

Appendix C

Computer-Assisted Telephone Interview (CATI) Questionnaire for Graduate Trainees

INTRO:
Hello, may I please speak to {INSERT FIRST NAME}?

01 PERSON ON THE TELEPHONE/PERSON COMING TO THE TELEPHONE
02 PERSON NOT AVAILABLE BUT CAN BE REACHED HERE
03 PERSON NOT KNOWN AT THIS NUMBER

PRETEST INTRODUCTION
Hello, my name is ______, and I'm calling on behalf of the National Academy of Sciences in Washington, DC. The Academy is conducting an assessment of some National Institutes of Health research training programs. You have been selected to help us out in testing the questionnaire because of your research experience in {YEAR} at {INSTITUTION}. We are interested in hearing your responses and assessing the flow of the questionnaire. We would really appreciate your help. The call should take less than 30 minutes. Before we begin, I would like to assure you that everything we talk about will be confidential. Your answers will only be used for evaluating the questions I will ask you, and they will never be reported in a way that can be linked back to you. Keep in mind, you may refuse to answer any question. You should also know that this call is being recorded for evaluation purposes.

INTRODUCTION
Hello, my name is ______, and I'm calling on behalf of the National Academy of Sciences in Washington, DC. The Academy is conducting an assessment of some National Institutes of Health research training programs. Recently, you received a letter inviting you to participate in a telephone interview to discuss your {ACADEMIC LEVEL} research experience in {YEAR}. The interview should take between 20 and 25 minutes. Is this a good time for you? Before we begin, I would like to assure you that everything we talk about is confidential. Your answers will only be reported in the aggregate, and will never be reported in a way that they can be linked back to you. They will only be disclosed to the researchers involved in this project, except as otherwise required by law. You may also refuse to answer any question. You should also know that this call may be monitored for the purposes of quality assurance.

Q2a SCREENER:
Because participants in this study were randomly selected, I need to confirm that you are the appropriate person to be answering these questions. Could you please tell me the last four digits of your Social Security number?

[IF NECESSARY: I only need the last four digits of your Social Security number, not the entire number. I am not able to see your social security number. My computer will compare the information you provide with the information we have on the selected study participants.]
01 RECORD RESPONSE

98 DON'T KNOW
99 REFUSED

Q2a2 SSN: __ __ __ __

(Q2oops) /IF NO MATCH, REFUSED, DON'T KNOW GOTO GOOD-BYE/

Great, we have a match. Let's begin the interview by talking about when your research was supported by {PROGRAM} at {INSTITUTION} in {YEAR}.

A.1 How did you hear about the {PROGRAM}? I'm going to read a list of ways you might have learned about the {PROGRAM}, please tell me all that apply to you.

[INTERVIEWER NOTE: READ LIST]

A. Trainee Awareness and Expectations

ga.1a Did you hear about it from an undergraduate professor?

01 YES
02 NO
98 DON'T KNOW
99 REFUSED

ga.1b Did you hear about it from an undergraduate academic counselor?

01 YES
02 NO
98 DON'T KNOW
99 REFUSED

ga.1c Did you hear about it from your graduate advisor?

01 YES
02 NO
98 DON'T KNOW
99 REFUSED

ga.1d Did you hear about it from departmental staff?

01 YES
02 NO
98 DON'T KNOW
99 REFUSED

ga.1e Did you hear about it from a faculty colleague or peer?

01 YES
02 NO
98 DON'T KNOW
99 REFUSED

ga.1f Did you hear about it from a close personal friend?

01 YES
02 NO
98 DON'T KNOW
99 REFUSED

ga.1g Did you hear about it from a notice on a bulletin board?

01 YES
02 NO
98 DON'T KNOW
99 REFUSED

ga.1h Did you hear about it from a scientific journal?

01 YES
02 NO
98 DON'T KNOW
99 REFUSED

ga.1i Did you hear about it from the Internet?

01 YES
02 NO
98 DON'T KNOW
99 REFUSED

ga.1j Or did you learn about it by some other means?

01 YES
02 NO
98 DON'T KNOW
99 REFUSED

/IF A.1 = 95 THEN ASK A.1.O, ELSE GOTO A.2/

ga1o How did you learned about the {PROGRAM}?

01 RECORD RESPONSE
98 DON'T KNOW
99 REFUSED

ga1how /TEXT LENGTH = 270/ ENTER RESPONSE: ____________________

ga2 At the time your research was supported by the {PROGRAM} at {INSTITUTION}, what was the highest degree you hoped to earn?

[INTERVIEWER NOTE: IF NECESSARY READ LIST]

01 MA/MS
02 Professional Master's
03 MBA
04 Ph.D.
05 MD
06 MD-Ph.D.
07 Other health degree (e.g., DDS, . . .)
08 Law degree
95 or some other degree
98 DON'T REMEMBER
99 REFUSED

/IF A.2 = 95 ASK A.2.O ELSE CONTINUE/

ga2o What was the highest degree you hoped to earn?

01 RECORD RESPONSE
98 DON'T REMEMBER
99 REFUSED

ga2what /TEXT LENGTH = 270/ RESPONSE: ______________________

ga4_1-ga4_13 When you were at {INSTITUTION} in {YEAR}, what were your career goals? I am going to read you a list of possibilities, please tell me all of the career goals that you had at that time. Were they:

[INTERVIEWER NOTE: READ LIST. SELECT ALL THAT APPLY]

/MUL = 8/

- 01 to practice medicine
- 02 to do clinical research
- 03 to do basic biological research
- 04 to do behavioral research
- 05 to do licensed clinical work at the Ph.D. level (e.g., Psychologist)
- 06 to work in the allied health professions (such as nursing, social work, paramedic, etc.)
- 07 to teach
- 95 or did you have some other goal that I did not mention?
- 97 NO SPECIFIC CAREER GOALS AT THAT TIME
- 98 DON'T KNOW
- 99 REFUSED

/IF A.4 = 95 ASK A.4.O ELSE CONTINUE/

g4ao Please tell me what other career goals you had at that time?

- 01 RECORD RESPONSE
- 98 DON'T KNOW
- 99 REFUSED

ga4what /TEXT LENGTH = 270/ RESPONSE: ______________________

ga5 During the time of your {PROGRAM} at {INSTITUTION} what did you see as the immediate next step in your career path? I am going to read you a list of options. Please choose one. Did you see your next step as . . .
[INTERVIEWER NOTE: PLEASE READ LIST]

- 01 getting a postdoctoral appointment
- 02 obtaining a faculty position at a college or university
- 03 getting a job in K-12 education
- 04 going on to medical school
- 05 getting a job in government
- 06 getting a job in the private sector
- 95 or obtaining some other position?
- 98 DON'T KNOW
- 99 REFUSED

/IF A.5 = 95 ASK A.5.O ELSE CONTINUE/

ga5o Please tell me what you saw as the immediate next step?

- 01 RECORD RESPONSE
- 98 DON'T KNOW
- 99 REFUSED

ga5what /TEXT LENGTH = 270/ RESPONSE: ______________________

ga6_1-ga6_8 What did you expect to gain from your {PROGRAM}program? I'm going to read a list of expectations, please tell me all the ones that applied to you at that time. Did you expect:

[INTERVIEWER NOTE: READ LIST. SELECT ALL THAT APPLY]

/MUL = 9/

01	to improve your research skills
02	to increase your chances of being admitted into medical school
03	to increase your chances of obtaining a postdoctoral appointment after graduate school
04	to establish a relationship with a mentor
05	to improve your teaching skills
06	to increase your chances of obtaining a teaching appointment after graduate school
07	to increase your chances of obtaining a research faculty appointment after graduate school
08	to finance your education
09	or to increase your chances at securing future grants and fellowships?
10	to improve your career options
97	DID NOT HAVE EXPECTATIONS (SKIP TO B.1)
98	DON'T KNOW (SKIP TO B.1)
99	REFUSED (SKIP TO B.1)

/SET VARIABLE EXPECTATIONS = number of responses provided in A.6/

ga7 Did you have any other expectations that I didn't mention?

01	YES
02	NO (SKIP TO A.8)
98	DON'T KNOW (SKIP TO A.8)
99	REFUSED (SKIP TO A.8)

/IF A.7 = 01 ASK A.7.O ELSE CONTINUE/

A.7.O What were they?

[INTERVIEWER NOTE: Respondent may provide up to 3 other expectations.]

ga7b1 01 /TEXT LENGTH = 70/ RESPONSE: _______________
ga7b2 02 /TEXT LENGTH = 70/ RESPONSE: ________________
ga7b3 03 /TEXT LENGTH = 70/ RESPONSE: ________________

/UPDATE VARIABLE EXPECTATIONS = number responses A.7 + A.7.O/
ga8_01-ga8_11. I am going to read you a list of expectations that you just mentioned you had for the {PROGRAM}. Please tell me which ones were not met.

/RECALL EXPECTATIONS FROM A.6 AND A.7.O, RANGE 1-10, LOOP BASED ON NUMBER OF EXPECTATIONS/

/START LOOP/

Was {RECALL {EXPECTATION X}} met?

01 YES
02 NO
98 DON'T KNOW
99 REFUSED

/WHEN LOOP # = #EXPECTATIONS, END LOOP/

ga8a_1 Could you tell me how or in what ways the{PROGRAM} did not meet your expectations?

01 RECORD RESPONSE
98 DON'T KNOW
99 REFUSED

GA8a /LENGTH = 240 CHAR/ RESPONSE: ______________________

B. Work and Finances

B.1 Switching gears, I would like to talk about sources of financial support.

gb2. During the time you received {PROGRAM}, did you have any additional sources of financial support?

01 YES
02 NO (SKIP TO B.3b)
98 DON'T KNOW (SKIP TO B.3b)
99 REFUSED (SKIP TO B.3b)

gb3a_1-gb3a_9. I am going to read a list of other funding sources you may have had while receiving {PROGRAM} in {YEAR}. Please tell me all that applied to your situation. Did you also have:

/MUL = 9/

[PLEASE READ. SELECT ALL THAT APPLY]

01 any scholarships
02 any loans (from any other source)
03 a job that paid a wage or a salary
04 any personal savings that you used to support yourself
05 help from a spouse or family support
06 a research grant or fellowship other than your {PROGRAM}
07 a teaching assistantship
08 a research assistantship other than your {PROGRAM}
95 or some other source of support that I haven't mentioned?
98 DON'T KNOW
99 REFUSED

/IF B.3.a = 95 ASK B.3.a.O ELSE CONTINUE/

gb3ao From what other source, or sources, did you receive support?

01 RECORD RESPONSE
98 DON'T KNOW
99 REFUSED

gb3awhat RESPONSE/TEXT 70/: ___________________________

gb3b_1-gb3b_9 Now I would like you to think about your graduate years, as a whole. I am going to read the same list of funding sources. Please tell me all the funding sources you used during graduate school. Did you have:

/MUL = 9/

01 any scholarships
02 any loans (from any other source)
03 a job that paid a wage or a salary
04 any personal savings that you used to support yourself
05 help from a spouse or family support
06 a research grant or fellowship other than your {PROGRAM}
07 a teaching assistantship
08 a research assistantship other than your {PROGRAM}
95 or some other source of support that I haven't mentioned?
98 DON'T KNOW
99 REFUSED

/IF B.3.b = 95 ASK B.3.a.O ELSE CONTINUE/

gb3bo From what other source, or sources, did you receive support during your graduate school years?

01 RECORD RESPONSE
98 DON'T KNOW
99 REFUSED

gb3bwhat RESPONSE/TEXT 270/: ____________________

gb4a What is your current status, with respect to {INSTITUTION}? I am going to read you a list of possibilities, please stop me when I reach the one that best describes your current status with respect to {INSTITUTION}.

[INTERVIEWR NOTE: PLEASE READ LIST, STOP WHEN RESPONDENTS PICKS]

01 I am still enrolled at {INSTITUTION} (SKIP TO B.5)
02 I left the {INSTITUTION} without getting a degree.
03 I graduated from the {INSTITUTION} with a Master's degree (SKIP TO B.5)
04 I graduated from the {INSTITUTION} with a Ph.D. (SKIP TO B.4b)
05 I transferred to another university and am still a student. (SKIP TO B.5)
06 I transferred to another university and then left without getting a degree
07 I transferred to another university and graduated with a Master's degree (SKIP TO B.5)
08 I transferred to another university and then graduated with a Ph.D. (SKIP TO B.4b)
09 I am currently on leave from {INSTITUTION}. (SKIP TO B.5)
95 OTHER
98 DON'T KNOW
99 REFUSED

/IF B.4a = 95 THEN ASK, ELSE CONTINUE/

gb4a0 How would you describe your current status with respect to {INSTITUTION}?

01 RECORD RESPONSE
98 DON'T KNOW
99 REFUSED

gb4ahow RESPONSE/TEXT 270/: ____________________

/IF B.4a = 02 or 06 ASK B.4a.O ELSE CONTINUE/

gb4a1 Tell me briefly, the reasons why you left without getting a degree?

01 RECORD RESPONSE
98 DON'T KNOW
99 REFUSED

gb4awhy /TEXT LENGTH = 270/ RESPONSE: ____________________

/IF B.4a = 04 or 08 ASK, ELSE CONTINUE/

gb4b_1-gb4b_5 What did you do after completing your Ph.D.? I am going to read you a list of possibilities, please tell me, please tell me which one, or ones, applies to you: Did you---

[INTERVIEWER NOTE: PLEASE READ LIST]

/MUL = 5/

01 secure a postdoctoral appointment
02 get a job in Academia
03 get a job in Government
04 get a job in the private sector
05 continue your education in some way
06 or none of these?
98 DON'T KNOW
99 REFUSED

gb5 Since your participation in the {PROGRAM}, have you been awarded any research grants on which you were the principal investigator?

01 YES
02 NO (SKIP TO B.6)
98 DON'T KNOW (SKIP TO B.6)
99 REFUSED (SKIP TO B.6)

gb5a1 How many research grants have you been awarded as principal investigator?

01 RECORD RESPONSE
98 DON'T KNOW
99 REFUSED

gb5a RANGE {1-500}_____________ NUMBER

gb6 Since your participation in the {PROGRAM}, have you been the first or senior author on any published research papers?

01 YES
02 NO (SKIP TO D.1)
98 DON'T KNOW (SKIP TO D.1)
99 REFUSED (SKIP TO D.1)

gb6a1 How many research papers have you been the first or senior author?

01 RECORD RESPONSE
98 DON'T KNOW
99 REFUSED

gb6a RANGE {1-500}____________ NUMBER

D. Research and Laboratory Experience

D.1 During the time you received the {PROGRAM}, how many people were in your principal investigator's, or PI's, research group?

[INTERVIEWER NOTE: A principle investigator (or PI) is the head of the lab or research group].

[INTERVIEWER PROBE: That is, on a typical day when the lab or office was full, about how many people worked there? IF NECESSARY: Your best guess is fine.]

/RANGE 1-50 / NUMBER: ____________

98 DON'T KNOW
99 REFUSED

d2 How many of the people in your PI's research group were underrepresented minorities?

[INTERVIEWER NOTE: Underrepresented Minorities include: African Americans, Hispanics, Native Americans, Pacific Islanders]

/RANGE 1-50 / NUMBER: ____________

98 DON'T KNOW
99 REFUSED

E. Mentor Demographics

E.2 While you were in the {PROGRAM}, was there someone who took a personal interest in and was supportive of, your research or career?

01 YES
02 NO (SKIP TO F.1)
98 DON'T KNOW (SKIP TO F.1)
99 REFUSED (SKIP TO F.1)

/IF E.2 = 01 THEN READ PRE.E3;/

PRE. E.3 For the purposes of the following questions, I am going to refer to this person who took an interest in and was supportive of your research career as a "mentor"

e3a Was your mentor male or female?

[INTERVIEWER NOTE: IF THERE IS MORE THAN ONE, ASK THEM TO PICK THE ONE THAT WAS MOST INFLUENTIAL AT THE TIME.]

01 MALE
02 FEMALE
98 DON'T KNOW
99 REFUSED

e4a Was your mentor Spanish, Hispanic, or Latino?

[DO NOT READ CATEGORIES]

01 YES Spanish, Hispanic, or Latino (incl: Chicano, Cuban, Mexican, Puerto Rican)
02 NO none of these categories apply
98 DON'T KNOW
99 REFUSED

[INTERVIEWER NOTE: PLEASE READ MAJOR CATEGORIES HEADINGS ONLY]

/MUL = 6/

[MULTIPLE RESPONSES ALLOWED]

01 White,
02 Black, African American
03 Asian, (incl: Asian Indian, Chinese, Japanese, Korean, Vietnamese)
04 Pacific Islander, Native Hawaiian or . . . (incl: Chamorro, Filipino, Guamanian, Samoan)
05 American Indian, Alaska Native,
95 Or some other race?
98 DON'T KNOW
99 REFUSED

/IF E5a_1-E5a_6 = 06 ASK, ELSE GOTO F.1/

e5ao OTHER TEXT: ______________________________

F. Principal Investigator -- Demographics

f1 Now, I would like to ask you about your PRINCIPAL INVESTIGATOR or PI, at the time you received the{PROGRAM}.

/IF E.2 = 01 ASK ELSE GOTO F.3/

f2 Were your mentor and Principal Investigator the same person?

01 YES (SKIP to G.1)
02 NO
98 DON'T KNOW (SKIP to G.1)
99 REFUSED (SKIP to G.1)

f3 Was your PI male or female?

01 MALE
02 FEMALE
98 DON'T KNOW
99 REFUSED

f4 Was your PI Spanish, Hispanic, or Latino?

[DO NOT READ CATEGORIES]

01 YES (Spanish, Hispanic, or Latino (incl: Chicano, Cuban, Mexican, Puerto Rican)
02 NO (none of these categories apply)
98 DON'T KNOW
99 REFUSED

f5_1-f5_6 What was your PI's race or ethnicity? Would you say . . .

[INTERVIEWER NOTE: PLEASE READ MAJOR CATEGORIES HEADINGS ONLY]

/MUL = 6/

[MULTIPLE RESPONSES ALLOWED]

01 White,
02 Black, African American
03 Asian (incl: Asian Indian, Chinese, Japanese, Korean, Vietnamese)
04 Native Hawaiian or Pacific Islander (incl: Chamorro, Filipino, Guamanian, Samoan)
05 American Indian, Alaska Native,
95 Or some other race?
98 DON'T KNOW
99 REFUSED

f5_o OTHER TEXT: ______________________________

G. Mentoring Experiences

G.1 Now, I would like to talk more about your PI, and what it was like to work with him or her?

g2 During the time of your {PROGRAM} award, how much encouragement for your research did your PI provide? On a scale of 1 to 5, where one represents abundant encouragement, and 5 represents no encouragement at all; please tell me where you would place your PI.

[INTERVIEWER NOTE: if respondent worked in more than one lab or research group during the time of their award, the response to this question should refer to the last lab or research group that the respondent spent the most time in, while the award was still active.]

01	ABUNDANT ENCOURAGEMENT FOR MY RESEARCH
02	
03	NEUTRAL
04	
05	NO ENCOURAGEMENT AT ALL FOR MY RESEARCH
98	DON'T KNOW
99	REFUSED

g3 Would you say that your PI was not good to work with, or was good to work with? On a scale of 1 to 5, where one represents very good to work with, and 5 represents not good to work with at all, please tell me how you would rate your PI?

01	VERY GOOD TO WORK WITH
02	
03	NEUTRAL
04	
05	NOT GOOD TO WORK WITH AT ALL
98	DON'T KNOW
99	REFUSED

G4) How active was your PI in the scientific community? That is to say did your PI publish research papers, present research at national conferences, win research grants, and so forth. On a scale from 1 to 5, where 1 represents very active in the scientific community and 5 represents not active at all, how would you describe your PI?

01	VERY ACTIVE
02	
03	NEUTRAL
04	
05	NOT ACTIVE AT ALL
98	DON'T KNOW/DON'T REMEMBER
99	REFUSED

g5 During the time of your {PROGRAM} award, how much assistance did your PI provide, in terms of helping you take the next step in your education or career path? Again, on a scale from 1 to 5, where 1 represents your PI provided a lot of assistance and 5 represents your PI provided no assistance at all, how would you rate your PI?

01 PROVIDED A LOT OF ASSISTANCE
02
03 NEUTRAL
04
05 PROVIDED NO ASSISTANCE
98 DON'T KNOW/DON'T REMEMBER
99 REFUSED

g6 How helpful would you say your PI was in helping you obtain grants, scholarships, fellowships, or other types of awards to support your research training? On a scale from 1 to 5, where 1 represents very helpful in securing funding and 5 represents not helpful at all, how would you rate your PI?

01 VERY HELPFUL IN SECURING FUNDING
02
03 NEUTRAL
04
05 NOT HELPFUL AT ALL IN SECURING FUNDING
97 NOT APPLICABLE
98 DON'T KNOW
99 REFUSED

g7 In general, would you say that your PI gave mostly good career advice or mostly poor career advice? On a scale from 1 to 5, where 1 represents giving really good advice and 5 represents giving very poor advice, how would you rate your PI?

01 VERY GOOD ADVICE
02
03 NEUTRAL
04
05 VERY POOR ADVICE
97 NOT APPICABLE
98 DON'T KNOW
99 REFUSED

H. Relationships

H.1 Now, I want you to try and think about different groups of people you may have interacted with while you were supported, by the {PROGRAM} at {INSTITUTION}.

h2a How frequently did you discuss your research with your PI? Did you discuss your research....

[INTERVIEWER: PLEASE READ THE LIST UNTIL THE RESPONDENT ANSWERS]

01 every day
02 once a week
03 2-3 times a month
04 once a month
05 once every three months
06 once every six months
07 once a year
08 or not at all
98 DON'T KNOW
99 REFUSED

h2b How frequently did you discuss your research with other people in your lab or research group? Would you say you discussed your research with them....

[INTERVIEWER NOTE: PLEASE READ THE LIST UNTIL THE RESPONDENT ANSWERS]

01 every day
02 once a week
03 2-3 times a month
04 once a month
05 once every three months
06 once every six months
07 once a year
08 or not at all
98 DON'T KNOW
99 REFUSED

h2c How frequently did you discuss your research with other research colleagues at {INSTITUTION}? Would you say you discussed your research with them....

[INTERVIEWER NOTE: PLEASE READ THE LIST UNTIL THE RESPONDENT ANSWERS]

01 every day
02 once a week
03 2-3 times a month
04 once a month
05 once every three months
06 once every six months
07 once a year
08 or not at all
98 DON'T KNOW
99 REFUSED

h3a Still thinking about the people whom you interacted with, while you were supported by the {PROGRAM} at {INSTITUTION}, tell me on a scale from 1 to 5, where 1 is distant and 5 is close, the quality of your relationship with your PI.

[IF NECESSARY PROMPT: Where 1 is distant and 5 is close?]

01 DISTANT
02
03 NEUTRAL
04
05 CLOSE
98 DON'T KNOW
99 REFUSED

h3b On a scale from 1 to 5, where 1 represents distant and 5 represents close, how would you characterize your relationship with the other members of your lab or research group?

[IF NECESSARY PROMPT: Where 1 is distant and 5 is close?]

01 DISTANT
02
03 NEUTRAL
04
05 CLOSE
98 DON'T KNOW
99 REFUSED

h3c On a scale from 1 to 5, where 1 represents distant and 5 represents close, how would you characterize your relationship with other research colleagues at {INSTITUTION}?

[IF NECESSARY PROMPT: Where 1 is distant and 5 is close?]

01 DISTANT
02
03 NEUTRAL
04
05 CLOSE
98 DON'T KNOW
99 REFUSED

h4a Still thinking about these same groups of people, now I would like you to rate them in terms of the influence they had on your career path. On a scale from 1 to 5, where 1 represents very little influence and 5 represents a great deal of influence how would you rate the influence your PI had on your career path?

[IF NECESSARY PROMPT: 1 represents very little influence and 5 represent a great deal of influence on your career path.]

01 VERY LITTLE INFLUENCE
02
03 NEUTRAL
04
05 GREAT DEAL OF INFLUENCE
98 DON'T KNOW
99 REFUSED

/IF H.4a = 04 OR 05 ASK H.4bO, ELSE GOTO H.4e/

h4b1 Tell me in what way your PI influenced your career path? Why do you think your PI had so much influence?

01 RECORD REPSONSE
98 DON'T KNOW
99 REFUSED

h4bo LENGTH = 240 CHAR/ RESPONSE: ______________________________

h4e How would you rate the influence of other members of your lab or research group on your career path?

[IF NECESSARY PROMPT: 1 represents very little influence and 5 represents a great deal of influence.]

01 VERY LITTLE INFLUENCE
02
03 NEUTRAL
04
05 GREAT DEAL OF INFLUENCE
98 DON'T KNOW
99 REFUSED

h4f How would you rate the influence of other research colleagues at {INSTITUTION} on your career path?

[IF NECESSARY PROMPT: 1 represents very little influence and 5 represents a great deal of influence.]

01 VERY LITTLE INFLUENCE
02
03 NEUTRAL
04
05 GREAT DEAL OF INFLUENCE
98 DON'T KNOW
99 REFUSED

h4g Still thinking back to when you were supported by the {PROGRAM} at {INSTITUTION},how long after leaving that lab or research group you were in did you remain in touch with your PI? I am going to read you a list of possibilities, stop me when I read one that describes how long you stayed in touch . . .

[INTERVIEWER: PLEASE READ THE LIST]

01 you did not remain in touch
02 less than six months
03 less than one year
04 between one and three years
05 between three and six years
06 greater than six years
98 DON'T KNOW
99 REFUSED

h4h Similarly, how long after leaving the same lab or research group did you remain in touch with other members of your lab or research group? I am going to read you a list of possibilities, stop me when I read one that describes how long you stayed in touch . . .

[INTERVIEWER: PLEASE READ THE LIST]

01 you did not remain in touch
02 less than six months
03 less than one year
04 between one and three years
05 between three and six years
06 greater than six years
98 DON'T KNOW
99 REFUSED

h4i Finally, how long after leaving the same lab or research group did you remain in touch with other research colleagues at {INSTITUTION}? I am going to read you a list of possibilities, stop me when I read one that describes how long you stayed in touch . . .

[INTERVIEWER: PLEASE READ THE LIST]

01 you did not remain in touch
02 less than six months
03 less than one year
04 between one and three years
05 between three and six years
06 greater than six years
98 DON'T KNOW
99 REFUSED

h5 Overall, do you believe the {PROGRAM} had an influence on your education?

01 YES
02 NO (SKIP TO H.6)
98 DON'T KNOW (SKIP TO H.6)
99 REFUSED (SKIP TO H.6)

/IF H.5 = 01 ASK H.5.O ELSE SKIP TO H.6/

h5a Please tell me how {PROGRAM} influenced your education?

01 RECORD RESPONSE
98 DON'T KNOW
99 REFUSED

h5ao /LENGTH = 240 CHAR/ RESPONSE: ______________________________

h6 Do you believe the {PROGRAM} had an influence on your career?

01 YES
02 NO (SKIP TO I.1)
98 DON'T KNOW (SKIP TO I.1)
99 REFUSED (SKIP TO I.1)

/IF H.6 = 01 ASK H.6O ELSE CONTINUE/

h6a1 Please tell me how the {PROGRAM} influenced your career?

01 RECORD RESPONSE
98 DON'T KNOW
99 REFUSED

h6ao /LENGTH = 240 CHAR/ RESPONSE: ______________________

I. Demographics

I.1 Now, I want to ask you a few questions about yourself and your family.

i2a At the time you received the {PROGRAM}, did you have a spouse or long-term partner?

01 YES
02 NO
98 DON'T KNOW
99 REFUSED

i2b At the time your {PROGRAM} was active, did you have any dependents?

[INTERVIEWER: a dependent is someone that the respondent supported financially and could legitimately claim on his/her income tax return].

01 YES
02 NO (SKIP TO I.3)
98 DON'T KNOW (SKIP TO I.3)
99 REFUSED (SKIP TO I.3)

i2c1 How many dependents did you have at that time?

01 RECORD RESPONSE
98 DON'T KNOW
99 REFUSED

i2c ENTER ____________ /RANGE =1-12/

i3 Is English your first language?

01 YES
02 NO
98 DON'T KNOW
99 REFUSED

i4 Are you Spanish, Hispanic, or Latino?

[DO NOT READ CATEGORIES]

01 YES (Spanish, Hispanic, or Latino incl: Chicano, Cuban, Mexican, Puerto Rican)
02 NO, NONE OF THESE CATEGORIES APPLY
98 DON'T KNOW
99 REFUSED

i5_1-i5_6 What is your race? Would you describe yourself as.....

[INTERVIEWER NOTE: PLEASE READ MAJOR CATEGORIES HEADINGS ONLY. SELECT ALL THAT APPLY]

/MUL = 6/

01 White,
02 Black, African American
03 Asian, (incl: Asian Indian, Chinese, Japanese, Korean, Vietnamese)
04 Pacific Islander, Native Hawaiian or..., (incl: Chamorro, Filipino, Guamanian, Samoan)
05 American Indian, Alaska Native,
95 Or some other race?
98 DON'T KNOW
99 REFUSED

[IF I.51 = 95 CONTINUE, ELSE SKIP TO I.6]

i5o OTHER TEXT: ______________________________

i6 What is the highest degree you received?

[INTERVIEWER NOTE: Please read list]

01 Associates Degree
02 BA/BS Candidate
03 BA/BS
04 MA/MS
05 MBA
06 Professional Master's
07 ABD
08 MD-Ph.D. combined
09 Ph.D. only
10 M.D. only
11 Other health degree (e.g., DDS, DVM, RN , NP . . .)
12 Law degree
95 Some other degree not mentioned.
99 REFUSED

/IF I6 = 95 ASK, ELSE CONTINUE/

i6o SPECIFY /TEXT = 70/________________________________

i7 Are you currently working in the biological or behavioral sciences?

01 YES
02 NO
98 DON'T KNOW
99 REFUSED

i8 Currently, how do you spend most of your productive daily hours Monday through Friday? I'm going to read you a list of options. Please choose one.

[INTERVIEWER NOTE: Please read list]

01 you are working (SKIP TO I.10)
02 you are looking for a job (SKIP TO I.9C)
03 you are a stay-at-home parent or full-time caretaker for a family member (SKIP TO I.9C)
04 you are pursuing a degree (SKIP TO I.9A)
05 you are currently on leave from a job/academic program (SKIP TO I.9C)
06 you are retired (SKIP TO I.10)
95 or are you doing something else? (SKIP TO I.9B1)
98 DON'T KNOW (SKIP TO I.9C)
99 REFUSED (SKIP TO I.9C)

i9a What degree are you pursuing, currently?

[INTERVIEWER NOTE: Please read list]

04	MA/MS
05	MBA
06	Professional Masters
08	MD-Ph.D. combined
09	Ph.D. only
10	MD only
11	Other health degree (e.g., DDS, DVM, RN, NP….)
12	Law degree
95	Some other degree not mentioned.
99	REFUSED

/IF I.8 = 95 THEN ASK, ELSE CONTINUE/

i9b1 How would you describe what you do with your most productive hours Monday through Friday? How would you describe what you are currently doing?

01	RECORD RESPONSE
98	DON'T KNOW
99	REFUSED

i9bo RESPONSE: /TEXT = 270/______________________

/IF I.8 = 01 DO NOT ASK, ASK OF EVERYONE ELSE/

i9c Have you ever worked?

01	YES
02	NO (SKIP TO INSTRUCTION BEFORE I.15a)
98	DON'T KNOW
99	REFUSED

i9d Have you ever held a full-time job?

01	YES
02	NO
98	DON'T KNOW
99	REFUSED

i10 What is (was) your most recent primary employment sector? Was it in . . . ?

[INTERVIEWER NOTE: Please read list]

01 education
02 government (SKIP TO I.12)
03 private sector (SKIP to I.13)
04 something else (SKIP to I.14)
98 DON'T KNOW (SKIP to I.15a)
99 REFUSED (SKIP to I.15a)

i11 Within the education sector, do you (or did you) primarily work at....

[INTERVIEWER NOTE: Please read list]

01 a U.S. medical school
02 a U.S. 4-year college or university
03 a U.S. junior, or community college
04 an elementary or secondary school
05 a foreign institution
98 DON'T KNOW
99 REFUSED

/IF I.4 = 01, or I.5 = 02,04,05 ASK I.15a, ELSE GOTO I.16/

i12 Within the government sector, do you (did you) primarily work for....

[INTERVIEWER NOTE: Please read list]

01 a foreign government
02 the U.S. federal government (i.e., civil service)
03 the U.S. military
04 a state government
05 a county or municipal government
98 DON'T KNOW
99 REFUSED

/IF I.4 = 01, or I.5 = 02,04,05 ASK I.15a, ELSE GOTO I.16/

i13 Within the private sector, do you (did you) primarily work ....

[INTERVIEWER NOTE: Please read list]

01 in industry or business
02 for a private research institute
03 for a nonprofit organization
04 or are you or were you self-employed
98 DON'T KNOW
99 REFUSED

/IF I.4 = 01, or I.5 = 02,04,05 ASK I.15a, ELSE GOTO I.16/

i141 How would you describe your most recent primary employment sector?

01 RECORD RESPONSE
98 DON'T KNOW
99 REFUSED

i14 /TEXT = 250 CHARACTERS/ RESPONSE: ____________________

/IF I.4 = 01, or I.5 = 02,04,05 ASK I.15a, ELSE GOTO I.16/

i15a Still thinking back to when you were supported by the {PROGRAM} at {INSTITUTION}, do you believe that being a minority individual in some way, affected your research training experience?

01 YES
02 NO (SKIP TO I.16)
98 DON'T KNOW (SKIP TO I.16)
99 REFUSED (SKIP TO I.16)

i15bo In what ways did your minority status affected your research training experience?

01 RECORD RESPONSE
98 DON'T KNOW
99 REFUSED

i15b /TEXT = 250 CHARACTERS/ RESPONSE: ____________________

i16 Are you an only child?

01 YES
02 NO
97 NOT APPLICABLE
98 DON'T KNOW
99 REFUSED

/IF I.16 = 02 ASK/
i17 Do your parents or any siblings have a bachelors (4-year) degree?

/IF I.16 = 01,97,98,99 ASK/
PreI.17Do either of your parents have a bachelors have a bachelors (4-year) degree?

01 YES
02 NO
97 NOT APPLICABLE
98 DON'T KNOW
99 REFUSED

/IF I.16 = 02 ASK/
i18 Do your parents or any siblings have a graduate degree?

/IF I.16 = 01,97,98,99 ASK/
PreI.18 Do either of your parents have a bachelors have a graduate degree?

01 YES
02 NO
97 NOT APPLICABLE
98 DON'T KNOW
99 REFUSED

i19 Still thinking back to the time your {PROGRAM} was active, how supportive would you say your parents were of your overall career goals? On a scale from 1 to 5, where 1 is not supportive at all, and 5 is extremely supportive, how would you rate the supportiveness of your parents for your career goals?

01 NOT SUPPORTIVE AT ALL
02
03 NEUTRAL
04
05 EXTREMELY SUPPORTIVE
97 NOT APPLICABLE
98 DON'T KNOW
99 REFUSED

/IF I.2a – 01, ASK I.20, ELSE GOTO J.1/

i20 Similarly, how supportive would you say your spouse or partner was of your overall career goals, at this same time? Remember, 1 is not supportive at all, and 5 is extremely supportive

01 NOT SUPPORTIVE AT ALL
02
03 NEUTRAL
04
05 EXTREMELY SUPPORTIVE
97 NOT APPLICABLE
98 DON'T KNOW
99 REFUSED

J. General questions

J.1 Finally, to finish the survey I want to ask you some general questions about the {PROGRAM}.

j2_1 What were the best features of the {PROGRAM}?

01 RECORD RESPONSE
98 DON'T KNOW
99 REFUSED

j2o /LENGTH = 240 CHAR/ RESPONSE: ____________________________

j3_1 What were the worst features of the {PROGRAM}?

01 RECORD RESPONSE
98 DON'T KNOW
99 REFUSED

j3o /LENGTH = 240 CHAR/ RESPONSE: ____________________________

j4 Do you believe the {PROGRAM} could be improved in any way?

01 YES
02 NO (SKIP TO J.6)
98 DON'T KNOW (SKIP TO J.6)
99 REFUSED (SKIP TO J.6)

j4_1 If you could make improvements to the {PROGRAM} what would they be?

01 RECORD RESPONSE
98 DON'T KNOW
99 REFUSED

j4o /LENGTH = 240 CHAR/ RESPONSE: ____________________________

j6 Is there anything else you would like NIH to know about the {PROGRAM}?

01 YES
02 NO (SKIP TO GOODBYE)
98 DON'T KNOW (SKIP TO GOODBYE)
99 REFUSED (SKIP TO GOODBYE)

j7o What would you like NIH to know about the {PROGRAM}?

/LENGTH = 240 CHAR/ RESPONSE: ____________________________

K. Goodbye

Those are all the questions I have for you today/tonight. I would like to thank you for taking the time to talk with me. Your participation is very important, and we greatly appreciate your input. The results of this study will be published in Summer 2004 and may be accessed for free at www.nap.edu.

Once again, thank you very much, and Good-bye.

GOODBYE1

We are only able to conduct this interview with people whom we can verify that they are indeed the selected respondent. Thank you very much for your time.

GOODBYE2
I am sorry, but I am having trouble pulling up your file at this time. Would it be possible for me to call you back at a later time?

01 YES (SCHEDULE A CALLBACK)
02 NO
98 DON'T KNOW (SCHEDULE A SYSTEM SCHEDULED CALLBACK 1 WEEK OUT)

Appendix D

Interview Instruments for Training Program Administrators

Program Administrator at Recipient Institutions (PARI)

Introduction

Thank you for agreeing to participate in the Assessment for NIH Minority Research/Training Programs project. The goal of this study is to assess and analyze NIH minority trainee educational and career outcomes, and to recommend improvements to the NIH coordinated tracking/information system of minority research/training programs and their participants.

In this interview, we are going to discuss various aspects of the training program. The results will help us determine:

- The ways and extent to which NIH minority research/training programs work
- Which features of minority programs have been the most successful in helping individual students and faculty members move a step forward toward productive careers as research scientists
- What programmatic, environmental, or other factors increase the likelihood of minority training programs and their participating trainees achieving success
- How to assess better NIH minority training programs

In this interview, we would like to discuss the ______________ program, which is funded though the __________ mechanism(s).

Do you know if this is a targeted or non-targeted program? Just to confirm, by *targeted* NIH is referring to mechanisms and programs designed for underrepresented minority trainees only. By *non-targeted*, NIH is referring to mechanisms and programs not specifically designed for underrepresented minority trainees.

A. Introductory Questions

A1: Briefly describe the history and evolution of the program at your institution or university.

A2: How does this program fit within the department at your institution or university?

A3: What are the stated program goals?

PROBE: How have the program goals changed over time?

A4: What is your role in the program?

PROBE: What percentage of your time at the institution, department, or university relates to the program?

PROBE: How long have you been in your current position?

PROBE: How long have you been administering this mechanism?

B. Trainee Recruitment

B1: How do you attract or recruit individuals to the training program?

PROBE: How does your department communicate the availability of the program to individuals?

PROBE: What is your role in the communication process?

PROBE: What is your role in announcing the availability of this research/training grant?

B2: What kinds of candidates do you wish to attract with this program?

PROBE: Describe the characteristics of the typical candidate

PROBE: Describe the characteristics of the ideal candidate.

B3. Do you take any special steps to recruit different kinds of trainees?
PROBE: From different gender groups?

PROBE: From different ethnic groups?

PROBE: Describe what steps you take.

B5: Do you think that any potential minority trainees are missed by the current recruitment strategy?

PROBE: What have you seen that helps you form this opinion?

B6: In your opinion, how could the dissemination of information about minority-targeted training programs be improved?

PROBE: Have there been changes in the way the program has been announced in the past?

PROBE: What would need to happen to implement the changes you suggest?

B7: What are you looking for when you select candidates?

PROBE: What criteria are used most often?

PROBE: What are the cues you see in candidates that lead you to recommend they be selected?

B8: How has your recruitment or selection approach changed since the program was started at your institution, university, or department?

C. Trainee Experience within the Program

C1: What challenges and issues confront students in the program?

C2: Describe a specific example of a student who was successful in the program.

PROBE: What factors about different trainees distinguish successful experiences from less successful experiences?

PROBE: Where would this student be, in terms of his/her career, if he/she did not participate in the program?

C3: Describe a specific example of a student who had difficulty in the program.

PROBE: What about the student, the program, and the surrounding context made it difficult for him/her?

PROBE: How were the issues resolved?

C4: How do you know when a student is having trouble in the program?

PROBE: What measures are in place to help students who begin to have trouble in the program?

D. Program Administration

D1: Describe how you interact with the trainees' sponsors or mentors at recipient institutions.

PROBE: Frequency?

PROBE: Duration?

PROBE: Depth?

PROBE: Other dimensions/qualities?

D2: Describe how you interact with the granting agency—NIH.

PROBE: Frequency?

PROBE: Duration?

PROBE: Depth?

PROBE: Other dimensions/qualities?

D3: From your experience, what can you tell me about the difference in contact between you as the Program Administrator and trainees with *individual* versus *institutional* awards?

PROBE: In what way is the nature of the contact different?

D4: From your experience, what can you tell me about the difference in contact between you as the Program Administrator and trainees in *targeted* programs versus *non-targeted* programs?

PROBE: In what way is the nature of the contact different?

D5: What would make the administration of the program more efficient or more effective?

PROBE: From an administrative perspective, what NIH policies if any, hinder the administration of this program?

PROBE: Are there any NIH policy changes that you would recommend?

PROBE: How would these policy changes make administration of the program more efficient or more effective?

D6: Has your institution, department, or university's focus on minority training changed over time?

PROBE: How has this focus changed?

PROBE: What has been the cause of these changes?

PROBE: How do these changes further or hinder NIH's goals related to minority research/training grant mechanisms?

PROBE: In your opinion, what is your institution, department, or university's level of commitment to minority research training programs?

E. Program Evaluation

E1: Tell me about the program and trainee outcomes.

PROBE: What percentage of potential applicants actually apply to the program?

PROBE: Of all applicants, what percentage is accepted?

PROBE: Of accepted applicants, what percentage actually enters the program?

PROBE: Of those who enter the program, what percentage completes the program?

E2: Is your program evaluated?

PROBE: Would you say this was a formal or informal evaluation?

PROBE: When was this?

PROBE: What were the findings?

PROBE: How else is the program evaluated?

PROBE: How did the findings influence the administration of the program?

PROBE: What other changes were made as a result of the evaluation?

E3: Describe any other major changes that have been implemented in this mechanism over time.

PROBE: What were the instigating reasons for these changes?

PROBE: What were the outcomes of having made these changes?

E4: Describe how you measure the attainment of the program's goals?

PROBE: What are the specific performance measures used?

F. Final Words

F1: Are there any other aspects of your training program that you think we should know about?

F2: Are there any issues that we haven't covered that should be discussed as part of our evaluation?

Conclusion

Thank you for participating.

Program Administrators at NIH Institutes and Centers (PAIC)

Individual Awards

Introduction

Thank you for agreeing to participate in the Assessment for NIH Minority Research/Training Programs project. The goal of this study is to assess and analyze NIH minority trainee educational and career outcomes, and to recommend improvements to the NIH coordinated tracking/information system of minority research/training programs and their participants.

In this interview, we are going to discuss various aspects of the training program. The results will help us determine:

- The ways and extent to which NIH minority research/training programs work
- Which features of minority programs have been the most successful in helping individual students and faculty members move a step forward toward productive careers as research scientists
- What programmatic, environmental, or other factors increase the likelihood of minority training programs and their participating trainees achieving success
- How to assess better NIH minority training programs

Just to confirm, by *targeted* NIH is referring to mechanisms and programs designed for underrepresented minority trainees, only. By *non-targeted*, NIH is referring to mechanisms and programs not specifically designed for underrepresented minority trainees.

In this interview, we would like to discuss the _____________ mechanism(s).

A. Introductory Questions

A1: Briefly describe the purpose of the mechanism, its history, and how it has changed over time.

PROBE: In your opinion what are the goals of the mechanism?

A2: Briefly describe your current role and how this mechanism is a part of that role.

PROBE: How long have you been in your current position?

PROBE: How long have you been administering this mechanism?

B. Trainee Recruitment

B1: How does your Institute or Center communicate the availability of training mechanisms to individuals?

B2: How do you communicate the availability of training mechanisms to institutions?

PROBE: What is your role in the communication process?

PROBE: What is your role in announcing the availability of this research / training grant?

B3. What kinds of candidates do you wish to attract with this mechanism?

PROBE: Describe the characterizes of the typical candidate

PROBE: Describe the characteristics of the ideal candidate.

B4: Do you take any special steps to recruit different kinds of trainees?

PROBE: From different gender groups?

PROBE: From different ethnic groups?

PROBE: Describe what steps you take.

B5: Do you think that any potential minority trainees are missed by the current recruitment strategy?

PROBE: If YES, Why?

B6: In your opinion, how could the dissemination of information about minority-targeted training mechanisms could be improved?

PROBE: Have there been changes in the way the mechanism has been announced in the past?

PROBE: What would need to happen to implement the changes you suggest?

C. Selection Criteria

C1: What are you looking for when you select candidates?

PROBE: What criteria are used most often?

PROBE: What are the cues you see in candidates that leads you to recommend they be selected?

D. Retention

D1: Describe how you interact with the trainees' sponsors or mentors at recipient institutions.

PROBE: Frequency?

PROBE: Duration?

PROBE: Depth?

PROBE: Other dimensions/qualities?

D2a—INDIVIDUAL AWARDS ONLY: Describe how you interact with individual trainees.

PROBE: Frequency?

PROBE: Duration?

PROBE: Depth?

PROBE: Other dimensions/qualities?

D2b—INSTITUTIONAL AWARDS ONLY: Describe how you interact with recipient institutions.

PROBE: Frequency?

PROBE: Duration?

PROBE: Depth?

PROBE: Other dimensions / qualities?

D3: From your experience, what can you tell be about the difference in contact between you as the Program Administrator and trainees with individual versus institutional awards?

PROBE: In what way is the nature of the contact different?

D4: From your experience, what can you tell be about the difference in contact between you as the Program Administrator and trainees in targeted programs versus non-targeted programs?

PROBE: In what way is the nature of the contact different?

D5: How does your Institute address trainee retention?

PROBE: What about trainees who do not complete their grant?

PROBE: What about trainees who leave the field or do not get a second grant?

D6: How do you learn about trainee attrition?

PROBE: Are you aware when a trainee leaves a training program without graduating, or quits the lab in which they were working?

PROBE: Is there any formal notification, such as a written or electronic form?

E. Program Evaluation

E1: Is your program evaluated?

PROBE: Would you say this was a formal or informal evaluation?

PROBE: When was this?

PROBE: What were the findings?

PROBE: How else is the program evaluated?

PROBE: How did the findings influence the administration of the program?

PROBE: What other changes were made as a result of the evaluation?

E2: Describe how you measure the attainment of the mechanism's goals?

PROBE: What are the specific performance measures used?

E2a—INSTITUTIONAL AWARD ONLY: Tell me about a recipient institution that in your opinion has been very successful in achieving the goals of this mechanism.

PROBE: What factors distinguish this successful case from other, less successful efforts at other locations?

E2b—INSTITUTIONAL AWARD ONLY: Tell me about a recipient institution that was less effective at achieving the goals of the mechanism.

PROBE: What strategies, if any, do you use to raise the performance of what might be considered less successful programs?

E3: Describe any other major changes that have been implemented in this mechanism over time.

PROBE: What were the instigating reasons for these changes?

PROBE: What were the outcomes of having made these changes?

F. Program Administration

F1: What would make the administration of the program more efficient or more effective?

PROBE: From an administrative perspective, what NIH policies if any, hinder the administration of this program?

PROBE: Are there any NIH policy changes that you would recommend?

PROBE: How would these policy changes make administration of the program more efficient or more effective?

F2: At your Institute or Center, who decides which minority-targeted mechanisms the Institute or Center will sponsor?

PROBE: To what extent are you Program Administrators included in the decision making process?

PROBE: To what extent are Program Administrators in general included in the decision making process?

F3: Has your Institute or Center's focus on minority training changed over time?

PROBE: How has this focus changed?

PROBE: What has been the cause of these changes?

PROBE: How do these changes as further or hinder NIH's goals related to minority research / training grant mechanisms?

F4: In your opinion, what is your Institute's level of commitment to minority research training programs?

G. Final Words

G1: Are there any issues that you would like to see this evaluation study address?

G2: Are there any other questions about this program that you think that we should be asking?

Conclusion

Thank you for participating.

Program Administrators at NIH Institutes and Centers (PAIC)

Institutional Awards

Introduction

Thank you for agreeing to participate in the Assessment for NIH Minority Research / Training Programs project. The goal of this study is to assess and analyze NIH minority trainee educational and career outcomes, and to recommend improvements to the NIH coordinated tracking/information system of minority research/training programs and their participants.

In this interview, we are going to discuss various aspects of the training program. The results will help us determine:

- The ways and extent to which NIH minority research/training programs work
- Which features of minority programs have been the most successful in helping individual students and faculty members move a step forward toward productive careers as research scientists
- What programmatic, environmental, or other factors increase the likelihood of minority training programs and their participating trainees achieving success
- How to assess better NIH minority training programs

Just to confirm, by *targeted* NIH is referring to mechanisms and programs designed for underrepresented minority trainees, only. By *non-targeted*, NIH is referring to mechanisms and programs not specifically designed for underrepresented minority trainees.

In this interview, we would like to discuss the ______________ mechanism(s).

A. Introductory Questions

A1: Briefly describe the purpose of the MECHANISM, its history, and how it has changed over time.

PROBE: In your opinion what are the goals of the MECHANISM?

A2: Briefly describe your current role and how this MECHANISM is a part of that role.

PROBE: How long have you been in your current position?

PROBE: How long have you been administering this MECHANISM?

B. Trainee Recruitment

B1: How does your Institute or Center communicate the availability of training mechanisms to individuals?

B2: How do you communicate the availability of training mechanisms to institutions?

PROBE: What is your role in the communication process?

PROBE: What is your role in announcing the availability of this research / training grant?

B2. What kinds of candidates do you wish to attract with this MECHANISM?

PROBE: Describe the characterizes of the typical candidate

PROBE: Describe the characteristics of the ideal candidate.

B3: Do you take any special steps to recruit different kinds of trainees?

PROBE: From different gender groups?

PROBE: From different ethnic groups?

PROBE: Describe what steps you take.

B4: Do you think that any potential minority trainees are missed by the current recruitment strategy?

PROBE: If YES, Why?

B5: In your opinion, how could the dissemination of information about minority-targeted training mechanisms could be improved?

PROBE: Have there been changes in the way the mechanism has been announced in the past?

PROBE: What would need to happen to implement the changes you suggest?

C. Selection Criteria

C1: What are you looking for when you select candidates?

PROBE: What criteria are used most often?

PROBE: What are the cues you see in candidates that leads you to recommend they be selected?

D. Retention

D1: Describe how you interact with the trainees' sponsors or mentors at recipient institutions.

PROBE: Frequency?

PROBE: Duration?

PROBE: Depth?

PROBE: Other dimensions?

D2: Describe how you interact with individual trainees.

PROBE: Frequency?

PROBE: Duration?

PROBE: Depth?

PROBE: Other dimensions?

D3: Describe how you interact with recipient institutions.

PROBE: Frequency? Duration? Depth? Other dimensions?

D3: Is the level of contact with trainees different with awards made to individuals, as opposed to institutions?

IF YES, PROBE: In what way is the level of contact different?
(frequency? duration? depth? All of these dimensions?)

D4: Of all the trainees, which do you have more contact with: those in targeted programs or those in non-targeted programs?

D5: How does your Institute address trainee retention?

PROBE: What about trainees who do not complete their grant?
PROBE: What about trainees who leave the field or do not get a second grant?

D6: How do you learn about trainee attrition?

PROBE: Are you aware when a trainee leaves a training program without graduating, or quits the lab in which they were working?
IF YES, PROBE: Is there any formal notification, such as a written or electronic form?

E. Program Evaluation

E1: Is your program evaluated?

PROBE: Formally?

PROBE: When was this?

PROBE: What were the findings?

PROBE: How did the findings influence the administration of the program?

PROBE: What other changes were made as a result of the evaluation?

PROBE: Informally?

PROBE: When was this?

PROBE: What were the findings?

PROBE: How did the findings influence the administration of the program?

PROBE: What other changes were made as a result of the evaluation?

E2: Describe how you measure the attainment of the MECHANISM'S goals?

PROBE: What are the specific performance measures used?

E4: Tell me about a recipient institution that in your opinion has been very successful in achieving the goals of the {MECHANISM}.

PROBE: What factors distinguish this successful case from other, less successful efforts at other locations?

E5: Tell me about a recipient institution that was less effective at achieving the goals of the {MECHANISM}.

PROBE: What strategies, if any, do you use to raise the performance of 'less successful' programs?

E6: Describe any other major changes that have been implemented in this {MECHANISM} over time.

PROBE: What were the instigating reasons for these changes?

PROBE: What were the outcomes of having made these changes?

F. Program Administration

F1: What would make the administration of the program more efficient or more effective?

PROBE: Are there any NIH policy changes that you would recommend?

IF YES, PROBE: How would these policy changes make administration of the program more efficient or more effective?

F2: From an administrative perspective, what NIH policies if any, hinder the administration of this program?

F3: At your Institute, who decides which minority-targeted mechanisms the Institute will sponsor?

F4: To what extent are Program Administrators included in the decision making process?

F5: Has your Institute's focus on minority training changed over time?

IF YES, PROBE: How has this focus changed?

F6: In your opinion, what is your Institute's level of commitment to minority research training programs?

G. Final Words

G1: Are there any issues that you would like to see this evaluation study address?

G2: Are there any other questions about this program that you think that we should be asking?

G3: How difficult was it to compile the documents we asked for?

Conclusion

Thank you for participating.

Appendix E

Survey Universe by Gender, 1970-1999

Stage	Program	Total	Male	Female	Unknown
UG	R25 Bridges to Baccalaureate	4,009	1,432	2,537	40
UG	T34 MARC U-STAR	831	287	502	42
UG	T34 NIMH COR	1,006	283	716	7
UG	T34 MARC HURT	4,428	1,621	2,723	84
GRAD	R25 Bridges to Doctorate	300	122	175	3
GRAD	R03 Dissertation	34	5	27	2
GRAD	T32 Inst Trng Grants (T)	995	356	605	34
GRAD	T32 Inst Trng Grants (UT)	7,875	3,452	4,066	357
GRAD	T35 Short-Term Trng Grants (T)	2,592	839	1,321	432
GRAD	T35 Short-Term Trng Grants (UT)	3,360	1,943	1,065	352
GRAD	F34 Predoc Faculty	10	3	6	1
PD	T32 Inst Trng Grants (T)	165	90	63	12
PD	T32 Inst Trng Grants (UT)	13,306	7,787	4,834	685
PD	T35 Short-Term Trng Grants (T)	26	16	5	5
PD	T35 Short-Term Trng Grants (UT)	51	37	14	0
PD	K08 Clinical Onc (T)	3	1	2	0
PD	K08 Clinical Onc (UT)	179	126	42	11
PD	K01 Indiv Research (T)	21	7	13	1
PD	K01 Indiv Research (UT)	65	19	34	12
PD	K01 Inst Research (T)	1	1	0	0
JF	K01 Indiv Research (T)	14	7	6	1
JF	K01 Indiv Research (UT)	54	25	24	5
JF	K01 Inst Research (T)	3	1	1	1
TOTAL		39,328	18,460	18,781	2,087

NOTE: T = Targeted Program; UT = Untargeted Program

Appendix F

Number of Trainees by Race or Ethnicity and Mechanism, for all NIH Institutes and Centers, 1999-2003

Mechanism	Year	White	Black	Asian	Hispanic	Native American	Pacific Islander	Race Unknown	Total
F31	1999	636	192	84	192	14	4	230	1,352
F31	2000	734	192	102	226	12	4	164	1,434
F31	2001	936	230	128	264	20	6	184	1,768
F31	2002	1,046	242	144	296	18	6	196	1,948
F31	2003	1,100	316	128	322	26	12	260	2,164
K01	1999	424	54	72	72	8	0	88	718
K01	2000	552	72	104	90	4	0	138	960
K01	2001	646	84	142	108	8	4	194	1,186
K01	2002	722	94	160	98	10	8	248	1,340
K01	2003	808	102	220	116	6	8	276	1,536
K08	1999	1,686	42	310	90	10	4	304	2,446
K08	2000	1,710	50	336	94	10	6	344	2,550
K08	2001	1,556	50	334	92	6	4	378	2,420
K08	2002	1,528	52	338	84	4	4	436	2,446
K08	2003	1,504	44	388	82	4	4	468	2,494
T32	1999	3,146	26	152	50	6	2	410	3,792
T32	2000	3,142	34	172	52	12	2	426	3,840
T32	2001	3,210	34	174	66	8	2	462	3,956
T32	2002	3,332	38	178	76	8	4	480	4,116
T32	2003	3,406	36	196	84	10	4	532	4,268
T34	1999	76	46	12	20	2	0	26	182
T34	2000	76	38	14	18	4	0	30	180
T34	2001	68	32	14	22	2	0	32	170
T34	2002	82	30	6	24	6	0	38	186
T34	2003	96	32	4	24	8	0	40	204
T35	1999	196	22	8	14	0	0	34	274
T35	2000	196	14	10	10	0	0	38	268
T35	2001	216	16	10	14	0	0	34	290
T35	2002	206	22	10	12	0	0	34	284
T35	2003	186	20	8	12	0	0	34	260
Totals		**33,222**	**2,256**	**3,958**	**2,724**	**226**	**88**	**6,558**	**49,032**

Appendix G

Trainee Percentages by Race or Ethnicity and Mechanism, for All Institutes and Centers, 1999-2003

Mechanism	Percent White	Percent Black	Percent Asian	Percent Hispanic	Percent Native American	Percent Pacific Islander
F31	47.04	14.20	6.21	14.20	0.30	17.01
F31	51.19	13.39	7.11	15.76	0.28	11.44
F31	52.94	13.01	7.24	14.93	0.34	10.41
F31	53.70	12.42	7.39	15.20	0.31	10.06
F31	50.83	14.60	5.91	14.88	0.55	12.01
K01	59.05	7.52	10.03	10.03	0.00	12.26
K01	57.50	7.50	10.83	9.38	0.00	14.38
K01	54.47	7.08	11.97	9.11	0.34	16.36
K01	53.88	7.01	11.94	7.31	0.60	18.51
K01	52.60	6.64	14.32	7.55	0.52	17.97
K08	68.93	1.72	12.67	3.68	0.16	12.43
K08	67.06	1.96	13.18	3.69	0.24	13.49
K08	64.30	2.07	13.80	3.80	0.17	15.62
K08	62.47	2.13	13.82	3.43	0.16	17.83
K08	60.30	1.76	15.56	3.29	0.16	18.77
T32	82.96	0.69	4.01	1.32	0.05	10.81
T32	81.82	0.89	4.48	1.35	0.05	11.09
T32	81.14	0.86	4.40	1.67	0.05	11.68
T32	80.95	0.92	4.32	1.85	0.10	11.66
T32	79.80	0.84	4.59	1.97	0.09	12.46
T34	41.76	25.27	6.59	10.99	0.00	14.29
T34	42.22	21.11	7.78	10.00	0.00	16.67
T34	40.00	18.82	8.24	12.94	0.00	18.82
T34	44.09	16.13	3.23	12.90	0.00	20.43
T34	47.06	15.69	1.96	11.76	0.00	19.61
T35	71.53	8.03	2.92	5.11	0.00	12.41
T35	73.13	5.22	3.73	3.73	0.00	14.18
T35	74.48	5.52	3.45	4.83	0.00	11.72
T35	72.54	7.75	3.52	4.23	0.00	11.97
T35	71.54	7.69	3.08	4.62	0.00	13.08
Totals	**67.76**	**4.60**	**8.07**	**5.56**	**0.18**	**13.37**